——— 2005-06 ———

Editors
Sidney Gottlieb and Richard Allen

Editorial Advisory Board
Charles Barr   Lesley Brill
Paula Marantz Cohen   Leonard J. Leff
Thomas M. Leitch   James Naremore

Founding Editor
Christopher Brookhouse

Editorial Assistant
Renata Jackson

Cover Design
Deborah Dutko

The *Hitchcock Annual* (ISSN 1062-5518) is published each spring. Editorial, subscription, and advertising correspondence should be addressed to: Sidney Gottlieb, Editor, *Hitchcock Annual*, Department of Media Studies, Sacred Heart University, Fairfield, CT 06825-1000. E-mail address: spgottlieb@aol.com

The cost for continuing subscribers is $10 per volume for individuals (outside the U.S. add $5.00 for postage) and $25.00 for institutions. Make checks payable to: *Hitchcock Annual*. All back issues are available, as are offprints of individual articles. Inquire for prices.

We invite articles on all aspects of Hitchcock and his work, and encourage a variety of approaches, methods, and viewpoints. For all submissions, follow the guidelines of the *Chicago Manual of Style*, using full notes rather than works cited format, and include two copies of the essay to be considered (only one of which will be returned) with return postage. Submissions may also be made by e-mail as attached files. The responsibility for securing any permissions required for publishing material in the essay or related illustrations rests with the author. Authors of articles with illustrations will be asked to contribute to covering the additional printing charges incurred by such illustrations.

The *Hitchcock Annual* is indexed in the *Film Literature Index* and *MLA International Bibliography*.

*The publication of this volume has been supported by grants from
the Graduate School of Arts and Sciences and the Tisch School
of the Arts, New York University, and from the Department of
Media Studies and Digital Culture, Sacred Heart University.*

HITCHCOCK ANNUAL
2005-06

THOMAS LEITCH

Hitchcock and Company

Although the torrent of Hitchcock commentary produced by the 1999 centennial of the director's birth may have crested, so much new work on the director has continued to appear that it makes sense to speak of Hitchcock studies as a field of study. My purpose in this essay is not to map that field—such an ambitious goal would require an entire book—but to indicate some ways in which it might be mapped. In particular, I'd like to review the circumstances under which it assumed at least some of the leading qualities of a disciplinary field, consider the shifting relations between Hitchcock studies and the larger field of film studies, and suggest several models for disciplinary studies I hope will help define the field more sharply. Unlike John Belton, whose recent review essay surveys the field in somewhat different terms, I am not mainly interested in what Hitchcock studies ought to look like.[1] So instead of evaluating particular contributions or laying down guidelines for future interventions, I'll try to create a picture of what Hitchcock studies actually does look like. The critics I cite will be representative—I'm especially interested in Robin Wood, perhaps the most influential of all Hitchcock commentators—but my roll-call will be selective rather than exhaustive.

All the questions I will be considering have their basis in a more fundamental question: Why Hitchcock? Out of all the filmmakers in all the film industries in all the world, why has Hitchcock spawned such a flood of commentary? Writing on the eve of the director's centennial, Gilberto Perez observed that Hitchcock "would have to be incomparably the greatest of all filmmakers to merit the amount of critical and academic attention bestowed on him."[2] What has Hitchcock done to deserve such close and sustained scrutiny? Is he really a greater or more important filmmaker than Griffith, Renoir, or Kurosawa?

Hitchcock is hardly the only celebrity director. My recent Google search of Hitchcock yielded 7,150,000 hits. That impressive-sounding number dwarfs the number of hits for Griffith (740,000), Renoir (978,000), and Kurosawa (2,290,000), but is outstripped by those of other directors like Quentin Tarantino (7,640,000), Peter Jackson (7,930,000), Clint Eastwood (10,400,000), Steven Spielberg (16,900,000), and Mel Gibson (136,000,000—though some of these may not deal primarily with Gibson as a director).

Nor is it clear from these figures that celebrity or popularity correlates with merit. The rise of Hitchcock studies does not mean that Hitchcock is the greatest of all filmmakers any more than the Google figures, which can vary dizzyingly from week to week, mean that Jackson and Tarantino are slightly greater, or Spielberg twice as great. What sets Hitchcock commentary apart is not its unprecedented volume or its subject's unique and incomparable greatness but several other distinctive features.

As Perez notes, Hitchcock is indisputably preeminent among filmmakers not in greatness or fame but in the quantity of critical attention he has attracted from outside and (mainly) inside the academy. Is the sheer volume of critical analysis of his work in essays and books, as opposed to Web pages, sufficient to constitute Hitchcock studies a disciplinary field in its own right rather than simply an area of specialization within film studies? The question of what makes a body of criticism into a discipline is a tricky one, and it may not be worth quibbling over whether Hitchcock studies is a discipline or a sub-discipline. The last section of this essay will have more to say about the nature of disciplines in general and the lessons Hitchcock studies offers for any attempt to define disciplines. For now, however, I'd like to begin with the hypothesis that disciplines grow not around bodies of information, however voluminous and well-organized, but around questions that generate more information and further questions, and the suggestion that the rise of Hitchcock studies has depended on the ability of Hitchcock's films to raise productive and far-reaching questions.

*   *   *   *   *

For as long as he was recognized as a trademark director, he offered obvious attractions as a subject for study. Early on in his career he became identified with a single popular genre, the suspense thriller, in which his preeminence remained unrivaled for forty years. Hitchcock's genius for self-promotion, despite his personal diffidence and his passion for guarding his privacy, made him a logical candidate for self-mythologizing even before his arrival in Hollywood placed at his service a publicity machine designed to recast successful individuals as iconic stars, distinctive, appealing, accessible, yet untouchable and remote. The franchising of his name and image in the 1950s to a weekly television series, a monthly mystery magazine, and a series of anthologies made his silhouette familiar to millions who had never seen a Hitchcock film. It would have taken a canny reader or viewer to realize that his ghoulishly witty trademark introductions to all three enterprises were ghostwritten by other uncredited hands. And what Robert E. Kapsis has called "Hitchcock's desire to be accepted by both mass and elite audiences,"[3] which shaped the production and publicity of *The Birds* and *Marnie*, coincided with François Truffaut's book-length series of interviews to vault Hitchcock into academic respectability at just the moment film studies were reaching a critical mass in American universities.

Hitchcock's fame was always of an unusual sort. He was never presented as the world's greatest filmmaker but more typically as a man of special and relatively narrow gifts, most notably a talent for scaring moviegoers, who also happened to be the world's most iconically distinctive, entertaining, and publicly available filmmaker, even if the darkly jolly image he presented to the public was as carefully controlled and in its way as inscrutable as Garbo's. Hitchcock was a favorite interview subject because he was so articulate and amusing, but his articulateness, as Truffaut's book made clear, was limited to favorite anecdotes and questions of craft rather than large conceptual or thematic claims. He was, in short, the director best suited for selling mass entertainment to the public through a persona that was itself a highly successful example of mass entertainment.

Unlikely as it might have seemed that such an entertaining figure would become the object of such intensive study, that is exactly what happened under the banner of the *politique des auteurs*. Through the efforts of 1950s French film reviewers seeking an alternative to the Tradition of Quality, whose merits were secured by their adaptation of literary masterpieces, Hitchcock became an obvious candidate for the proposition that directors rather than studios or screenwriters or authors of the properties on which films were based provided the shaping intelligence behind their films. No matter who wrote or released or starred in them, Hitchcock's films were always instantly recognizable as his own by their common genre, their continued preoccupation with mothers and staircases and icy blondes, and the director's trademark cameo appearances, which served the invaluable function of keeping his image before the public without committing himself to saying anything in particular.

None of these publicity devices, however, would have been successful if they had not been supported by the body of Hitchcock's work. The director had the advantage of having been a filmmaker since the days of silent features. He absorbed essential lessons of expressionist cinema—the uses of decoupage to convey unvoiced emotions, as when Mrs. Verloc stabs her husband to death in *Sabotage*; the power of telling visual details like the Professor's half-finger in *The 39 Steps*; the need to keep the screen, as he told Truffaut, "charged with emotion"[4]—from the time he spent in Germany and the German films he watched so attentively. Setting to work in English-language cinema, he established his professional credentials just as the coming of talkies would make English world cinema's dominant language, then moved to America and his greatest popular successes. By the time he was championed by Truffaut and his *Cahiers du Cinéma* colleagues Eric Rohmer and Claude Chabrol, Hitchcock had made an impressive number of thrillers on both sides of the Atlantic. Virtually all of them were highly entertaining and commercially successful. Most were readily available for rental in 16mm prints, just as they would later be available for purchase on videotape and DVD.[5]

In addition to providing a retrospective view of a filmmaking career virtually coeval with the rise of commercial cinema, Hitchcock's films managed to be both immediately accessible and endlessly discussable. Ironically for a director enlisted against the Tradition of Quality, Hitchcock made films with many literary virtues. His signatures were tight plotting consistent with often breathtaking set-pieces, mordant humor, a consistent sense of irony, and an enviable mastery of the rhetoric of cinema, its ability to play on the audience's powers of reasoning and emotion.

The director's chosen genre, the suspense thriller, was based on the paradox that the unknown and the menacing could best be approached through a tightly scripted formula. In Hitchcock's hands, however, the thriller became both more obvious and more devious. It telegraphed its twists and turns through the director's well-known preference for suspense over surprise and his signature obsessions with shared guilt, sexual repression, and increasingly compromised innocents. At the same time, Hitchcock complicated the sentimental appeal of wholesome American teenager Charlie Newton in *Shadow of a Doubt* by making her unwillingly complicit with her murderous uncle, and the patriotic appeal of amateur spy Alicia Huberman in *Notorious* by turning the American agent T.R. Devlin from her lover into her procurer. He undercut the resolutions of *Rear Window, To Catch a Thief, The Wrong Man, Psycho,* and *The Birds* by their increasingly destabilizing final scenes.

The most obvious feature Hitchcock provided Hitchcock studies was an *oeuvre* that was extensive, entertaining, and surprisingly varied. Hitchcock's work, which amounted to both a primer and an anatomy of suspense, was both appealing on first view and rewarding to study in closer detail. Because of Hitchcock's well-advertised, if not entirely credible, insulation from the influence of other filmmakers since his apprentice days, his career amounted to a self-contained body of work that could be mastered even by scholars and students reluctant to immerse themselves in the increasingly thorny problems of film studies as the larger field developed in the 1960s and 1970s. Even more important, however, was the ability of Hitchcock's films to provoke debate by raising productive questions that would define and redefine the field. Apart from noting the ambiguous endings of *Vertigo* and *The Birds,* virtually none of the films' original reviewers had raised the possibility of interpretive cruxes in the films, which seemed to move from tense problems through a series of variously exhilarating adventures and set-pieces to strong and unambiguous resolutions. Nonetheless, Hitchcock's films turned out to be surprisingly hospitable to productive reinterpretation. What was at stake in each new round of interpretation was not only the meaning of a given film and its place in the director's career, but, as often as not, questions about the nature of that career and of Hitchcock studies generally.

The first and best known of these questions was raised by Robin Wood in 1965: "Why should we take Hitchcock seriously?"[6] To the question at the heart of his debate with *Sight and Sound* journalist Penelope Houston—should we take Hitchcock seriously?[7]—Wood added a single word that preserved the question of paramount urgency (could Hitchcock be usefully addressed in the terms heretofore reserved for such relatively elitist forms as the novel?) at the same time as it flung wide the doors of Hitchcock studies by making it possible to address the question on many different fronts (Hitchcock as craftsman, as artist, as moralist, as observer of human behavior, as explorer of the psyche).

Raymond Durgnat attempted, in *The Strange Case of Alfred Hitchcock*, to chart "a middle road between those [like Houston] for whom Hitchcock is a Master, but a Master of nothing, and those [like Wood] for whom Hitchcock is regularly rather than occasionally a profound and salutary moralist."[8] Durgnat's conclusion that Hitchcock was "an aesthetic virtuoso" in the minor tradition of "Aesthetes, Decadents and Symbolists" whose most notable exemplar is Oscar Wilde provoked still further debate about the nature of Hitchcock's achievement through its insinuation that the question of whether Hitchcock was an artist could be answered in more interesting ways than yes or no.[9]

The heart of Wood's 1965 monograph was not his general defense of Hitchcock but his readings of seven key Hitchcock films from *Strangers on a Train* through *Marnie*. Looking beyond *Psycho*'s success as "Hitchcock's ultimate achievement to date in the technique of audience participation,"[10] he emphasized the ways in which the audience's identification with Marion Crane and Norman Bates implicated them morally in what might have seemed nothing more than funhouse horrors, revealing a psychological insight he found as penetrating as Shakespeare's analysis of evil in *Macbeth* and Conrad's in *Heart of Darkness*. Rejecting the leading theories of the meaning of the birds that attack Bodega Bay, he called them "a concrete embodiment of the arbitrary and unpredictable . . . a reminder . . . of the possibility that life is meaningless and absurd."[11] The delicacy and complexity of these readings served two functions. One was to advance such a powerful case for Hitchcock's artistry that Wood's opening question was effectively settled. The other, equally important, was to lay the groundwork for a continuing and fruitful dialogue in which critics convinced that Hitchcock should be taken seriously debated the interpretation of films whose meanings had once seemed self-evident.

The question of why Hitchcock should be taken seriously was only the first of several key questions to animate Hitchcock studies by opening interpretive debates that led in turn to further general questions. Wood himself, responding to Tania Modleski's *The Women Who Knew Too Much,* raised a second pivotal question in a 1982 essay reprinted in the expanded version of his seminal volume: "Can Hitchcock be saved for feminism?"[12] This question addresses Laura Mulvey's widely influential 1975 essay "Visual Pleasure and Narrative Cinema," which had pronounced Hitchcock a stellar example of the sadism and fetishistic scopophilia through which the patriarchal gaze Mulvey identified as dominant in cinema neutralized the castrating threat of the female subject.[13] Increasingly radicalized by what he took to be increasingly reactionary Anglo-American politics, his self-identification as a gay film critic, and Modleski's attack on his attempt "to reestablish the authority of the artist—to 'save' Hitchcock"[14]—Wood rejects his own earlier humanistic description of "romantic love" as "some eternal and unchangeable 'given' of 'the human condition.'"[15] Opening a debate with himself allows Wood to maintain the focus on his earlier premise (*Vertigo*'s analysis of romantic love) while making his terms more psychoanalytic and political. At the same time, he launches a counterattack on Modleski's "attitude toward personal authorship" as "shot through with a disingenuousness that is by no means personal to her but endemic to the entire semiotic/structuralist school."[16] Although Wood rarely responded directly to other Hitchcock scholars, his engagement with Modleski through his argument with his own earlier interpretation of *Vertigo* helped confirm the status of both Hitchcock's work and interpretation generally to the larger field of film studies.

Wood's rereading of *Vertigo* seeks to shift the ground of Hitchcock studies in two crucial ways. One, which Wood acknowledges at length, is to propose Hitchcock as a test case for Peter Wollen's influential argument about the distinction between filmmakers as putative authors or agents and the auteurs that emerge as an effect of the discourse, products of "a kind of decypherment" of the salient structural elements of their *oeuvre*.[17] The relation between Hitchcock and "Hitchcock," to use one commonly accepted way to mark this distinction, has provided perhaps the single most productive instance of this relation. But there is an equally important shift that Wood does not explicitly acknowledge: the shift from an intrinsic question (what are Hitchcock's films like?) to an instrumental question (what can we do with Hitchcock's films?). The examination of Hitchcock's particular sexual politics would continue in D.A. Miller, Theodore Price, Robert Corber, Lee Edelman, and Robert Samuels.[18] The more general debate about the relation between Hitchcock the agent and "Hitchcock" the product of external forces moved to the center of both Hitchcock studies and film studies, where it remains today. The equally tenacious question about the relation between explaining Hitchcock and using Hitchcock, however, has never been squarely confronted.

A third debate, and the one most widely known outside the circle of Hitchcock specialists, was provoked by Donald Spoto's *The Dark Side of Genius: The Life of Alfred Hitchcock*. Rejecting the portrait that Hitchcock's authorized biographer, John Russell Taylor, had drawn of the director as a good-natured professional given to humorous pranks and epigrammatic remarks,[19] Spoto reconfigured Hitchcock as a tormented soul whose films expressed as clearly as his practical jokes his fears of physical inadequacy, his sexual longing, and his sadistic drive to establish his authority by controlling his professional colleagues, especially a storied series of blonde leading ladies. Although the primary orientation of Spoto's book was biographical, he drove home his argument by emphasizing the sadistic elements in films as different as *The 39 Steps, Frenzy,* and the unrealized project *The Short Night,* elements which assumed a new and darker importance in Hitchcock studies.[20]

Spoto's account of Hitchcock's private fantasies and their cinematic display may or may not have been accurate, but it had a galvanizing effect on the field. Commentators recoiling from Spoto's sadistic, misogynistic portrait of the director could dispute his account of the facts, claim that his psychoanalysis was reductive, argue for a sharper distinction between Hitchcock and "Hitchcock," or go back to the films for another look. One of the most judicious resulting reinterpretations of Hitchcock was Lesley Brill's *The Hitchcock Romance*, which, while disclaiming any biographical insight, argued that Hitchcock was not "an exotic sadist," but "deeply conventional, thoughtful, and rather soft-hearted" in his exploration of love as "the most common" cure for "the maladies of being human."[21] In Brill's reading of Hitchcock, films like *North by Northwest, To Catch a Thief,* and *The Trouble with Harry* become both more optimistic and more central to the director's career. Brill's attempt to find a balance between love and irony in Hitchcock's films prefigures Patrick McGilligan's analogous attempt to find such a balance in the director's life.[22] The middle ground McGilligan seeks between Taylor and Spoto is no more likely to resolve the debate than Brill resolved the question of Hitchcock's irony or Durgnat resolved the question of his artistic status once and for all.

Each of these debates has produced further commentary that has used reinterpretations of specific Hitchcock films to push past the boundaries of the original questions even as it has left those questions behind. Hitchcock's success among academic film scholars has largely silenced earlier claims that art is incompatible with commercially successful filmmaking. Whether or not Hitchcock's films offer a prophetic vision of late twentieth-century feminism, it is clear that their shifting and often contradictory attitudes toward assumptions about gender binaries and gendered behavior handsomely repay close study. And however autobiographical the nightmares of Hitchcock's cinema may be, whatever Hitchcock may or may not have said to Tippi Hedren on the set of *Marnie,* it seems clear that the relation between Hitchcock's life and work that Spoto opened to scrutiny is both an unsettled question and one well worth pursuing.

*　*　*　*　*

This brief survey of Hitchcock criticism strongly suggests that the development of Hitchcock studies so far has been governed by four rules that are applicable to the development of any emerging disciplinary field:

1. *The field is defined and developed by a series of productive debates.* These debates often begin with yes-or-no questions that immediately arrest commentators' attention by defining a pivotal issue concisely (Should we take Hitchcock seriously? Can Hitchcock be saved for feminism? Is Hitchcock basically an inveterate ironist or a sentimentalist who believes in happy endings? Are his films the expression of a tortured and torturing soul or the product of a hard-working professional collaborating with other professionals?), but what makes them productive is their ability to generate responses that open the debates to wider questions precisely because they are not reducible to yes or no.

2. *The field gains strength from its subject's receptiveness to reinterpretation and regeneralization.* English teachers routinely assure their students that *Hamlet* will be different every time they read it—a key feature of Hitchcock's as well as Shakespeare's masterpieces, as shown by Wood's rereading of *Vertigo*, which pointedly takes issue with his earlier reading. The potential strength of a disciplinary field is vastly increased by the possibility of productive disagreements with oneself and others. Even though *Coriolanus* may be, as T.S. Eliot once tartly announced in pressing its claims against those of *Hamlet*, "Shakespeare's most assured artistic success,"[23] it has neither provoked as much commentary as *Hamlet* nor loomed as large in Shakespeare studies or popular notions of Shakespeare because, as Eliot concedes, it is not as "interesting," as endlessly reinterpretable.

3. *The most influential interventions in the field are those that present the subject in ways that provoke further debate rather than those that seek to close off debate.* This is why Spoto's biography, for all its oversimplifications and shortcomings, is likely to remain more important than McGilligan's: because Spoto's portrait of Hitchcock as a neurotic, sexually-entranced manipulator is simply more compelling, not least because of its power to provoke debate that is more than dissent. McGilligan's more judiciously drawn Hitchcock is neither as interesting as Spoto's nor as likely to lead to further interesting discussions of the director and his work.

4. *The more vigorous these debates are, the more firmly established the field becomes.* In field studies as in business and politics, nothing succeeds like success. Discussion begets discussion because the more interesting earlier commentators are likely to have found Hitchcock's work, the more interesting later commentators are likely to find Hitchcock studies, which now includes not only the films themselves, along with contemporary reviews and interviews, but a growing body of increasingly sophisticated earlier commentary.

Hence Gilberto Perez's impatience with what he takes to be the overvaluation of Hitchcock misses a vital point. At a critical moment in the rise of a new disciplinary field, the production of discourse changes from an inhibition—how is it possible to say anything new about Hitchcock in the light of everything that's already been written about him?—into a spur. Each new commentary opens the door to further commentaries, not simply on the founding texts, but on earlier commentaries, in the manner of the midrashic commentaries generations of rabbis devoted to sacred scripture and its accumulated layers of interpretation. Behind the practice of midrash is the faith that the Bible is an inexhaustible text capable of supporting, indeed requiring, literally endless commentary.

A more cynical contemporary version of this faith is Stanley Fish's remark on the founding of the Spenser Society, modeled on the Milton Society, that "it is the business of these societies first to create the work and second to make sure it will never get done."[24] Fish, who has put in his share of time on the boards of such learned societies, is certainly entitled to his opinion that the result is a makework mentality. It would be more judicious, however, to observe that the imperative that governs all disciplines, the very sign of disciplinarity, is to develop a momentum that makes further discussion seem logical and desirable. All disciplines that establish themselves successfully reach a critical mass that generates further commentary. When Sidney Gottlieb, surveying the dazzling variety of "Hitchcocks" that commentators have proposed, wonders why "we still have not had a full treatment of the comic Hitchcock,"[25] his question amounts to a challenge. It is instructive that the two contributors to Hitchcock studies that come closest to answering that challenge since Gottlieb issued it—Susan Smith and James Naremore—make no attempt to exhaust the subject and indeed whet the appetite for more.[26] The more that gets written about Hitchcock, the more there is to say.

This rule has particular force in the rise of a disciplinary field newly emerging from the shadow of a better-established parent field. It has been a signal contribution of Hitchcock studies to borrow a series of debates from film studies, then redefine and energize them in ways that depend specifically on Hitchcock's example. In turning now to three of these debates, I'll review their early history, note the ways they intersect with broader disciplinary problems, and emphasize in each case one particular recent contribution that best summarizes the nature of the debate and indicates its most likely future direction.

* * * * *

The first of these debates reflects the rise of New Historicism in literary studies. The return of so many film scholars to studio archives and other primary material has revived the age-old debate between historical scholarship and interpretive criticism. Do we learn more about Hitchcock from collecting new information about the circumstances under which his films were planned, produced, and publicized, or by looking more closely at the films themselves? This debate is played out most dramatically in monographs on individual films. On one side are the production studies of *Psycho, Vertigo,* and *Marnie* by Stephen Rebello, Dan Auiler, and Tony Lee Moral that take their methodological cue from Leonard J. Leff's pioneering study of Hitchcock's relationship with David O. Selznick.[27] On the other are a growing list of critical studies of individual films: James Naremore and Raymond Durgnat on *Psycho,* Stefan

Sharff and John Fawell on *Rear Window,* Tom Ryall on *Blackmail,* Camille Paglia on *The Birds,* Charles Barr on *Vertigo*—to which may be added recent collections edited by John Belton and Robert Kolker, and Philip J. Skerry's even more narrowly focused analysis of *Psycho*'s shower scene.[28]

Many of these monographs attempt to straddle the line between historical scholarship and interpretation. Rebello, Auiler, and especially Moral all offer interpretive insights into the films they are examining. Although Paglia, Fawell, and especially Sharff avoid any consideration of the production history of the films they are analyzing, most other interpretive critics investigate these factors in more or less detail. The most influential intervention in this debate, however, and the most important volume on Hitchcock published in the last ten years, is Bill Krohn's *Hitchcock at Work.*

The importance of Krohn's work, an oversized, heavily illustrated series of essays on the production histories of Hitchcock's American films, with special emphasis on *Saboteur, Shadow of a Doubt, Notorious, Strangers on a Train, Rear Window,* the 1956 *Man Who Knew Too Much, Vertigo, North by Northwest, Psycho,* and *The Birds,* lies in its power to recast Hitchcock in a new light. Not content to examine studio production files for materials about the circumstances under which Hitchcock worked, Krohn combines his research with his critical sensitivity to particular scenes in particular films to present a powerful new portrait of the director. The most instructive contrast is with Dan Auiler's *Hitchcock's Notebooks,* which assembles a vast amount of production material on several Hitchcock films without imposing a pattern on it that would present a coherent new view of the director.[29] In a prologue to his volume, Krohn lists a series of truisms about the filmmaker that his book will attack:

> Before making a film, Hitchcock "made the film on paper" in the screenplay. Translating the screenplay to celluloid was for him a necessary but boring activity, never a creative one. . . . It's all in the script, even the camera angles. . . . Every angle, every camera move,

was storyboarded. . . . The picture was already edited
in the camera. . . . There was no room for
improvisation. . . . Every Hitchcock film is spun out of
a single form, which often appears in the title
sequence. . . . Hitchcock filmed everything on a
sound-stage so that he could control every detail and
create a stylized vision of the world.[30]

Krohn proceeds to recount hundreds of occasions on which
Hitchcock departed from his screenplays and storyboards,
invented or deleted scenes on the set, encouraged actors and
actresses to improvise dialogue and bits of business, devised
new camera setups or editing rhythms, and changed films still
further in post-production. The result is an intervention
comparable to Spoto's pivotal recasting of Hitchcock's
biography: a new portrait of the director's working methods
that challenges received wisdom and lays the ground for a
new round of debates about the relation between standard
industry practice and the working habits of Hitchcock, long
assumed even by other Hollywood filmmakers to be "a
brilliant exception whose famous method worked for him, but
only for him."[31]

The second debate most important in recent work on
Hitchcock also concerns the director's apparent
exceptionalism: the question of whether Hitchcock can most
profitably be studied in isolation from other filmmakers or in
the context of other directors, writers, and thinkers whose
work influenced him. A peculiar feature of Hitchcock studies
from its earliest days was its confidence, following many of
the director's own public pronouncements, that Hitchcock
was the sole proprietor of a private island, the suspense
thriller, on which he reigned supreme. The corollary, that
expertise in Hitchcock did not require a detailed familiarity
with film history or theory, was fostered in several different
ways. Few of the earliest commentators on Hitchcock were
academics with degrees in film history or theory because they
arrived on the scene before the flood. The film-by-film
surveys by Robert A. Harris and Michael Lasky (*The Complete*

Films of Alfred Hitchcock), Donald Spoto (*The Art of Alfred Hitchcock: Fifty Years of His Motion Pictures*), and Gene D. Phillips (*Alfred Hitchcock*), along with Maurice Yacowar's *Hitchcock's British Films*, all treated Hitchcock as a self-contained subject.[32] Robin Wood, who rarely cited other critics in his work, wrote at length on structuralist semiotics only to mark his distance from it.

Signs of a new willingness to contextualize Hitchcock instead of treating him as a self-contained subject appear as early as Elisabeth Weis's *The Silent Scream*, which uses the soundtracks of a number of Hitchcock films to explore a range of possibilities in the manipulation of sound open to all filmmakers, and especially Tom Ryall's *Hitchcock and the British Cinema*, which generally eschews close analysis in favor of an examination of the social, economic, institutional, and generic contexts in which Hitchcock worked in England.[33] Charles Derry positions Hitchcock as the exemplary practitioner of a genre far more extensive than his own work.[34] Paula Marantz Cohen reads Hitchcock's cinematic families through two contexts that she contends the director inherited from Victorian culture: a psychological conception of character and the importance of an active and formative female subjectivity.[35] When Charles Barr in *English Hitchcock* returns to the early films Yacowar had surveyed in 1977, he notes two vital differences in his approach: his emphasis on Hitchcock's specifically national context, his Englishness, and on the contexts provided by the director's lively interest in the playwrights and novelists from whom he learned the principles of story construction.

Still another context invoked by recent commentators is Hitchcock's relationships with the collaborators his own self-publicizing systematically eclipsed. Apart from Charles Barr's examination of Hitchcock's work with screenwriters Eliot Stannard and Charles Bennett, Steven DeRosa has explored Hitchcock's most enduring partnership with an American screenwriter in *Writing with Hitchcock: The Collaboration of Alfred Hitchcock and John Michael Hayes*; Royal S. Brown and Steven C. Smith have both analyzed Hitchcock's collaboration

with the composer Bernard Herrmann; and Patricia
Hitchcock O'Connell has provided a memoir of Hitchcock's
wife and closest collaborator in *Alma Hitchcock: The Woman
Behind the Man.*[36]

The most ambitious attempt to date to place Hitchcock in
a broader context is John Orr's *Hitchcock and Twentieth-
Century Cinema.* Indeed Orr's title is too limiting, since the
single most important figure in Orr's intertextual analysis is
the eighteenth-century Scottish philosopher David Hume.
Building on Hume's rejection of essentialist notions of human
nature in favor of a thoroughgoing perceptual empiricism,
Hitchcock, argues Orr, devises stories that dramatize the fear
of "perceptual collapse" through the radical defamiliarizing
of melodramatic situations, so that "the force of unexpected
experience completely breaks down the power of custom and
convention, of our normal ways of seeing."[37] Though his
highly selective contexts make him less persuasive than
Krohn in presenting a new Hitchcock, Orr is likely to
provoke further studies seeking to broaden or correct his
welcome attempt to establish Hitchcock's place in twentieth-
century cinema.

The third and most important debate in Hitchcock studies
continues Robin Wood's quarrel with semioticians who had
rejected the notion of the director, or indeed of any alleged
author, as creator. What is the relation between Hitchcock the
staid Cockney in the black suit and Hitchcock the trademark
who is at least partly an effect rather than a cause of his own
discourse? To put it more briefly, what do we mean by
Hitchcock (or "Hitchcock")?

More than any other question, this one has from the
beginning defined the relation between Hitchcock studies and
the broader discipline of film studies. Hitchcock rose to early
prominence in American university courses on film because
he was the exemplary auteur, the director who could most
convincingly be defended as the maker of meaning in
individual films and across his entire career. Hardly had
Hitchcock been defined as the exemplary auteur, however,
than the more general notion of authorship came under attack

by structuralism, psychoanalytically-inflected semiotics, and apparatus theory. Now the question was not whether Hitchcock was the sole or dominant creative force behind his films but whether it was defensible to talk about any individual creative force at all. Ironically, Hitchcock's reputation as an auteur, the primary force behind the film's authorship, was secure; it was authorship itself that was in doubt.

As the focus of academic film criticism shifted from the identification, evaluation, and analysis of auteur directors to the question of whether anyone could be an author, Hitchcock seemed at times the last exemplar of the filmmaker as creative agency, the sole exception to the prevailing tenor of film studies and therefore a refuge for scholars like William Rothman, who insisted that the director was the primary agent who shaped the meanings of his films and found signs of his authorship persistently inscribed in motivic visual patterns, especially the series of four hard verticals (/ / / /) that appear most explicitly in the exterior shot that introduces the courthouse sequence in *Psycho*.[38] Even during this period, however, Modleski's comments on Wood's attempt to save Hitchcock for feminism show that his authorship was hardly immune from attack. Kapsis's volume on Hitchcock reconfigured the debate over his status as auteur by shifting its grounds to the specific practical steps Hitchcock himself had taken to construct his own public image. In Kapsis's analysis, both Hitchcock and "Hitchcock" were crucial; it was the nature of the connection between them that was open to debate.

Apart from Kapsis's redefinition of the relation between Hitchcock and "Hitchcock" and Rothman's exhaustive analysis of the traces of the director's authorship in *The Lodger, Murder!, The 39 Steps, Shadow of a Doubt,* and *Psycho,* the most important contribution to the debate over the status of Hitchcock's authorship is the collection of documents compiled by Sidney Gottlieb in *Hitchcock on Hitchcock: Selected Writings and Interviews* and *Alfred Hitchcock: Interviews.*[39] Covering a wider and more diverse range of subjects and occasions than Truffaut's celebrated series of interviews, these pieces show the director dispensing practical dicta, self-mythologizing anecdotes, and unexpectedly shrewd and precise self-assessments. The result is a more nuanced portrait than ever before of Hitchcock intermittently turning himself into "Hitchcock." At the same time, Slavoj Žižek has for over ten years been considering the nature of the textual signs in Hitchcock's films that establish his authorship, his status as the "subject supposed to know,"[40] in a sense quite remote from his agency.

The most ambitious recent book on the question of Hitchcock's authorship is Tom Cohen's two-volume *Hitchcock's Cryptonomies: Secret Agents* and *War Machines*, which pushes beyond Žižek to make the idea of authorship tangential and indeed inimical to its project. In tracking the "secret writing systems that traverse [Hitchcock's] work" but cannot be decoded or reconciled by means of any generic or semiotic grammar, Cohen finds the director impossible to define as an authorizing agent, a traditional author, or a label for a coherent signifying system. Although "the long-held premise of cinema studies has been predicated on privileging a visual ideology, an aesthetic ideology," Cohen maintains that Hitchcock's "secret agents" elude these ideological systems. Hence " 'Hitchcock' from this perspective appears less an *oeuvre* in film history—more or less 'modernist,' more or less auteurist—than an unsettled event within the archeology of 'global' image culture."[41]

As this brief summary suggests, Cohen's account of Hitchcock's authorship is not only hermetic in its critical rhetoric but deeply paradoxical. Hitchcock is the anti-author whose function is to authorize images that resist reduction to any system of meaning. Hitchcock's secret agent is for Cohen the anti-maker of meaning. At the same time, Hitchcock is Hitchcock, whose work is uniquely distinctive because of its traversal by the secret agents that undermine the tyranny of semiotic and disciplinary systems. Cohen's Hitchcock, who is both utterly representative of contemporary visual culture and uniquely exempt from its strictures, irresistibly brings to mind Wood's response to Modleski's attack on Hitchcock's authorship: "If one is not concerned with the personal nature of the work (which does not at all preclude a concern with its representativeness, as a product of its culture)—with the individual stamp that distinguishes it from other Hollywood movies—then why write a book on *Hitchcock's* films at all? Why *this* grouping of films other than other groupings (films made in the same period, within the same genre, on similar subjects, etc.)?"[42]

Clearly, Cohen is seeking to use Hitchcock rather than to understand him; the determined solipsism of his project makes the very word "understand" sound naïve. But it remains unclear from Cohen's analysis whether he is seeking to penetrate Hitchcock's work as a uniquely licensed field of secret agents or a representative example of a process that continues in all visual signifying systems. So the question of the relation between Hitchcock and "Hitchcock" leads first to the question of whether Hitchcock is to be plumbed for the distinctive rewards his work offers or pressed into some larger project, and finally to the question of whether there is any useful distinction to be made between Hitchcock's films and any other films—or, as Cohen makes clear, between Hitchcock's secret agents and the even broader field of "teletechnics that wire epistemologies and define the human, within which 'cinema' marks an exorbitant and self-marking hiatus."[43]

Cohen's work constitutes either a frontier or an impasse in Hitchcock studies. Its opaque language is unlikely to inspire much direct response. In the absence of the sort of intermediaries who provided the commentary that made Raymond Bellour's untranslated essays available to English-speaking scholars,[44] Cohen seems more likely to mark a road not followed in Hitchcock studies. On the other hand, whatever power he may have to provoke productive debate, the indispensable hallmark of the most influential work in the field, could lead to a reconfiguration of Hitchcock studies that amounts both to a dissolution (making Hitchcock's work merely exemplary of the secret agents that undermine the iron rule of genre and grammar throughout visual culture) and a wider redefinition (relocating Hitchcock from film studies to visual culture). Despite Hitchcock's oft-quoted assurance to Ingrid Bergman that "it's only a movie," the work of the movies' most firmly established auteur may end by being used to dissolve film studies into the brave new world of interactive media.[45]

* * * * *

The course of Hitchcock studies as it has developed so far has been marked by features that can best be described by four retrospective models, each of them predicated on a different way critical authority is established and diffused. These models in turn suggest some general conclusions about the way the field has been organized and may change in the future.

The first and most obvious of these is the academic model in which power flows from the most prestigious research institutions. Influential scholars win tenure by the authority of their critical contributions to or transformations of a given discipline, which is confirmed by the kinds of funding—faculty lines, administrative costs, office space—that establish it as a department with sub-disciplines that correspond to university courses. Non-academics who successfully intervene in the field are frequently rewarded by the academic appointments that institutionalize their authority.

This is an excellent model for film studies as it is presently constituted, but a highly suspect model for Hitchcock studies. Aside from the fact that serious interest in Hitchcock predates the rise of film studies as an academic discipline and that no university recognizes Hitchcock studies as a discipline,[46] the field does not even fit neatly into the larger academic discipline of film studies because so much of its energy has consistently been provided by amateurs outside film studies, often outside the professoriate. All of Hitchcock's most influential early defenders were journalists—Truffaut, Rohmer, and Chabrol in France and Andrew Sarris in America—and only Sarris entered the ranks of the university.

Hitchcock studies continues to occupy a place that overlaps film studies but is not entirely contained by it. A great deal of valuable work on Hitchcock has come from outside film studies. Peter Bogdanovich and Stefan Sharff are filmmakers. Robert Kapsis and Murray Pomerance are sociologists. J. Lary Kuhns is a mathematician.[47] Peter Conrad is only the most recent of many Hitchcock commentators to come from literary studies.

Conrad's book *The Hitchcock Murders* illustrates still another way in which Hitchcock studies has occasionally departed from the model of an academic discipline: its freedom from footnotes. In most academic disciplines, the surest way to assert one's authority is to cite one's predecessors, indicating familiarity with their work as a point of departure. Conrad, by contrast, dismisses Hitchcock scholarship as the "bogus cerebration" of "conscientious axe-grinders."[48] Impatient with the empty abstractions of Hitchcock criticism, he dispenses with citation, basing his gamble on the fact that valuable new perspectives have frequently entered Hitchcock studies from outside the academy and been normalized by the discipline's centripetal force. Far more than film studies itself, Hitchcock studies has long been open to the work of amateurs like Christopher Brookhouse, the founding editor of the *Hitchcock Annual*, and Ken Mogg, the independent Australian scholar who edits the occasional journal *The MacGuffin* and presides over its affiliated website.

Clearly, the academic model does not adequately describe the development of Hitchcock studies to date. An alternative model is less institutional and more authoritarian: the theological model in which power flows from a single source (God, the Pope, the Bible) to infuse the followers beneath. This is the model Mogg evidently assumes when he attacks McGilligan on his website as "an interloper to Hitchcock studies" whose biography is "less definitive than some of us had hoped for." The principal evidence for this negative judgment offered by Mogg is that McGilligan *"completely ignores* [Mogg's book] *The Alfred Hitchcock Story,* which summarises half a lifetime's findings about Hitchcock and his films by someone said [by Dan Auiler] to know 'more about Alfred Hitchcock and his milieu than any other film critic.' "[49] In other words, Mogg is attacking McGilligan's attempt to produce a definitive biography of Hitchcock, the last word on Hitchcock whose authority is beyond question, on the grounds that it ignores Mogg's definitive interpretation of Hitchcock's work.

Under a theological model of Hitchcock studies, both McGilligan or Mogg could reasonably aspire to produce definitive work on the director, the final word that would be written into canon law or perhaps even assume scriptural authority itself. Putting aside claims McGilligan never makes to definitive status, however, Mogg's counterclaims remain problematic. Even though his MacGuffin website shows that he is both impressively well-informed about Hitchcock and avid to seize on any new facts about the production histories of his films to elaborate his own interpretations of them, Mogg is rarely receptive to the claims of high theory or individual interpretations that conflict with his. And his own critical orientation, which reads Hitchcock's films largely as dramatizations of "the life-force — or rather the life-and-death-force" — that Arthur Schopenhauer called "the cosmic Will" has evolved remarkably little despite half a lifetime's exposure to Hitchcock commentary.[50]

Nor is it clear that a definitive reading of Hitchcock's life and work, even if it were possible, would be desirable. Such work, if it were recognized as such, would surely mark the end of Hitchcock studies by rendering all further labor superfluous. A critic like Conrad might acidly observe that pulling the plug on Hitchcock studies would be all to the good, assuming of course that it were pulled after Conrad's own contribution. But the end of productive debate about Hitchcock's films, apart from dealing a mortal blow to Hitchcock studies, would make Hitchcock's films unavailable as further spurs to critical thinking about all sorts of subjects: the manufacture of fear and suspense, the opposition between good and evil, the relation between entertainment and art, the nature of authorship in the cinema and elsewhere.

A theological model of disciplinary studies is based on authoritative criticism whose force is ultimately authoritarian. But the simple absence of definitive studies of Hitchcock's life and work is no guarantee of freedom from such authori-tarianism in a third model of disciplinary studies based on Michel Foucault's work on the birth of the modern prison. In *Discipline and Punish,* Foucault argues that the rise of so-called enlightened prisons in the beginning of the nineteenth century, prisons which punished their inmates by incarceration rather than physical torture, did not end authoritarian control over the body but merely diffused and internalized its operations, making possible "the meticulous control of the operations of the body." The new prisons sought to discipline inmates through a process of spatial and temporal regimentation and the development of panoptic architectural models that encouraged prisoners to behave themselves properly because they could never be sure they were not under observation by unseen warders. A vital implication of Foucault's analysis is that the modern prison is a model for "factories, schools, barracks, hospitals." So-called humanistic disciplines of study, in Foucault's view, operate by enforcing "the power of the Norm," a disembodied but authoritarian model of normative behavior toward which all contributions to the field, like all prisoners, postulants, and schoolchildren, are urged and so urge themselves.[51]

It would be hard to deny the power of this model to explain a great deal of disciplinary field studies, especially given Foucault's insight that power is ultimately productive rather than suppressive. Recent developments in Hitchcock studies, however, indicate that a fourth model may be still more appropriate: a quasi-scriptural model that is less like the Catholic Church or Foucault's panoptic prison than like the rabbinic study of scripture that yielded endless midrashic commentaries of variable and contested authority, none of them the last word. The practice of such a group might be called Hitchcock and Company. This label is not meant to imply the corporate structure of a centrally controlled "Hitchcock Ltd." or "Hitchcock Inc.," but a more decentralized structure: a network of Hitchcock commentators—historians and interpreters, academics and amateurs, fans and professionals—joined only by their shared interest in Hitchcock. Perhaps the closest mercantile analogue is Friends and Family, the network that allowed MCI cell phone customers to obtain reduced rates on calls they made to other cell phone users they enlisted to sign up for the network. Closer analogies can be found online, in eBay and MySpace, which facilitate the self-presentations and transactions of their participants without subordinating them to corporate interests and corporate control. The ever-expanding network of Hitchcock studies is the best guarantee that it will fulfill Sidney Gottlieb's prescription to "keep de-centering activities at the center of Hitchcock studies (an irony I fully intend)."[52] Hitchcock and Company is more radically decentered than the academic and theological models, and less invisibly coercive than the model of Foucault's prison. In following the disciplinary model that places the lowest priority on discipline, it offers in turn an appealing model for any number of longer-established fields.

Even if Tom Cohen is incorrect in his implication that Hitchcock's work will help dissolve the relatively parochial field of film studies in the more capacious discipline of media studies, this is one area in which his prediction is rapidly coming true: the way the Web has expanded and transformed the possibilities of networking. These possibilities, of course, have been available in many other fields besides Hitchcock studies, from Indiana University's VICTORIA listserv for scholars of nineteenth-century British literature to DorothyL, a listserv for readers of detective fiction. Each of the models I have described has generated websites of its own. The scholarly model is perhaps best exemplified by the page listing Alfred Hitchcock resources at the University of California,

Berkeley (www.lib.berkeley.edu/MRC/hitchcockbib.html) and the site the Museum of Modern Art established in connection with its 1999 Hitchcock exhibit (www.moma. org/exhibitions/1999/hitchcock). Ken Mogg's MacGuffin site at www.labyrinth.net.au/~muffin is clearly informed by a combination of the theological and the panoptic models. Mogg archives a great deal of earlier work by various hands, produces a daily column focusing most often on interpreting specific details in Hitchcock films, and keeps an untiring eye out for new video releases or critical studies in order to pronounce judgment on them.

A surprising number of Hitchcock sites, even those created by fans rather than scholars, follow one of these three models because they are designed to disseminate information rather than generate it. But the midrashic model, which encourages interaction through forums and message boards, lives in sites as different as The World of Alfred Hitchcock (www.ahworld.net/pages/news.php) and the Internet Movie Database's Hitchcock page (www.imdb.com/name/nm0000033), both of which diminish the gap between scholars, fans, and novices by encouraging and incorporating feedback that makes their readers writers as well.

In The Gender of Modernism, Bonnie Kime Scott proposes replacing the hierarchical canon of modernist writers with a web that traces "the connections that emerge among them" and concludes after discussing several implications of these connections (through acquaintance, mutual contact with publishers, reviews and critiques) that "our understanding of modernism depends on an inadequate number of sources and is accordingly sketchy and oversimplified."[53] Hitchcock studies could well be reconfigured in an analogous way, not by emphasizing Hitchcock's connections to other filmmakers—though Orr offers a fascinating experiment along these lines—but by emphasizing the kinds of connections among Hitchcock commentators the Web is beginning to make easier and more visible. The goal would not be to award prizes to the commentators with the most connections. Instead, we would do well to recognize that they derive their authority from the quality of these connections, their continued ability to provoke debates about Hitchcock, thrillers, cinema, narrative, and the visual world that keep his work alive for everyone who takes pleasure in sharing Hitchcock's company.

Notes

I wish to express my profound gratitude to Richard Allen and Sidney Gottlieb for their comments on an earlier draft of this essay.

1. See John Belton, "Can Hitchcock Be Saved from Hitchcock Studies?" *Cineaste* 28, no. 4 (2003): 16-21.

2. Gilberto Perez, *The Material Ghost: Films and Their Medium* (Baltimore: Johns Hopkins University Press, 1998), 9.

3. Robert E. Kapsis, *Hitchcock: The Making of a Reputation* (Chicago: University of Chicago Press, 1992), 82.

4. François Truffaut, *Hitchcock,* revised edition (New York: Simon and Schuster, 1984), 61.

5. Indeed, Universal, Warner Bros., and Criterion, the most important producers controlling DVD releases of Hitchcock's films, have not only been generally scrupulous in their remastering of archival prints and their selection of supplementary materials, but have released the disks in boxed sets that emphasize Hitchcock's authorship as a selling point.

6. Robin Wood, *Hitchcock's Films* (London: Zwemmer, 1965), 9; rpt. in *Hitchcock's Films Revisited* (New York: Columbia University Press, 1989), 55.

7. Reconsidering his original question in 1989, Wood noted that "At that stage in the evolution of film criticism, the meaning would not have been significantly different if I had written `Should we take Hitchcock seriously?' " (371).

8. Raymond Durgnat, *The Strange Case of Alfred Hitchcock, or The Plain Man's Hitchcock* (London: Faber and Faber, 1974), 39.

9. Durgnat, *The Strange Case of Alfred Hitchcock,* 61, 58.

10. Wood, *Hitchcock's Films Revisited,* 146-47.

11. Wood, *Hitchcock's Films Revisited,* 154.

12. Wood, *Hitchcock's Films Revisited,* 371.

13. Laura Mulvey, *Visual and Other Pleasures* (Bloomington: Indiana University Press, 1989), 21-24.

14. Tania Modleski, *The Women Who Knew Too Much: Hitchcock and Feminist Theory* (New York: Methuen, 1988), 3.

15. Wood, *Hitchcock's Films Revisited*, 377; cf. 109.

16. Wood, *Hitchcock's Films Revisited*, 375.

17. Peter Wollen, *Signs and Meaning in the Cinema* (London: Secker and Warburg, 1969), 104.

18. See D.A. Miller, "Anal *Rope*," *Representations* 32 (Fall 1990): 114-33; Theodore Price, *Hitchcock and Homosexuality: His 50-Year Obsession with Jack the Ripper and the Superbitch Prostitute: A Psychoanalytic View* (Metuchen: Scarecrow, 1992); Robert Corber, *In the Name of National Security: Hitchcock, Homophobia, and the Political Construction of Gender in Postwar America* (Durham: Duke University Press, 1993); Lee Edelman, "Piss Elegant: Freud, Hitchcock, and the Micturating Penis," *GLQ* 2, nos. 1-2 (1995): 149-77, and *"Rear Window's* Glasshole," in *Out Takes: Essays on Queer Theory and Film,* ed. Ellis Hanson (Durham: Duke University Press, 1999), 72-96; and Robert Samuels, *Hitchcock's Bi-Textuality: Lacan, Feminisms, and Queer Theory* (Albany: State University of New York Press, 1998).

19. See John Russell Taylor, *Hitch: The Life and Times of Alfred Hitchcock* (New York: Pantheon, 1978).

20. See Donald Spoto, *The Dark Side of Genius: The Life of Alfred Hitchcock* (Boston: Little, Brown, 1983), 148-49, 513-14, 542-45.

21. Lesley Brill, *The Hitchcock Romance: Love and Irony in Hitchcock's Films* (Princeton: Princeton University Press, 1988), xiii, 3.

22. See Patrick McGilligan, *Alfred Hitchcock: A Life in Darkness and Light* (New York: HarperCollins, 2003).

23. T.S. Eliot, "Hamlet and His Problems" (1920), rpt. in *The Sacred Wood: Essays on Poetry and Criticism,* 7th ed. (London: Methuen, 1950), 99.

24. Stanley Fish, "No Bias, No Merit: The Case Against Blind Submission" (1979), in *Doing What Comes Naturally: Change, Rhetoric and the Practice of Theory in Literary and Legal Studies* (Durham: Duke University Press, 1989), 171.

25. Sidney Gottlieb, *Hitchcock on Hitchcock: Selected Writings and Interviews* (Berkeley and Los Angeles: University of California Press, 1995), xxiii.

26. See Susan Smith, *Hitchcock: Suspense, Humour and Tone* (London: British Film Institute, 2000), and James Naremore, "Hitchcock and Humor," *Strategies* 14, no. 1 (May 2001): 13-25.

27. See Stephen Rebello, *Alfred Hitchcock and the Making of Psycho* (New York: Dembner, 1990); Dan Auiler, Vertigo: *The Making of a*

Hitchcock Classic (New York: St. Martin's, 1998); Tony Lee Moral, *Hitchcock and the Making of* Marnie (Metuchen: Scarecrow, 2003); and Leonard J. Leff, *Hitchcock and Selznick: The Rich and Strange Collaboration of Alfred Hitchcock and David O. Selznick in Hollywood* (London: Weidenfeld and Nicolson, 1987).

28. See James Naremore, *Filmguide to* Psycho (Bloomington: Indiana University Press, 1973); Raymond Durgnat, *A Long Hard Look at "Psycho"* (London: British Film Institute, 2002); Stefan Sharff, *The Art of Looking in Hitchcock's* Rear Window (New York: Limelight, 1997); John Fawell, *Hitchcock's* Rear Window: *The Well-Made Film* (Carbondale: Southern Illinois University Press, 2001); Tom Ryall, *Blackmail* (London: British Film Institute, 1993); Camille Paglia, *The Birds* (London: British Film Institute, 1998); Charles Barr, *Vertigo* (London: British Film Institute, 2002); *Alfred Hitchcock's* Rear Window, ed. John Belton (Cambridge: Cambridge University Press, 2000); *Alfred Hitchcock's* Psycho: *A Casebook*, ed. Robert Kolker (New York: Oxford University Press, 2004); and Philip J. Skerry, *The Shower Scene in Hitchcock's* Psycho: *Creating Cinematic Suspense and Terror* (Lewiston, NY: Mellen, 2005).

29. See Dan Auiler, *Hitchcock's Notebooks* (New York: Avon, 1999).

30. Bill Krohn, *Hitchcock at Work* (London: Phaidon, 2000), 11, 12, 14, 15.

31. Krohn, *Hitchcock at Work,* 10.

32. See Robert A. Harris and Michael S. Lasky, *The Complete Films of Alfred Hitchcock* (New York: Citadel, 1976; revised ed., New York: Carol, 1999); Donald Spoto, *The Art of Alfred Hitchcock: Fifty Years of His Motion Pictures* (New York: Doubleday, 1976; 2nd ed., 1992); Gene D. Phillips, *Alfred Hitchcock* (Boston: Twayne, 1984); and Maurice Yacowar, *Hitchcock's British Films* (Hamden, CT: Archon, 1977).

33. See Elisabeth Weis, *The Silent Scream: Alfred Hitchcock's Sound Track* (Teaneck: Fairleigh Dickinson University Press, 1982), and Tom Ryall, *Hitchcock and the British Cinema* (Urbana: University of Illinois Press, 1986; rev. ed., London: Athlone, 1996).

34. See Charles Derry, *The Suspense Thriller: Films in the Shadow of Alfred Hitchcock* (Jefferson, NC.: McFarland, 1988; rev. ed., 2001).

35. See Paula Marantz Cohen, *Alfred Hitchcock: The Legacy of Victorianism* (Lexington: University Press of Kentucky, 1995).

36. See Charles Barr, *English Hitchcock* (Moffatt: Cameron and Hollis, 1999); Steven DeRosa, *Writing with Hitchcock: The Collaboration of Alfred Hitchcock and John Michael Hayes* (London: Faber and Faber,

2001); Royal S. Brown, "Hitchcock, Herrmann, and the Music of the Irrational," *Cinema Journal* 2, no. 2 (spring 1982): 14-49; Steven C. Smith, *A Heart at Fire's Center: The Life and Music of Bernard Herrmann* (Berkeley and Los Angeles: University of California Press, 1991), 191-273; and Patricia Hitchcock O'Connell and Laurent Bouzereau, *Alma Hitchcock: The Woman Behind the Man* (New York: Berkley, 2003).

37. John Orr, *Hitchcock and Twentieth-Century Cinema* (London: Wallflower, 2005), 29.

38. See William Rothman, *Hitchcock—The Murderous Gaze* (Cambridge: Harvard University Press, 1982).

39. Gottlieb, ed., *Hitchcock on Hitchcock*; and *Alfred Hitchcock:: Interviews* (Jackson: University of Mississippi Press, 2003).

40. Slavoj Žižek, Introduction to *Everything You Always Wanted to Know About Lacan (But Were Afraid to Ask Hitchcock)* (London: Verso, 1992), 10.

41. Tom Cohen, *Hitchcock's Cryptonomies: Secret Agents* (Minneapolis: University of Minnesota Press, 2005), xi, xii.

42. Wood, *Hitchcock's Films Revisited*, 375-76.

43. Cohen, *Hitchcock's Cryptonomies: War Machines* (Minneapolis: University of Minnesota Press, 2005), 264.

44. See Raymond Bellour, *The Analysis of Film*, ed. Constance Penley (Bloomington: Indiana University Press, 2000).

45. Adaptations of Hitchcock's work to interactive digital media have ranged from the archival—Lauren Rabinovitz and Greg Easley's CD-ROM *The Rebecca Project* (New Brunswick: Rutgers University Press, 1995), available for individual purchase; Kapsis's *Multimedia Hitchcock* (1999), a museum installation also on CD-ROM; and Stephen Mamber's *Digital Hitchcock,* an installation at UCLA's Film and Television Archive—to the more experimental installations Federico Windhausen reviews in "Hitchcock and the Found Footage Installation: Müller and Girardet's *The Phoenix Tapes*," *Hitchcock Annual* 12 (2003-04): 100-25.

46. The University of Southern California, however, does have an Alma and Alfred Hitchcock Professorship of American Film, currently held by Drew Casper.

47. See Murray Pomerance, *An Eye for Hitchcock* (New Brunswick: Rutgers University Press, 2004); and J. Lary Kuhns, "Hitchcock's *The Mountain Eagle*," *Hitchcock Annual* 7 (1998-99): 31-108.

48. Peter Conrad, *The Hitchcock Murders* (New York: Faber and Faber, 2000), xi.

49. See www.labyrinth.net.au/%7Emuffin/mcgilligan1_c.html.

50. Ken Mogg, *The Alfred Hitchcock Story* (London: Titan, 1999), 4.

51. Michel Foucault, *Discipline and Punish: The Birth of the Prison*, trans. Alan Sheridan (New York: Pantheon, 1978), 137, 228, 184.

52. Sidney Gottlieb, Introduction to *Framing Hitchcock: Selected Essays from the* Hitchcock Annual, ed. Sidney Gottlieb and Christopher Brookhouse (Detroit: Wayne State University Press, 2002), 17.

53. Bonnie Kime Scott, ed., *The Gender of Modernism: A Critical Anthology* (Bloomington: Indiana University Press, 1990), 9, 12.

Sidney Gottlieb

Hitchcock on Griffith

Throughout his career Hitchcock was an avid film watcher, and on several levels his films bear the traces of his deep immersion in the ongoing history and development of filmmaking. His characteristic "touches" and innovations all have a lineage, sometimes complex and subtle, other times strikingly obvious and direct. His works regularly include visual homages, witty allusions and borrowings, and extended recapitulations and transformations of key films (*Potemkin*, *Variety*, and *Diabolique*, for example), as well as imaginative contests with important filmmakers (such as Lang and Antonioni), illustrating the extent to which he was focused on and energized by a creative engagement with film history. T.S. Eliot's notion of the fundamental link between tradition and the individual talent applies to Hitchcock just as surely as it does to Shakespeare, and to claim that Hitchcock's cinema is composite and backward- as well as forward-looking, communal and dialogic rather than solitary, usefully reformulates rather than attacks and undermines his originality and greatness. And while Eliot and Shakespeare are useful touchstones in this regard, perhaps I should use cinematic rather than literary reference points: two of the most Hitchcockian modern filmmakers—Godard and Scorsese—are so not only because of their use of some of Hitchcock's distinctive and recognizable techniques, notions of vulnerable and volatile characters, and vision of the perils of modernity, but because of their shared passion for film history, embedding this history in their films in inventive and provocative ways. These three all know that even creatively original films are often made substantially out of other films, and that individuality is supported by a bedrock of other individuals one can stand on and push against. Each knows that a good way to history is through film history, and that one's own films to some extent have already been made by others.

But (strikingly unlike Godard and Scorsese) Hitchcock did not frequently praise other filmmakers, talk about cinematic influences, or specifically acknowledge predecessors (or contemporaries) that had an impact on him. Perhaps this is tied in with what some critics see as his general reticence to share credit and public attention with his cinematic competitors and even with his closest and most substantial and reliable co-workers, often causing rifts with such valuable but underappreciated contributors as Eliot Stannard, John Michael Hayes, and Bernard Herrmann. Or perhaps he felt that the most suitable "discourse of acknowledgment" was sufficiently written into the films themselves, by way of visual imitation, parody, homage, or transformation, and need not be otherwise highlighted or specified in interviews and essays (as he did do for other kinds of Hitchcock "moments" of stylistic subtlety and virtuosity, where he delighted in alerting the audience and crediting his own ingenuity). And yet there were a few key exceptions when it came to naming names: for example, Hitchcock was not at all reticent about repeatedly mentioning Murnau—as is well known, while he was in Germany in 1924 assisting on Graham Cutts's *The Blackguard*, he observed Murnau working in the same studio on *The Last Laugh* and was lastingly affected by this experience—and he routinely brings up Pudovkin, although primarily as a theorist, when he speaks about montage as being the essence of pure cinema.[1] Last among the major influences specifically acknowledged by Hitchcock, and perhaps least credited and examined by critics and scholars, is D.W. Griffith, referred to regularly in his statements on film and to my knowledge the only director to whom Hitchcock devoted an entire essay, filled with praise, analysis, and both implicit and explicit indications of a deeply felt kinship.

Hitchcock's essay on Griffith, titled "A Columbus of the Screen," was published in the February 21, 1931 issue of *Film Weekly*, and as far as I can tell has been virtually unnoticed since then. I have never seen it cited or otherwise referenced, and was unaware of it when I was assembling *Hitchcock on Hitchcock*, otherwise I surely would have included it as one of his important essays on film.[2] (I came across it serendipitously after the publication of that collection while continuing to troll through microfiches of early film periodicals at the British Film Institute, an activity that I am confident will unearth additional fugitive pieces written by Hitchcock.) To redress that omission, I reprint the essay in full below. In addition to making this interesting piece more easily accessible, the occasion of reprinting it also allows me an opportunity to comment on how the essay reveals some of what Griffith represents for and means to Hitchcock, and also to talk briefly about other elements of the Hitchcock-Griffith connection that I hope will be the subject of further critical examination.[3]

Hitchcock is not known as a writer of "puff" pieces (except, of course, about himself and his own works), and he did not routinely join in the time-honored ritual of lending his name to the publicity efforts of other directors or writing blurbs for their newly-released films. At first glance, this essay may seem to be an exception. As the introductory heading announces, it was "Inspired by *Abraham Lincoln*," Griffith's latest film, "now at the London Pavilion," and what the heading goes on to describe as Hitchcock's "striking tribute to its Director" is indeed filled with hyperbolic praise, including a description of the film as "one of the most moving and essentially true works of art ever accomplished." Some of the essay seems to be little more than gleanings from a studio pressbook, repeating "facts" about Griffith's many occupations before he became a director (and getting at least one minor thing wrong: rather than still a "comparative youth" of "not yet fifty-one," Griffith had just turned fifty-six years old), rehashing familiar cinematic legends (like the one about audiences responding to his close-ups by yelling "Where are their feet?"), and embellishing what Richard Schickel calls one of Griffith's "usual outlandish claims for himself" associated with the promotion of this film, that he had read 180 books on Lincoln (Hitchcock says 182), attesting to his intellectual vigor and the historical credibility of his work.[4] Art of lasting value can sometimes result when poems are made from other poems, and films from other films, but nothing good can come of publicity made from other publicity.

Yet there is much more to Hitchcock's essay than hyperbole and refried promotional material. While his high praise for the film may strike us as somewhat unwarranted, it was very much in line with the critical response at the time: Schickel surveys what he calls the "superb reviews" in the New York press and concludes that they were not only generously sympathetic to a troubled director seemingly on the rebound but properly appreciative of "the genuine merits of the film."[5] And in any event, Hitchcock's essay is only incidentally about *Abraham Lincoln*, which is mentioned only in passing, and press-release information about Griffith's life. He is much more centrally concerned with spelling out and ruminating on the details of Griffith's legacy: his influence, innovations, and perhaps most of all his archetypal status as the "Director," a heroically determined and resourceful but also perennially vulnerable figure struggling for his art, often against the industry and the audience.

Part of what makes the essay so valuable is that Hitchcock clearly takes his subject personally: without ever mentioning it directly, his focus is primarily on Griffith's legacy to him, in terms of their shared techniques, conception of film, and artistic obstacles, and his portrait of the "Old Master" is simultaneously a sketch of an emerging new "Master" of cinema who is alternately bold and justifiably anxious. Hitchcock is described in the headnote to the *Film Weekly* essay as "England's most famous film maker," but at the time it came out, he was between successes, several years past *Blackmail* and several years before his breakthrough spy thrillers, mired in *The Skin Game* and *Number Seventeen*, and in general "running for cover" during a period in which he was, as Donald Spoto notes, "confused and professionally adrift."[6]

With all this perhaps weighing on him, it is not surprising that Hitchcock would be particularly attuned to Griffith as both a cautionary figure, a reminder that "a man who has built up for himself such a giant reputation has an uphill task to keep that reputation intact," and also an inspirational model, "a man whose career the world thought finished" but who proved capable of a return to his past greatness.

The main drama of Griffith's life that appears in Hitchcock's essay has nothing to do with his drinking, failed personal relations, or bad business decisions, all of which were prominent and unfortunate elements of Griffith's life at this time, but instead revolves around his art, especially the vagaries of fame and creativity, and is envisioned in almost mythological terms. The essay begins with a personification of "The Film Public," described literally as all-powerful: "the final judge of our efforts, the arbiter of our destiny, and the be-all and end-all of our professional existence"—a vision of the public that surfaces repeatedly in Hitchcock's interviews and writings as he considers the difficulties he faced in attempting to make the kind of films he wanted to. Somewhat ominously, this power is wielded to caricature and even efface the director: the public "imagines a shadowy figure with a megaphone bawling confused orders, and leaves it at that."

This is only the first of the forces conspiring to relegate the director to insignificance, but, as Hitchcock tells the tale, a worthy hero springs forth to engage in the ongoing battle: "A giant, this man Griffith, as successful pioneers must be." The title of the essay alerts us to one of the predominant metaphors that Hitchcock will use—Griffith as an adventurous traveler—and he returns regularly to this figure of him as the discoverer of a new continent and as a man on the move, even to this day not only dreaming of but embarking on "great new voyages." While Columbus is to some extent a good name for such a figure (not himself an American as of course Griffith was, but at least associated with America), the character Hitchcock presents is actually more like Ulysses, not just a sailor or captain, but a heroic warrior, characterized by "fighting spirit," "driving force and independence."

Hitchcock uses martial and heroic terms to pull the director out of the shadows of the cinematic apparatus and picture him as a "romantic figure, ready to capture the imagination." This last phrase is purposefully double-edged: it simultaneously describes the role of the director as that of capturing the imagination on film and also suggests that great directors are thereby themselves characters of dramatic interest. Griffith is such an exemplary figure, "incomparably the greatest," and not only a subject of deserving praise but also, perhaps even more important, a key pathfinder and model for Hitchcock as he charts his course and creates his own persona. Hitchcock's appreciation of Griffith is, to be sure, a central part of this essay, rather than merely a sub-text or an incidental occasion for him to talk about another topic, but it is also the take-off point for something a bit more far-reaching: one of Hitchcock's early and most sustained arguments for the legitimacy of the director as auteur,[7] framed in high romantic and high Victorian terms as a custodian and vehicle of the imagination and as a beleaguered but capable leader, determined, like Tennyson's Ulysses, to strive, to seek, and not to yield.

The uncomprehending audience represents not only an uncaring body, disregarding and disrespecting the director perhaps because it is too enamored of the "players" who appear in front of the "veil," but also a monster of inertia, a "mass of regulated opinion." Having become accustomed to a certain kind of cinema, they fix its forms and conventions, and act as though "moving pictures had attained their final level and their ultimate, perpetual form" by 1907. Griffith rises against this, by his "creative ability" and "uncanny foresight" and also by his tremendous energy: he has both "perception" and persistence, and this combination allows him to "insist upon experiments and carry them out successfully." Griffith is Hitchcock's compelling example of how a great director is defined by singularity and innovation, not repetition or even mastery of convention, a key argument in defining the auteur and also affirming that cinematic art should be perennially dynamic, and must always be approached in a spirit of freshness and inventiveness, a spirit Hitchcock would later often summarily describe as "avoiding the cliché."

Not surprisingly, Hitchcock notes that inertia also often characterizes those who work on films as well as those who watch them, but the example he concentrates on is not one we would expect. He mentions Griffith's renowned cameraman, Billy Bitzer (normally thought of as one of Griffith's greatest allies and creative partners) as an obstacle to be overcome as the director attempted to pioneer the use of the close-up. At least in Hitchcock's version of the story, Griffith evidently had to at first go ahead without Bitzer to do what he wanted and bring the camera closer to his subjects in order "to show expression on the human face": "This was so wild, so fantastic, so utterly impossible an idea that Billy Bitzer, the all-powerful cameraman, threatened to walk out if it were proceeded with. It *was* proceeded with, and Bitzer *did* walk out—and the first close-up was recorded by his successor!" Whether or not this is historically accurate, in telling the story this way Hitchcock is able to emphasize that the introduction of the close-up was politically (using the term broadly) as well as stylistically "revolutionary" (Hitchcock's own word): that is to say, it is as important an advance in the power of the director as it is in the development of the artistic resources of film.

It is true that the rise in a director's control over a film came at the expense of the cameraman, who was often the primary shaping force of early films, but Hitchcock's description of the situation when Griffith turned to directing— "the all-important personage in a studio was the cameraman, and a director was rather less than the dust beneath his tripod-foot"—is not only somewhat exaggerated and melodramatic but strikingly adversarial. This is consistent with Hitchcock's image of Griffith as a heroic warrior, whose innovations are framed as battles, but it gives a rather skewed and partial view of the Griffith-Bitzer relationship—and perhaps an intriguing preview of Hitchcock's more than occasionally jealous and adversarial attitude toward his own cinematographers, whom he later banishes from the realm of film by famously and not entirely jokingly repeating "I wish I didn't have to shoot the picture."

Hitchcock's focus on Bitzer also draws attention away from Griffith's far more threatening adversaries. The archetypal enemy of the heroic director is, one would think, the studio, a circumstance perhaps acknowledged implicitly, by a nod and a wink, in a cryptic allusion to the "hundred new problems" that "had arisen" for Griffith while making his latest film, but otherwise conspicuous by its absence in this essay, apart from a few quick references to Griffith's bold disregard of presumably studio-imposed budget restrictions when it came to forging his art. This is a serious oversight, not only in reckoning with Griffith's struggles and achievements throughout his entire career but even more specifically appreciating his truly heroic success in making *Abraham Lincoln* against all odds, which is to say despite the relentless interference and pressure of his current studio, described in chilling detail by Schickel.[8] In his essay, Hitchcock examines a variety of key artistic dilemmas and strategies directly relevant to Griffith and also to his own activities and evolving image of himself as a filmmaker, but he did not peer very deeply into the critical and problematic relationship between the director and the studio. However even if he has a somewhat foreshortened view here, or for some reason or another feels that there are some subjects not to be broached directly on this occasion, Hitchcock nevertheless powerfully conveys his deep appreciation for Griffith's remarkable success at overcoming many of the forces both in front of as well as behind the screen that worked against a cinema of experiment and innovation.

A particularly interesting dimension of the essay is Hitchcock's brief enumeration of Griffith's most significant innovations and quick mention of the specific films that best embody his legacy. In doing this, Hitchcock was, whether he was aware of it or not, following Griffith's own lead: in an early bit of self-promotion Griffith had taken out an advertisement in the *New York Dramatic Mirror*, identifying himself as the "Producer of all great Biograph successes, revolutionizing Motion Picture drama and founding the modern technique of the art."[9] The ad also specifies a few of the "innovations which he introduced and which are now generally followed by the most advanced producers," followed by a list of some of his most noteworthy films. Hitchcock's choices of which techniques and films to highlight are very revealing.[10] The close-up, as mentioned above, is the technique he features, and it seems to represent Griffith's most vital assertion of what Hitchcock, without using the term, seems to be defining as "new" cinema, adventurous and resolutely visual. The "new" cinema most discussed at this time was the sound picture, and when Hitchcock notes somewhat elliptically that the close-up has "surmounted the obstacle of the talkies" he is in effect enlisting Griffith as one of his great allies in the struggle to forge and preserve what he will later call "pure cinema," routinely contrasted with "pictures of people talking." Griffith's legacy to "pure cinema" is spelled out even more clearly later in the essay where Hitchcock links the close-up with another one of Griffith's "discoveries in the realm of cinematography": the reaction shot (not mentioned by Griffith in his ad), first seen, according to Hitchcock, in the film *The Barrel*. These two techniques give film "its first mobility and thus its first advantage over stage plays."

Hitchcock's references to techniques and films get briefer as he goes along, which is a shame, particularly when he comes to mention Griffith's *The Avenging Conscience*. Perhaps the most intriguing and tantalizing reference in the entire essay is his identification of this film as "the forerunner and inspiration of most of the modern German films, to which we owe so much artistically." Much indeed has been made of Hitchcock's debt to German films and filmmaking practices of the Weimar period,[11] but in this one short sentence Hitchcock turns us to a deeper source of what we normally think of as his expressionism and a more complex chart of influence than we usually draw. In the very least, we need to expand our understanding of the American influence on

Hitchcock (something which he repeatedly called attention to by saying he was "American-trained")[12] to include more than "modern" production techniques and studio organization and a smoothly paced narrative style; and we may find it useful to follow up on Hitchcock's hint that Griffith influenced him in a refracted and mediated way, via German films, as well as directly.

Now is not the time to do a detailed analysis of *The Avenging Conscience,* but it is worth mentioning a few aspects of it that may have made it a particularly critical film for Hitchcock. It is based primarily on two works by Poe, "The Tell-tale Heart" and "Annabel Lee," the latter quoted throughout the film and used to add elements of frustrated erotic desire to a story of inscrutable obsession — a Hitchcockian formula if ever there was one. Hitchcock was a great lover of Poe, and Griffith was undoubtedly a key figure in helping him find ways to give cinematic form to the elements of Poe that he admired. The film effectively, even poetically, uses darkness, shadows, and chiaroscuro lighting effects, and the main character played by Henry Walthall is a precursor of a recurrent figure in Hitchcock, a tortured man and furtive murderer, one who (at least apparently, until much of the action is shown to be a hallucinatory fantasy) has killed, hidden the body, and lives undiscovered in "normal" society. Hitchcock did not need to go to *The Cabinet of Dr. Caligari* or *Nosferatu* to find these elements to weave throughout many of his most important works, including *The Lodger, Shadow of a Doubt,* and *Psycho.*

Finally, some of the special effects used by Griffith to create mystery, terror, and a sense of the uncanny may have been useful to Hitchcock as he attempted to evoke similar moods: for example, the double-exposures used to show the haunting of the main character in *The Avenging Conscience,* although by no means unique to Griffith, may well lie somewhere behind Hitchcock's use of this technique in *The Pleasure Garden,* where at the end of the film Levett is revisited by the image of a native woman he has drowned. This is not a particularly subtle technique, and later was far surpassed by Hitchcock's inventive use of unseen presences haunting a character or environment (as in *Rebecca*) and more complex attempts to show the interaction of concrete and imaginary worlds (as in *Vertigo*), but Griffith is nonetheless a major contributor to Hitchcock's increasingly adventurous visualizations of the mysterious, the invisible, and the uncanny.

In addition to his insightful comment on *The Avenging Conscience*, Hitchcock notes other important "discoveries" made by Griffith, not only in cinematography (for example, soft focus in *Broken Blossoms*) but also in personnel: he gives a long list of very well-known actors and actresses associated with Griffith, and the subtle insinuation is, I think, that he not only discovered but helped create them. The intimation here that directors not only use but make stars, and play a major role in the transformation of a Gladys Smith into a Mary Pickford, is echoed repeatedly in many of Hitchcock's later pronouncements on his own relations with his featured players.

But for Hitchcock, perhaps Griffith's greatest contribution to cinema comes as a result of the cumulative force of his many innovations and discoveries, and is summarized as the overall effect of his signature film, *The Birth of a Nation*: "With this picture, at one stroke, the director obtained popular recognition of the new art-form." Hitchcock's argument here is compressed but each term and metaphor he uses is extremely suggestive. The world infantilizes the cinema, but Griffith forces it to "publicly acknowledge" not only the maturity but the "legitimacy of the child." This "great step forward" comes because audiences accept that film is not only an art form (presumably rather than a mere commodity or low attraction) but one that deserves and draws mass attention and patronage. Hitchcock spent a lifetime arguing as well as attempting to demonstrate that film could appeal to low and high, mass audiences as well as critics; that it could be a blend of old and new, conventional as well as avant-garde; that it could make money and be a vehicle of personal expression, creativity, and vision; and that it could challenge and disturb as well as please and satisfy. All this, though spelled out only in shorthand here, marks the "perfection of . . . entertainment," the highest reach of film, and the specific and enduring legacy of Griffith.

In the stirring conclusion of this essay, Hitchcock works himself up into a kind of rhetorical passion rare in his writings as he intones Griffith's name, almost funereally— "Remember David Wark Griffith"—and reminds us that his signature is to this day written "in plainly traceable form" in every film that we watch, and that he is the perennial torchbearer for filmmakers, deserving the respect of all filmwatchers "as the man who has contributed more than any other" to the development of cinema. For a person usually so reticent about crediting and celebrating another filmmaker's achievement, the concluding peroration—indeed the tone of the entire essay—is extraordinary. Perhaps the ultimate tribute from one filmmaker to another is Godard's simple statement, on behalf of himself and all other filmmakers, about Orson Welles (interestingly, just after pairing Welles with Griffith): "All of us, always, will owe him everything."[13] Many years before Godard, Hitchcock found his own way to say virtually the same thing in his praise of Griffith as "the first in his line who really mattered."

Notes

1. I would also add Chaplin to this brief list. Hitchcock more than occasionally mentioned Chaplin, and the connection between the two is very intriguing. It would be well worth studying Hitchcock's appreciation of Chaplin's narrative economy, auteurial control, "presence," and individual style; the substantial influence on him of *A Woman of Paris*; and their shared dark sense of humor, Cockney attitudes (despite the attempt of each to be "cosmopolitan" and worldly, they never lost all traces of provinciality), and grim "take" on the world. Chaplin's influence on Hitchcock is not nearly as deep as Griffith's, but it is substantial and rarely discussed.

2. Sidney Gottlieb, ed., *Hitchcock on Hitchcock: Selected Writings and Interviews* (Berkeley and Los Angeles: University of California Press, 1995).

3. I discuss Hitchcock's technical and stylistic, thematic, and conceptual debts to Griffith in detail in a companion piece to this present essay, titled "Hitchcock and Griffith."

4. Richard Schickel, *D.W. Griffith: An American Life* (New York: Simon and Schuster, 1984), 556. As will be evident in what follows, I rely heavily on Schickel's remarkably well-documented and insightful study for information about Griffith.

5. Schickel, *D.W. Griffith*, 556.

6. Donald Spoto, *The Dark Side of Genius: The Life of Alfred Hitchcock* (New York: Ballantine Books, 1984), 149.

7. From very early in his career Hitchcock was outspoken about the central importance of the director of a film. For example, at a meeting of the London Film Society in 1925, he argued for the star-status and high visibility of the director: "*We* make a film succeed. The name of the director should be associated in the public's mind with a quality product. Actors come and actors go, but the name of the director should stay clearly in the mind of the audiences (quoted in Spoto, *The Dark Side of Genius*, 80). And in another early essay, "Films We Could Make" (1927), while making a case for what he called "One-Man Pictures," he suggested that films are the "babies" of a director "just as much as an author's novel is the offspring of his imagination. And that seems to make it all the more certain that when moving pictures are really artistic they will be created entirely by one man"; reprinted in *Hitchcock on Hitchcock*, 167.

8. Schickel, *D.W. Griffith*, 552-56.

9. This ad is reprinted in facsimile and discussed in David Cook, *A History of Narrative Film*, fourth edition (New York: W.W. Norton and Co., 2004), 63, and also nicely analyzed in Schickel, *D.W. Griffith*, 202-03.

10. What he chooses to leave out is also interesting. This is a short essay and we should not expect Hitchcock to give a comprehensive account of Griffith and his influence, but it is at least worth noting some of the most striking and in some respects surprising omissions here. There are at least three characteristic elements of Griffith's films valued very highly by Hitchcock (as we know from other writings and interviews) not mentioned in this essay, even in passing: Hitchcock does not talk here about the chase, which in a much later interview he describes as "the core of the

movie" (see his essay with that title, reprinted in *Hitchcock on Hitchcock*, 125-32); he doesn't mention suspense, a central part of Griffith's films, as he notes in his "Lecture at Columbia University" (1939), reprinted in *Hitchcock on Hitchcock*, 272, and of course a defining mark of his own films—although not so much the ones he had made by the time he wrote this essay; and he doesn't bring up montage (either in general as the linking of bits of film, or more specifically in terms of Griffith's signature mode of intercutting), which comes to be the key component in his definition of "pure cinema."

11. See, for example, Sidney Gottlieb, "Early Hitchcock: The German Influence," *Hitchcock Annual* 8 (1999-2000): 100-30; Joseph Garncarz, "German Hitchcock," *Hitchcock Annual* 9 (2000-01): 73-99; Thomas Elsaesser, "Too Big and Too Close: Alfred Hitchcock and Fritz Lang," *Hitchcock Annual* 12 (2003-04); and Hitchcock's own comments on the subject in an interview with Bob Thomas, "Alfred Hitchcock: The German Years" (1973), reprinted in *Alfred Hitchcock: Interviews*, ed. Sidney Gottlieb (Jackson: University of Mississippi Press, 2003), 156-59.

12. See, for example, Hitchcock's comments on being "deeply entrenched in American cinema" in François Truffaut, *Hitchcock* (New York: Simon and Schuster, 1985), 124-25.

13. Cited as the epigraph in Joseph McBride, *What Ever Happened to Orson Welles? A Portrait of an Independent Career* (Lexington: University of Kentucky Press, 2006), vi. As McBride notes, Godard made this statement in *The Orson Welles Story*, a 1982 BBC television documentary produced by Leslie Megahey and Alan Yentob.

ALFRED HITCHCOCK

A Columbus of the Screen

The Film Public—that Public which is the final judge of our efforts, the arbiter of our destiny, and the be-all and end-all of our professional existence—rarely lifts aside the thick veil before which the players perform, to catch a glimpse of the personality behind. It imagines a shadowy figure with a megaphone bawling confused orders, and leaves it at that—and it is just as well that it should be so, for the director is not usually a romantic figure, ready to capture the imagination.

Incomparably the Greatest

However, there are exceptions; and incomparably the greatest of these is David Wark Griffith, who has just completed his twenty-third year in connection with moving pictures, and who, in spite of his comparative youth—he is not yet fifty-one—is known affectionately and even reverently throughout the film world as "The Old Master."

A giant, this man Griffith, as successful pioneers must be. It is not only, or even chiefly, the hard work and the thought, the creative ability and the almost uncanny foresight for which we are indebted to him, but the fighting spirit which prompted him to force his way against opposition, to overcome prejudice, and to bore his persistent path through the mass of regulated opinion which held, in 1907, that moving pictures had attained their final level and their ultimate, perpetual form.

Reprinted from *Film Weekly*, February 21, 1931, p. 9, with several small errors silently corrected.

Driving Force and Independence

As to his qualifications, he certainly touched life at many points, as newspaper reporter, dramatic critic, actor, book salesman, free-lance journalist, "puddler" in an ironworks, rust-scraper, hop picker, dramatist, film actor, scenario writer, and, finally, director—albeit this last in the days when the all-important personage in a studio was the cameraman, and a director was rather less than the dust beneath his tripod-foot. However, Griffith has the distinction of having been the first of his line who really mattered, for he had not only the perception of greater things in the future of the screen, but the driving force and independence with which to insist upon experiments and carry them out successfully.

In these days of hundreds of thousands of pounds being lavished on a single film it is almost incredible that there should have been a serious split, amounting to a major crisis, in the old Biograph Company because Griffith kept his unit on location for half the night and ran the total cost of a production up to ten pounds! Yet that was considered mad extravagance in those groping days.

And this was nothing to the upheaval caused by his revolutionary suggestion that shots should be taken close enough to show expression on the human face. This was so wild, so fantastic, so utterly impossible an idea that Billy Bitzer, the all-powerful cameraman, threatened to walk out if it were proceeded with. It *was* proceeded with, and Bitzer *did* walk out—and the first close-up was recorded by his successor!

Bitzer's judgment seemed vindicated when the audience, thinking there was something wrong with the picture, hooted and yelled, "Where are their feet?" but the close-up has survived their disfavour, and even, though with greater difficulty, surmounted the obstacle of the talkies.

His Discoveries

During his association with Biograph, D.W. Griffith tried out quite a number of players whom he considered promising, among them being a pretty girl named Gladys Smith, who afterwards adopted the screen name of Mary Pickford; two sisters named Gish; Blanche Sweet, Owen Moore (who afterwards married Mary Pickford), Alice Joyce, Lionel Barrymore, Mabel Normand, Mack Sennett, Henry B. Walthall, Richard Barthelmess, and Constance Talmadge.

A formidable array—but even more vitally important than these were his discoveries in the realms of cinematography. In a film called "The Barrel," long forgotten except as pure history, Griffith first cut away from a scene to show the reaction of bystanders. This, together with the close-up, gave the film its first mobility and thus its first advantage over stage plays.

Then, after he left the Biograph Company and found himself, in association with Mutual Reliance, actually in command of a sizeable sum of money, he "splashed" twenty-thousand pounds on "The Birth of a Nation."

A Great Step Forward

With this picture, at one stroke, the director obtained popular recognition of the new art-form. "The cinema," the world persisted, "is in its infancy"—oblivious of the fact that it was then twelve or fourteen years old. But the legitimacy of the child was publicly acknowledged, and that was a great step forward.

In "Hearts of the World" we had our first war picture. In "Broken Blossoms" (his first film with United Artists) we made the acquaintance of soft focus.

Hardly any filmgoer of to-day has ever heard of "The Avenging Conscience," but that picture made in the first year of the War, was the forerunner and inspiration of most of the modern German films, to which we owe so much artistically.

A long series of arduous voyages into uncharted seas, and explorations of unknown territories . . . and at last the traveller, weary but full of honours, put his slippered feet on the fender and began to dream. And in his dream he saw possibilities of great new voyages; gradually the old power came into his brain, the old joy of conquest into his heart, and the Old Master, the man whose career the world thought finished, set sail again and made "Abraham Lincoln," one of the most moving and essentially true works of art ever accomplished.

The Old Fighting Spirit

It was not an easy voyage. A hundred new problems had arisen; and a man who has built up for himself such a giant reputation has an uphill task to keep that reputation intact. But he tackled the job with his old fighting spirit and his old thoroughness (he is said to have read 182 accounts of the life of Lincoln before beginning to outline the story)—with such result as the world will acclaim.

Remember David Wark Griffith; every time you go to the cinema you enjoy, in some indirect but plainly traceable form, the fruits of his labours; to the vast multitude of filmgoers he is the man who has contributed more than any other to the perfection of their entertainment; and to us who are endeavouring to explore new territories and to carry on his torch he is the honoured Head of our profession.

James M. Vest

The Making of Downhill
and Its Impact on Hitchcock's Reputation

Relatively few details about the making of *Downhill* appear in Hitchcock biographies or even in such specialized studies as Maurice Yacowar's *Hitchcock's British Films*, Charles Barr's *English Hitchcock,* and Bill Krohn's *Hitchcock at Work*.[1] This scholarly inattention is largely due to the relative unavailability of pertinent documentation for consultation and of the film for viewing. It may also reflect the wildly diverging sentiments expressed by those who have seen *Downhill*, including paradoxical comments by the filmmaker himself. Barr considered it "not a film with a strong claim to being rescued from obscurity," whereas John Russell Taylor judged it to be "one of [Hitchcock's] liveliest and most joyously inventive silent films"; its director thought of it as a minor work based upon a "rather poor" play that nevertheless afforded opportunities to "experiment" cinematographically.[2]

One of the most underestimated of Hitchcock's films, *Downhill* merits attention on several accounts: for the creative *élan* it elicited from its cast and crew, for its cinematic daring, and for the light it sheds on a crucial moment in British filmmaking and on the careers and personal lives of Alfred and Alma Hitchcock. *Downhill's* planning and production schedule coincided not only with Hitchcock's status as an emerging director and as husband to one of the industry's most promising editors, but also with the movie industry's upheavals in 1926-27, with the advent of cinematic sound, with rampant protectionist concerns in

Britain, and with a bold internationalizing tactic on the part of Gainsborough Pictures.

The present essay uses sources contemporary with the production, many of them long overlooked, to fill lacunae concerning the making of *Downhill*. It aims to contribute to a fuller understanding of Hitchcock's working conditions and of his inventiveness at a turning point in his career. In the process it underscores the need for increased attention to Hitchcock's earliest films, particularly those made in collaboration with producer Michael Balcon, in the hope that they may become more widely available for viewing and studying.

Gainsborough Pictures in the Mid-1920s

Nearly three years before *Downhill* went into production, Balcon acquired from Famous Players-Lasky the cavernous building that would become Gainsborough Studios, a former power plant on Poole Street in the north London borough of Hackney, beside the misty Islington Canal.[3] That building provided 6,250 square feet of interior filming space on two levels, connected by a heavy-duty elevator. Moreover, Balcon gained access to state-of-the-art technology including advanced arc and spot lighting as well as Bell & Howell cameras offering superior focusing flexibility and steadiness. With the facility, Balcon inherited a first-rate production crew, among them technicians versed in up-to-date practices. He also profited from the talents of well-known cinematographer Claude L. McDonnell, as well as those of a set decorator and title designer with aspirations for directing, Alfred Hitchcock. Early in 1927 they would all collaborate on *Downhill*.[4]

Long an outspoken proponent of British film production in the widest possible context, Balcon addressed the challenges of making films "not only for this country, but for the world," the alternative being, in his terms, "a lamentable leveling down" of production standards.[5] Referencing American-made films, he issued a call for British movies to "comply with the accepted standards of picture production" and strove to respect that dictum in his work at Gainsborough. Balcon wanted to make films that could be distributed internationally. Those broad-ranging concepts as well as some of the practical problems they encountered would be reflected in *Downhill*'s emphasis on foreign settings and on cinematic experimentation.

In summer 1926 Picadilly Pictures, co-owned by Balcon in partnership with American actor Carlyle Blackwell, acquired all of Gainsborough's shares. Problems arose when financier C.M. Woolf, who bankrolled production for most Gainsborough films, became chairman of Piccadilly and compelled Balcon to have Gainsborough's product distributed by his own company, W. & F., which handled British distribution only. Balcon became increasingly concerned about Gainsborough's restrictive relationship with Woolf and loss of international market. In March 1927, while *Downhill* was in production, Woolf sold W. & F. to Gaumont-British, the largest producer-exhibitor in Britain. Amid these maneuvers Balcon's sense of independence diminished, and he and Hitchcock, both of whom valued creative freedom, actively sought alternatives. By that summer Hitchcock was working full-time for newly-formed British International Pictures. Within a few months, Gainsborough Studios became Gainsborough Pictures Ltd., with Woolf accompanied in the boardroom by Maurice Ostrer of Gaumont-British. By April 1928 Gainsborough was a wholly-owned subsidiary of Gaumont-British.[6]

Adding to the sense of instability in the industry was the Cinematograph Films Act of 1927, popularly known as the Quota Bill, intended to encourage an increase in British film production so as to combat the onslaught of American pictures. The resulting advent of "quota quickies" and ensuing hotly-debated issues of "quality vs. quickies" dominated discussions in trade magazines for months.[7]

The production history of *Downhill* reflects its relationship to the emerging low-cost "quickie" culture as well as some departures from that culture. It was made with economy on a tight schedule. Stringent conditions are evident in some of its sets, in its editing, and in its abrupt ending.[8] Moreover, the production schedule for Hitchcock's next picture necessitated completing some footage for *Downhill* while on location for *Easy Virtue*. Overlapping productions were common but challenging, and in this instance the overlap contributed to problems of continuity.

Difficulties inherent in times of corporate flux, of governmental and industrial pressures, and of grueling production schedules converged in *Downhill*, which eventually emerged in a form that managed to reflect creativity fostered by stress. Knowledge of its production history can enhance appreciation of its attention to emotional and psychological content, to narrative irony and visual impact, to economy and innovation—traits characteristic of its producer and director.

Preproduction at Islington
and a Honeymoon on the Continent

The final weeks of 1926 were remarkable for Hitchcock, both personally and professionally. On December 2 he married his highly respected colleague Alma Reville in the opulent Brompton Oratory in Kensington. The marriage of this "clever and very likeable couple" was reported in *Kinematograph Weekly*, along with assurance that Mrs. Hitchcock would not retire totally from filmmaking.[9] Meanwhile at Gainsborough plans were coalescing for filming the stage play *Down Hill*, authored by Ivor Novello and Constance Collier under the pen name David L'Estrange.[10] The "probable" commitment to the cinematic project of the play's co-author and male lead was reported on the Hitchcocks' wedding day and confirmed within a fortnight.[11] On December 16, Gainsborough teasingly announced that a film version of the play was soon to be directed by a "big name," and a week later that name was revealed.[12]

While the newlyweds were honeymooning in Paris and Saint Moritz, preparations for filming proceeded in London. By the end of December Novello had signed a contract with

Gainsborough to make three films in 1927.[13] His first project would be to recreate the role of the falsely-accused Roddy Berwick in *Down Hill*, under Hitchcock's direction. Negotiations for the rights to that play were concluded on January 3, 1927. At this point the original title was elided into the single word that would designate the film. In assigning rights to Gainsborough, Collier and Novello insisted that their collective pseudonym David L'Estrange should appear prominently on the film's main title. Consequently, moviegoers' contact with *Downhill* would begin with a statement reflecting the priorities and exigencies of the movie industry in early 1927:

C.M. Woolf and Michael Balcon

present

IVOR NOVELLO

in

DOWNHILL

by David L'Estrange

with

ISABEL JEANS

Directed by

ALFRED HITCHCOCK

COPYRIGHT 1927 BY GAINSBOROUGH PICTURES LTD.

The fact that the director's name appeared in relatively large lettering was a reflection of Hitchcock's emerging prominence and a feather in his cap.[14]

From the start, the schedule was tight, with production slated to begin in mid-January. A screenplay had to be finalized, sets designed and constructed, location sites coordinated, and players hired. When the Hitchcocks returned from their honeymoon and took up residence in the apartment at 153 Cromwell Road—near Brompton Oratory and the Royal Albert Hall—which would be their home base until 1939, *Downhill* was moving into high gear at Gainsborough.

First there was the adaptation of the theatrical play into a suitable screenplay. Conceived for the stage as a series of tableaux, the story needed to be refitted for the screen. The plot centers on Roddy Berwick, an upper-class public school student-athlete with a flair for the histrionic, whose supposed dishonor—he gallantly assumes the burden of guilt for his roommate, who is accused of getting a girl pregnant—leads to a life of increasing degradation, initially in the theaters of London, then in a cabaret in Paris, and finally in a hovel on the docks of Marseilles. Eventually he returns to welcoming arms in England and is exonerated. In the Novello-Collier play, Roddy is presented as a temperamental, spoiled son of *nouveaux-riches* parents; his devoted friendship for his roommate, Tim, carries him through a series of difficulties toward a fresh start in America.

This basic story line was radically modified in a twenty-page filmic treatment prepared for Gainsborough by Ivor Montagu, a prime mover of the London Film Society who had served as final editor on *The Lodger*. Montagu's treatment presented Roddy as a race-car driver, given to piano playing and drugs, eventually brought to his senses by a suitable love interest in the person of his headmaster's daughter. Alert to the importance of music in cinema and anticipating synchronized sound, Montagu proposed that a musical leitmotif should be incorporated into this picture in the form of a recording of a "flowing melody, in a minor key . . . provided by Mr. Novello," to be played in theaters to accompany scenes of Roddy at the piano.[15] Given the constraints of time and technology, the sonorization plan was scrapped, along with Montagu's convoluted narrative, in favor of a non-musical screenplay by Eliot Stannard that retained the basic story line of the original play while accentuating visual elements emphasizing physical activity and geographic and mental dislocation.[16]

With a screenplay nearing completion, set design could advance toward construction. Gainsborough's dual stage areas, each two stories tall, allowed for simultaneous construction of several sets, and that space was used effectively in making *Downhill*. Hitchcock himself had experience in set design, and one can readily imagine him influencing the decor for this project. Among the sets constructed were an art-deco foyer for a modern London flat, its high-ceilinged bedroom and parlor, a stolid drawing room for the Berwick mansion, a spacious Parisian dance hall, an outsized and expressionistically-lit hovel in Marseilles, a multi-functional candy shop with inviting back rooms, a ship's hold, a dormitory suite, stairwells, and an imposing headmaster's office with (apparently) leaded windows that would figure prominently in publicity for the film.

Throughout January actors were hired with dual projects in mind. Robin Irvine, Isabel Jeans, Ian Hunter, and Violet Farebrother signed on for two films in tandem. Irvine would assume the role of Tim Wakeley, Roddy's weak-willed roommate in *Downhill*, and would then become the male lead in *Easy Virtue*. Farebrother would participate in two brief, unflattering sequences in the former production in anticipation of a substantial role in the latter. Jeans, who had previously starred with Novello in Gainsborough's *The Rat* (1925) and *The Triumph of the Rat* (1926), would become the female lead both in *Downhill*, as the saucy spendthrift actress Julia Blue, and in *Easy Virtue*, as the much-maligned Larita Filton. By February it was determined that Hunter would play Julia's self-serving companion, Archie, in the first film and the plaintiff's lawyer in the second.[17]

Among the staff, scenarist Stannard continued his long-term professional relationship with Hitchcock while Claude McDonnell, cinematographer on several projects for Gainsborough, prepared to shoot this pair of films. *The Picturegoer* made much of the latter's contributions to these projects, calling him "one of the finest cameramen in Europe."[18] Ivor Montagu was slated to serve as editor and creative consultant on both pictures, but a tiff about an "impossible" Hitchcockian camera trick in a taxicab interfered with their collaboration.[19] Frank Mills was assigned to the production as assistant director, a role filled in previous Hitchcock films by Alma Reville.

It was not apparent at first that Hitchcock should direct both movies. Although the *Easy Virtue* project was heralded in early January, the name of its director was not released to the press until late February, when *Bioscope* announced: "Alfred Hitchcock, the brilliant young director, who is on the final stages of *Downhill*, will commence work, immediately on completion of this film, on Noel Coward's *Easy Virtue*."[20]

Chief among the participants in *Downhill* who did not carry through to *Easy Virtue* was the male lead. Novello may have exercised his contractual right of refusal, preferring the principal role in the film version of another Coward piece, *The Vortex*, under the direction of Adrian Brunel. It is possible that Novello took umbrage at published reports that in *The Lodger* Hitchcock had succeeded in transforming him from a mere "screen matinee idol" into "an actor."[21] *Downhill* would be his last picture with Hitchcock.

Most of *Downhill*'s other players were on the payroll as of mid-January. Among them were Norman McKinnel, cast as Roddy's father, and Ben Webster, who would play the headmaster. By late January they were joined by Sybil Rhoda, the youthful Stoll Award winner who would play Tim Wakeley's sister. Casting the finagling Archie proved difficult. The name of Miles Mander, who had appeared in *The Pleasure Garden*, was mentioned, then dropped. Finally, well into February, Hunter's participation was confirmed and casting was complete.[22]

Gainsborough's reputation for getting value for money in its players was upheld in this production. Annette Benson, just back from a five-month assignment in France, was forced to gear up quickly for the role of the impassioned, high-stepping confectioner's assistant, Mabel; and Barbara Gott would do double duty as Mme Michet, "La Patronne" of the Paris dance hall sequences, and also as an unnamed woman in the segments set in Marseilles.[23]

In this context it is likely that, in the name of economy among other motives, Hitchcock contemplated making a cameo appearance in *Downhill*, as he had done in *The Lodger* and would do again in *Easy Virtue* and subsequent films. If he indeed followed through on that idea, that footage appears to have gone missing.

In its February 3 issue *Bioscope* published photos of Novello and Irvine costumed for their roles in *Downhill*, and an article on the same page confirmed the gradual completion of casting for secondary roles in that film, noting that "Lilian Braithwaite is to play a mother role and Jerrold Robertshaw and Gladys Jennings have been given parts."[24] That article ended with a comment which attested to the interest that this production and Hitchcock's growing reputation as director held within the industry. It stated that aspiring director Basil Dean "spent some time watching Mr. Hitchcock at work" in preparation for *The Constant Nymph*, which Dean would direct for Gainsborough that summer, assisted by Alma Reville. The article concluded that Dean's time observing Hitchcock would be "well spent." At least in some circles, Hitchcock was now viewed as an exemplar, and his current project held interest as a potential model for other filmmakers.

Production

Kinematograph Weekly's January 20, 1927 issue confirmed that "Alfred Hitchcock has now begun the Gainsborough production of *Downhill*."[25] *Bioscope* reported the start date as Monday, January 17, and noted a week later that Hitchcock had "made excellent progress on *Downhill* . . . in the public school [interiors] and village scenes, which form the opening sequence of the picture." Soon thereafter *Kinematograph Weekly* reported that "Claude McDonnell, at the camera, has already obtained much fine quality, and the studio atmosphere, in moist mid-January, was clear as crystal."[26] Principal photography continued until mid-March, with supplemental footage added into early April.

Early in the production period Gainsborough released two other Hitchcock films. *The Pleasure Garden* began its commercial run on January 24, and *The Lodger* followed on February 14. Together, they served to focus considerable attention on the director's current project. *The Pleasure Garden* furthered the reputation of "this capable director" in professional circles, while *The Lodger* met with great public success, and both films contributed to growing interest in Hitchcock's ability to appeal to a "popular" audience and to attract a "better class" of viewers to the cinema.[27]

Amid talk of Hitchcock's recent efforts, contemporary trade publications shed light on aspects of *Downhill*'s production schedule. In early February *Kinematograph Weekly*'s Patrick L. Mannock reported on his visit to two sets: the headmaster's office on the ground floor, where Mannock witnessed the filming of the accusation scene, and the candy shop on the larger second level, where shooting had recently ended.[28] *The Picturegoer* also commented on the accusation scene in its chatty way: "We recently watched Ivor Novello start off on his perilous journey 'downhill,' in the film of that name, when, as a college boy, he faced the wrongful accusations of Annette Benson, who plays a local vamp . . . with charm and vigor."[29]

Bioscope reported frequently on the production's progress, with special emphasis on segments featuring public transport: filming of the Underground sequence was accomplished around midnight on Saturday, February 26, at the Maida Vale station, with the aid of a crew of electricians and assistants, it reported, and the scenes involving the omnibus were shot on March 18.[30] The subway sequence captivated commentators and held a special appeal for the director. Although in subsequent interviews Hitchcock pointed out the heavy-handedness of showing his protagonist's physical descent into the Underground, his recollections of the circumstances surrounding this shoot remained among his most cherished. Since the sequence had to be filmed when trains were not running, Hitchcock, Novello, and crew arrived around midnight. The director was on his way home from a fancy theatrical premiere to which he had worn formal attire. He delighted in recounting how he directed this scene dressed in "white tie and top hat" and called it "the most elegant moment of direction I've ever had."[31]

Bioscope commented at length on the party that Gainsborough threw on March 10 for press and exhibitors on the dance hall set constructed for the film. "To celebrate the completion of Alfred Hitchcock's *Downhill*," the correspondent reported, studio executives organized a midnight cabaret that continued into the wee hours: "At a quarter to four the following morning, a big crowd was still dancing to the music provided by W. Trytel's band."[32] Among the revelers were director Adrian Brunel and Constance Collier as well as Novello, Jeans, and Hunter. During the course of the evening Hitchcock had his own sort of fun, hinting inscrutably at a "surprise ending" for his film.

The popular film magazine *Picture Show* dispatched veteran writer Edith Nepean to Islington to report on "the new Alfred Hitchcock film."[33] Nepean chronicled developments during production, sometimes revealing details about particular props or costumes or cinematic processes. For example, color-conscious readers would learn that the talisman school cap that made thirty-four-year-old Novello look "sixteenish at most" was blue-striped. On a subsequent visit Nepean, intrigued to catch Novello doing a scene representing delirium, described the event in considerable detail: "A gramophone was wailing a plaintive air, the cameraman was moving hither and thither, the set was closed in with black velvet, and Ivor was going through . . . delirium, delight, terror." This "tiny intimate scene," the reporter opined, was "just a wee bit for *Downhill*" that nevertheless would count heavily in "a big production."

Kinematograph Weekly also sent a correspondent to the set twice and ran a publicity photo featuring Novello and Jeans in its March 10 issue. That same publication documented the final exterior British location shoots for the film on Sunday, March 27—a "school Rugby match at Ashbridge Park," in which the director was assisted by "the good will of some Oxford undergraduates"—and also announced Hitchcock's departure for France three days later to wrap shooting for this film and to begin *Easy Virtue*.[34]

*Retakes and Cuts: Traces of a Torn Curtain,
a Smashed Vase, and a Broken Chair*

The *Picturegoer*'s April 1927 issue ran an article titled
"Downhill with Ivor," featuring E.E. Barett's reflections on his
excursions to Gainsborough Studios to observe filming. His
first visit occurred during the early days of production. At the
office of the headmaster, Barett watched as Benson's Mabel
accused Novello's Roddy, in a "spirited and fiery manner," of
not having done right by her.[35] Having worked herself into a
"state of trembling hysteria," she was escorted out of the
office, and the camera stopped. Almost immediately "Ivor lost
that hangdog expression," and the perky actress stepped back
onto the set, "smil[ing] upon her victim of a moment before."
Between takes she confided to Barett, "Yes, I'm the girl that
causes all the trouble" in this film. After an adjustment of
lighting, the encounter was reshot, with Benson "going
through the whole scene once again, with enthusiastic
hatred."

On his second visit some days later, Barett witnessed a
fight scene between Novello and Ian Hunter.[36] Barett was
startled by the sight of Novello's hand protruding through a
top hat, a casualty of battle. Barett was also impressed by a
protective wooden frame surrounding the camera, leaving
only a "small, square hole" for shooting. Hunter had just
"dragged down" a curtain. He now stood holding a chair,
which "on the word of command" he threw at Novello, who
dodged it. The chair broke at his feet, then was reassembled
by crew members and thrown again. Some half-dozen retakes
later, when "the chair was so weak that it literally couldn't
stand," the scene was judged completed. Next Novello hurled
a large, fancy vase directly at the carefully protected camera.
When the porcelain smashed on the wooden frame, he was
supplied with another vase and then "repeated the routine in
the interest of a better shot." Barett concluded that Hitchcock
was looking for gags to enliven the "banal" plot, attempting
to create a "comedy angle" calculated to add "humorous
touches."

Although relatively little of the fight scene survives in extant prints, there is ample evidence to support several of Barett's observations. Roddy is shown discovering Archie's hat and making a fist over it, but his violent thrust is missing. Similarly the curtain in question is clearly visible throughout the sequence, covering the glass door that connects the parlor to the bedroom; however, by the end of the fight it is rumpled, dangling on its disconnected rod. The shot of Archie tearing at it has been eliminated. Although no evidence of the chair smashing survives, Barett's observations concerning the broken vase are supported indirectly. *Bioscope*'s Herbert Thompson confirmed:

> One of the big scenes in *Downhill* . . . is a fight between Roddy . . . and Archie. . . . Although the fight is waged in all seriousness, Hitchcock's direction should turn it into a piece of genuine comedy. The fight is watched anxiously by Roddy's wife, but not because of concern for either of the combatants, her horrified expressions during its progress being entirely due to the breakage of her pet possessions.[37]

It would appear that such breakage did indeed occur, but was eliminated in editing, leaving only a brief segment showing the rescue of a single fragile object, filmed from several angles. In all known prints Julia salvages a large vase from a wooden pedestal while the two men tussle nearby. She cradles it in her arms, then carries it to an adjacent room, presumably to prevent it from coming to harm. Although Roddy's angry vase-pitching is absent from all prints, they do show Archie lying amid debris scattered on the floor, including some ceramic shards that could result from a broken vase.

In Hitchcock's 1937 essay on "Direction," the filmmaker corroborated Barett's observations, adding some detail:

> [In *Downhill*] there was a sequence showing a quarrel between Hunter and Novello. It started as an ordinary

fight; then they began throwing things at one another. They tried to pick up heavy pedestals to throw and the pedestals bowled them over. In other words I made it comic. I even put Hunter into a morning coat and striped trousers because I felt that a man never looks so ridiculous as when he is well dressed and fighting. This whole scene was cut out; they said I was guying Ivor Novello. It was ten years before its time.[38]

It appears that some sequences Hitchcock wanted for ironic or comic effect were filmed but then deleted in editing, while others were retained (among them episodes involving the spitwad kid at Roddy's school, Archie's character-defining super-ciliousness and sneezing, and the Parisian cabaret scenes depicting faded humanity).

Visiting the set, Barett was aware of the comedic quality inherent in what was being enacted and also alert to the personalities around him. He was taken with the sight of Isabel Jeans, "seated on a couch near the set, an interested spectator," wearing "a wonderful gold negligée, trimmed with brown fur, and a wig of short, yellow curls." His report clarified the stages of the fight sequence as conceived and filmed:

Miss Jeans . . . is present when the two men start to fight. As the heat of the battle grows, and the furniture begins to suffer, she gets into a state of extreme agitation. She implores them frantically to stop—not because she fears for the safety of either of the contestants, but because she doesn't want to see her happy home completely wrecked. Then as . . . the fight grows even more fast and furious, she gradually collects all the most cherished vases and ornaments, and takes them out of the room.

Perhaps more than one "cherished" object was initially involved, perhaps not, since the hyperbole evident in this description of what was clearly not a "happy home" might well extend to encompass the generalizing plurals. Barett's enthused account now turned to Jeans's active part in the proceedings:

> When the camera was turned on Miss Jeans for her work in the fight scene, the two men stood on one side to watch, and she had to go through all the pantomime of dodging the chairs and other missiles that were thrown, while she ran round in a frantic effort to save her property, with nothing but the whirring camera in front of her. The vehemence with which she stamped her foot at nothing, and implored it to stop fighting, could not have been more realistic if the two men had been battering each other to pieces in front of her eyes.

After this description of scenes now lost came details of another, the misdirected vase toss:

> Ivor had once more taken the floor. In spite of her tearful pleadings, he had seized one of Julia's beloved vases and was preparing to hurl it at Ian Hunter—or rather at a little mark on the wooden screen that protected the camera. He missed the bull's eye at his first shot, and hit the lens of the camera, so he was promptly supplied with another vase and prepared for another shot.

One could readily imagine the producers' reactions to such reports of methods that put at risk costly equipment, not to mention actors, in pursuit of footage subsequently scrapped.

Inspired by wide-eyed admiration for the participants and for the process of filmmaking, Barett's commentary provides an account of portions of what Hitchcock and Stannard wanted to convey. Barett's write-ups of his visits to the set round out our knowledge of what lay behind the edited version that eventually reached screens. Scenes of chair breaking and vase throwing may have been suppressed because they were judged too long, too complicated, or too brutish. Following Hitchcock's lead, Barett offered this view of the artistic merit of the venture which he had witnessed unfolding: "The whole of the fight scene is relieved with subtle humorous touches . . . because, as Mr. Hitchcock remarked, 'You can't treat two men fighting in a flat in lounge suits seriously. The scene must be funny.' "

Barett concluded that Hitchcock liked to give "highbrow" treatment to a "lowbrow" story and that this venture promised to be one of the director's most "original." Hitchcock's "clever direction" could overcome the weaknesses of the "banal" plot, but perhaps not conflicts with the front office or with his consulting editor, Montagu, who preferred to trim footage perceived as excessive. Barett asserted that in this film Hitchcock "has given his characteristic bent for symbolism full play," citing two examples: the escalator scene in the Maida Vale Station and the night club sequence in Paris. Like other commentators, Barett was taken with the intriguing technical details of the Maida Vale shoot, accomplished with arc lamps "juiced" by generators on trucks stationed outside; however, he was uniquely perspicacious in pursuing the visual impact of the resulting "remarkable lighting effects" that served to reinforce symbolic overtones of the scene. As for the dance hall sequence, Barett found in it "subtle humor and [a] sense of symbolism" achieved by presenting "not the ordinary nightclub" typically shown on the screen but a compelling, if extravagant, "skit on nightclub life."

Vestiges of a Compromising Morning After

Additional sources of evidence concerning changes effectuated during the making of *Downhill* include photographs taken during production. Among these are production stills and publicity photos. Several of the latter appeared in contemporary publications, including one in the

April 1927 *Picturegoer* that has no parallel in known prints of the film. Covering one-third page, it shows Jeans recumbent on a sofa adorned with overstuffed pillows. She is wearing a fancy, strapless, beaded dress. She smiles coquettishly at Hunter, who is leaning over her with his hands near her bodice, fingering her pearl necklace. The caption identifies the scene as a "playful passage . . . in *Downhill*." The decor matches that of the parlor in the Avondale Mansions apartment in London. Perhaps this scene was meant to be part of the costume party segment, apparently slated to occur between the scene of Julia and Roddy's truncated kiss in their bedroom and her discussion with Archie there. It does not appear in preserved copies of the film.

Fay Filmer, a *Picture Show* correspondent who visited the set of *Downhill* during production, reported finding Novello "dressed in a dull red costume of the Medici period, and wearing a wig of long black hair and a moustache" for a scene with Isabel Jeans.[39] Like the smashed chair, this disguise did not figure in known copies of the finished film. The scene could have been planned for the theatrical segment or perhaps for the proposed costume party at the newlyweds' flat.

The BFI Stills Collection contains two photographs that may illuminate this situation. Against a backdrop distinguished by a staircase visible in two sequences in extant prints, they show revelers in disguise relaxing in the foyer of Roddy's and Julia's apartment, several of them nearly horizontal, arms akimbo. Among them are Julia and Archie in prone positions anticipatory of comparable scenes near the beginning of *Notorious* and the end of *To Catch a Thief*. This sequence appears to have been based on the party depicted in the second act of the Novello-Collier stage play.[40] As scripted for the film, it was probably intended to precede the chair-breaking and vase-throwing. Like those scenes, this fairly elaborate set piece was carefully planned, cast, and costumed. But was it filmed? Were there technical problems? Was it too static? Too somber? Too explicitly associated with the alcohol and drug usage so prominent in both the stage version and the Montagu treatment and consistently toned down for the movie? Was it too controversial, like the coffin?

The Memorable Missing Coffin

When Hitchcock spoke with François Truffaut about *Downhill* in 1962, he recalled with pleasure a sequence that he particularly liked for its sense of irony, communicated visually. Set in a Parisian cabaret, it ended, according to Hitchcock, with a shot of a coffin:

> There I experimented a bit. I showed a woman seducing a younger man. She is a lady of a certain age, but quite elegant, and he finds her very attractive until daybreak. Then he opens the window and the sun comes in, lighting up the woman's face. In that moment she looks dreadful. And through the open window we show people passing by carrying a coffin.[41]

Hitchcock apparently envisioned the scene as the movie existed in his mind rather than on screen, and his memory of events differs from the film in several details. On screen there is no suggestion that Roddy finds the solicitous "poetess" attractive; he merely responds to her apparently sympathetic interest in him. Nor is it he who opens the windows to admit the morning sun, that function being performed by anonymous employees of the dance hall. The windows open onto a nearly featureless exterior distinguished only by a grill of iron bars (reminiscent of the one that figured prominently near the end of *The Lodger*) and distant buildings. There is no cortege in sight. What comes through clearly in Hitchcock's recollection, however, is his enthusiasm for experimentation and his desire to convey an ironic vision juxtaposing revelry and its somber aftermath.

This conception of the abrupt intrusion of stark reality may have been inspired by Sean O'Casey's *Juno and the*

Paycock, which was originally registered as a stage play in England the same month as the play *Down Hill*, the two works appearing side by side in the Lord Chamberlain's Register of plays for December 1925. Hitchcock would film O'Casey's play for British International in 1929. Its second act concludes with a scene depicting a cortege near a festive gathering. As a band of celebrants regale themselves around a newly purchased gramophone, the scene devolves into the intonations of a funeral procession. Sounds of raucous singing give way to the drone of a cortege passing outside the window.[42] Elements of this scene in the play are dramatically enhanced in the film where Hitchcock's camera hovers intently at the open window through which the funereal sounds seem to emanate. The window is shown but not the mourners or the coffin, those details being left to the audience's imagination.

In *Downhill* the nightclub windows are opened onto an empty street scene. What happened to the phantom cortege? Contemporary reports throw light on production problems that may have contributed to its disappearance. When *Kinematograph Weekly*'s P.L. Mannock wrote about *Downhill*'s final days of studio filming he commented on a nightclub scene involving "persons past their prime—a subtle commentary on the alleged wildness of youth."[43] Mannock also reported hearing of a "mild but firm refusal, on quite reasonably superstitious grounds, in my opinion, of the studio carpenters to supply Hitchcock with a coffin for a brief scene." Indeed the coffin may have been omitted because of superstitions, or out of concern for possible transgressions of taste, or because of the cost of setting up and shooting that scene. Before dismissing Hitchcock's recollection as flawed, however, one should note that in preserved prints that shot ends abruptly after the windows are opened and could have been subject to postproduction shearing. If the scene with the coffin was indeed shot as Hitchcock described it, then it may have been eliminated for reasons of appropriateness, or for technical or editorial reasons, like the broken chair and vase.

In his *Picturegoer* article of April 1927, Barett described seeing other portions of the cabaret sequence being shot with a large number of actors and with multiple retakes. In the Parisian dance hall, Barett claimed, Hitchcock's "subtle humour and sense of symbolism" evoked "a most unusual club environment." Instead of the wild flappers and jazz-mad youths often depicted as habitués of idealized night clubs, Hitchcock "naturalistically" showed a collection of ordinary "excitement-craving" people, "beyond their prime." Barett speculated that, with "over two hundred extras" dancing to the music of a "jazz band composed of rather decrepit-looking old men," this sequence should be among "the most amusing in the whole film." He did not mention the coffin scene, which would surely have struck this symbolism-conscious observer, had he witnessed it. This lacuna may support the supposition that it was either filmed another day and deleted, or not filmed at all.[44]

Kinematograph Weekly reported that interior shooting for *Downhill* was completed the week of March 10 and that exterior shooting in Britain wrapped on March 27, three days before Hitchcock's departure for France to complete final shots for this film and begin *Easy Virtue*.[45]

Finale in France and Postproduction

Following Gainsborough's basic operating principle that "no extravagance" would be permitted, *Downhill* and the studio's next project, *Easy Virtue*, were conceived in tandem and produced as a pair. Since tight schedules were in force, the final footage for the former was shot in France, while the latter was beginning production with the same director and several of the same players. The fact that these shoots occurred in France reinforced another emerging Gainsborough hallmark. As Seaton and Martin put it, "*Downhill* provided the first intimation of Gainsborough's long-standing and at times obsessional involvement with life across the Channel. A trip to France was always on the cards."[46]

Taylor provided a picturesque account of the circumstances surrounding last-minute footage that remained to be filmed after Hitchcock had moved to the Riviera for *Easy Virtue*, including shots of Novello staggering through what appeared to be East London docklands:

> Novello came down very grandly, checked into the Hotel de Paris in Nice for one night, gave a lot of interviews there in his suite, and then, having got that out of the way, vanished to a very humble pension for the rest of his time on location. The shots were done on the flat roof of the pension, with a couple of men holding a painted backdrop of the London docks while Novello walked on the spot in front of it in the bright Mediterranean sunlight and the natives looked on incredulously, speculating as to what on earth these crazy Englishmen could be doing. (86)

As production was concluding in France, *Bioscope* ran a half-page photograph from the dining hall sequence over the caption "New British Productions."[47] During April and May, *Picture Show*'s effusive Edith Nepean offered a series of reports of her on-the-set encounters with the stars of *Downhill*: Novello, Jeans, Hunter, Braithwaite, McKinnel, and Benson were subjects of breathless accounts that kept *Downhill* fresh in the minds of readers and built anticipation for the film's release.[48] Nepean was especially impressed with a scene involving Jeans and Hannah Jones, as her dresser: "Isabel Jeans' black silky shingled hair was covered with a piquant 'cupid effect' curly fair wig, which made her look extremely youthful. It also added to the charm of her little oval face and the sparkle of her wonderful brown eyes. She was wearing a perfectly adorable black chiffon peignoir with wide hanging sleeves, edged with black fox." Nepean was so taken with this sight that she returned to it two months later in these terms: "Jeans [was] clad in the flimsiest and most seductive of negligée garments, her black hair covered by a supremely fascinating gold wig. . . . [She] was lolling back in an attractive fashion in her dressing room, whilst that other great little artiste, Hannah Jones, possessor of the sweetest of Welsh voices, was arranging Isabel Jeans' hair. And lots of fun they had together, these two." Intrigued by stars and glamour, Nepean remained indifferent to the director, whom she never interviewed and twice misidentified as George Hitchcock.[49]

Meanwhile final editing continued under the watchful eye of Ivor Montagu. According to Montagu, this phase was accomplished at odd moments around his daytime job at Gainsborough, when he was called upon to "supervise scripts" and "repair wrecks."[50] It is unclear how much of the final editing was Montagu's and how much was done by T. Lionel Rich, who received screen credit as editor.[51] The task involved combining footage from several sources, managing carefully-coordinated dissolves, manipulating multiple exposures, assembling visual collages for the delirium sequences, inserting close-ups and title cards, and much more. It is probable that portions of the montage were completed while Hitchcock was engaged on *Easy Virtue*.

Attention to continuity was sporadic. The tackler who brings Roddy to the ground in the opening sequence disappears abruptly when a more flattering shot of Novello is inserted, and at the Parisian cabaret La Patronne effectuates a similar disappearing act. One of the film's most impressive sequences, a theater scene featuring Roddy, Julia, Archie, and several dancers in a musical comedy, relies on cross-cutting of images filmed at different times from different angles: one shot clearly shows a cigarette case that subsequently becomes a focus of interest. However, in other shots the case is nowhere to be seen. Hitchcock's dictum that "if anybody did notice, nobody would mind" seems apt since, despite the mismatches, this sequence remains, through its effective blending of action and illusion, one of the most admired segments of the film.[52]

During this phase was assembled one of the earliest misleading flashbacks in the Hitchcock canon—the accusation scene at the headmaster's office—in which dynamic, complex editing vividly conveys Mabel's embellished account of events at Ye Olde Bunne Shoppe.[53] Presenting the story subjectively, this montage superimposes over her accusatory features previously unseen footage, thus simultaneously emphasizing her particular perspective and revealing inconsistencies with what the audience has witnessed previously. Edited with different emphases, different components, and different contexts, these shots communicate a revisionist story. Instead of the more objective long and medium shots of the "real time" sequence, here are sensual, suggestive close-ups. In this reworking, the dramatic inconsistencies of Mabel's tale are accentuated for viewers through double exposures and dissolves that manipulate important elements in new ways. Instead of a recap, this is a thorough recasting, emphasizing the most incriminating aspects of her yarn through new footage of events at the confectioner's shop. A canted shot of a spinning phonograph record gives way to a close-up of a dancing couple's feet disappearing through a beaded curtain. Another new shot shows the passing of money across the top of the cash register, from a male hand to a female hand, presented in slow, sensual close-up, with no reference to the innocent circumstances originally surrounding that payment for candy. In the earlier scene, Roddy plopped down the currency and removed his hand before Mabel's approached it; as presented here the cash seems to constitute a lingering bond between them. Next comes a full-screen close-up of the sign announcing the shop's closing hours, followed by a large image of the shop's "CLOSED" sign, suggesting a compromising situation within. These previously unseen images are shown over Mabel's trance-like face to emphasize their context of denunciation through rank fabulation.[54]

Aligned with these subjective, revisionist editing techniques is an impressionistic collage of images later in the film representing Roddy's delirium, which viewers may recognize as incongruous and, once again, purposely misrepresentational. In this unsettling montage, visualizations of his wild imaginings contain several scenes that do not match what has been shown before: Roddy dancing with the Poetess at the Parisian cabaret; seeing her along with other figures from his past around a table, mocking him; picturing a gramophone record with a label quite different from the one previously seen at the candy shop; imagining Tim and Mabel disappearing together into that shop; mistaking a sailor or a policeman for his father. These scenes of mental distress are reinforced by a mélange of shipboard scenes with super-imposed images of the whirling phonograph record associated with Mabel as well as by wharf and street scenes presented from Roddy's confused point of view. The bits of film that eventually constituted these visual highlights of *Downhill's* denouement required considerable manipulation and creative editing.[55]

In accordance with industry practice in the mid-1920s, the final edited master was subjected to tinting. The results were considerably more subtle than in previous Gainsborough releases, particularly *The Rat*, which featured a brightly colored opening sequence as well as segments where bold blue or sepia tinting came and went arbitrarily, sometimes obscuring the images. Hitchcock proceeded with discretion, instructing the lab technicians to tint segments of *Downhill's* delirium scenes pale green, thereby giving that sequence an unreal, somewhat nauseous appearance appropriate to a rough sea voyage. In doing so, Hitchcock claimed, he eschewed the more common practice of blurring the margins of such images to suggest an unstable inner vision.[56]

Trade Shows and Initial Responses

The editing and laboratory work on *Downhill* were completed with alacrity, and within six weeks it passed the Board of Film Classification review. Its London trade show took place a few days later, on May 24, at 3 P.M. at the Hippodrome, "by reserved ticket only."[57] Over the next few days it was shown to potential exhibitors in Birmingham, Liverpool, and Cardiff; and Novello and Jeans were in attendance at a special trade screening and luncheon in

Glasgow.[58] The front cover of *Kinematograph Weekly*'s May 5 issue featured the accusation scene from *Downhill*, and two weeks later that publication's calendar of London trade shows included publicity stills from the film. *Downhill* was heralded with great fanfare: "Hitchcock's best effort and a triumph for Novello" said *Kinematograph Weekly*'s reviewer, and the next week the same critic judged the direction to be "thoughtful and imaginative," and several scenes to be "characteristically clever."[59] *Bioscope* ran a half-page publicity photograph of Jeans. and Hunter over a caption that confirmed the importance of this homegrown director: "Alfred Hitchcock's Latest British Film."[60]

Not everyone was so kind. *Downhill*'s earliest commentators reacted negatively to the film's lack of narrative continuity, to what one reviewer called a sense of encountering a "separate supporting star cast in practically every reel," to characters that appeared only to "fade away."[61] *Kinematograph Weekly*'s coverage of the week's trade shows cited *Downhill*'s "clever treatment in adaptation of a rather weak and sordid stage play" and predicted that its drawing power would be its "star and interesting direction."[62] Reviewer Lionel Collier noted that Hitchcock's "clever pictorial touches" and "expert handling and imaginative production" made "a distinctly weak" story interesting: "In his depiction of delirium Hitchcock has achieved some wonderfully good effects." Although the visualization of the faded "poetess" struck Collier as "practically nauseating," he added the caveat that "this is, of course, due to the story," rather than the director, "whose depiction of depravity is certainly as realistic as was obviously demanded."

Shortly after the London trade show, *Bioscope*'s May 26 issue headed its "Box Office Film Reviews" section with a large photo of Jeans and Hunter behind foregrounded liquor bottles over the caption "Alfred Hitchcock's latest production . . . *Downhill*."[63] *Bioscope*'s anonymous reviewer asserted that this screen adaptation of the successful stage play had been refitted "with an ending to suit popular taste."[64] The reviewer added, with reserve, "It is more by the brilliant treatment of the director and the excellent work of the artists engaged that this film is likely to appeal to the public than by the strength of its story." A principal selling angle would be "the name and clever direction of Alfred Hitchcock." A separate notice in *Bioscope*'s business section stated that *Downhill* "displays all the ingenuity and knowledge of technique which caused *The Lodger* to be regarded as a milestone of British production. Mr. Hitchcock . . . [combines] artistry with box-office appeal." This notice ended with the promising statement that *Downhill* had already been booked for a special pre-release run in October at one of London's prominent cinemas, the Plaza.

The Emerging "Hitchcock Touch"

In the interim Hitchcock's name was frequently before the public, to his great pleasure, since he acknowledged this to be the best route toward directorial independence and leverage with different studios.[65] In May, the first issue of a new magazine called *Cinema World* ran an article entitled "The Men who Make the Film," in which Hitchcock figured prominently. A photograph of him, head tilted jauntily, was accompanied by a mention of his "just completed" project, *Downhill*, and this assessment of his work: "Mr. Hitchcock is one of the very few . . . who have mastered the intricacies of the camera [and the] production side of making films, as well as directing. In the opinion of leading critics, he is the most progressive British producer, and all his productions show clear thinking and breadth of treatment."[66]

At the time *Downhill*'s trade screenings were scheduled around the United Kingdom, *Easy Virtue* was in post-production, Hitchcock's earlier Gainsborough film *The Mountain Eagle* was going into commercial release, and the director was making his move to British International Pictures (BIP).[67] He completed *Easy Virtue* in May and by June was engaged in his next project, based on an "original scenario" for "a screen version of his own story" about boxing, *The Ring*. He would film it at BIP's large, up-to-date facility near Elstree in Hertfordshire. The announcement of Hitchcock's two-year contract was made by BIP chairman John Maxwell at the Glasgow luncheon following the trade showing of *Downhill*.[68]

During that summer Hitchcock continued to juggle multiple assignments while working assiduously to keep his name and face before the public. In mid-June, *Bioscope's* British Film Issue offered full-page photographs of Britain's foremost filmmakers. While Graham Cutts and other directors chose to be pictured with open collars and cigarettes, Hitchcock appeared in suit and tie, looking contemplative. Whereas Cutts's image was accompanied by a listing of thirteen films he had directed, Hitchcock's page presented only his visage and a circular labyrinthine design which, if deciphered by the curious, spelled his name.[69] Hitchcock was making his intriguing, idiosyncratic mark, and the industry was taking note. In that same issue, an article by Herbert Thompson on "Creative Artists and their Methods," included an entry on his work. "He has a brilliant mind," it stated. "He thinks in terms of the screen—a rare quality—and, being the possessor of a vast technical knowledge, he is able to secure the exact effect he wants with the minimum amount of trouble."[70] The encomium ended with these words: "Hitchcock, with his original methods of treatment and his fine sense of drama, is one of the directors best qualified to lead the British attack on world markets."

The June issue of *Picturegoer* featured a "symposium" on the topic "Have we the talent?" that canvassed six of "England's leading producers and directors," among them Hitchcock and Balcon.[71] Each responded to a series of questions prompted by the Quota Act, including:

1. Are there in existence today, in this country, the players, producers, scenarists, and technicians needed to make the sixty good films per annum which the quota demands?
2. If not where are they to be recruited?

Balcon's answer was laconic: "In my opinion, there are sufficient players, directors, etc., to make the sixty good films per annum which the quota demands." Hitchcock's more fulsome response, which concluded the article, expressed considerable reserve:

> We must, I am afraid, face the unfortunate fact that there is not the personal material at hand for making sixty feature pictures a year. The British studio industry has never been big enough to give employment to very many people, with the result that there have been limited opportunities for developing artists by experience. We have often been forced to employ stage stars who, in too many instances, regard film work as a fill-in for pocket-money. Thus film acting has never been taken sufficiently seriously, and discipline has been often lacking. . . . Good direction—the real cause of America's wealth of talent—is also a vital factor in making stars, even out of amateurs.

With its emphasis on "personal material" and "amateurs" this statement anticipates Hitchcock's frequently cited comments about actors being conceptualized as "cattle," or perhaps more appropriately as the related term, capital. Reflecting his recent experiences and his move to British International, these statements reveal a decidedly negative view about British options (a perspective shared by two of the six respondents polled, the others being moderately optimistic) and perhaps offer indications that, at this stage of his career, Hitchcock was actively surveying options, in Britain and in Hollywood.

In mid-August *Kinematograph Weekly* published the long-awaited results of a film questionnaire circulated by theater-owner Sidney L. Bernstein among patrons of his chain of cinemas.[72] Respondents were asked, among other items, to name their favorite director. Hitchcock's name appeared, along with D. W. Griffith and Cecil B. De Mille, among the top five directors listed by male respondents. Women's responses to that question did not include Hitchcock in the top five, but substituted the name of his colleague and early supervisor at Gainsborough, Graham Cutts. These results attested to Hitchcock's growing name recognition, at least among men.

Other magazines reported at length on Hitchcock's current project, *The Ring*, and on the upcoming trade showing of *Easy Virtue*.[73] Photos and sketches of Hitchcock appeared in the daily press, spreading his renown and his distinctive image. A caricature first published in the *Evening Standard* was reproduced in *Bioscope*.[74] It shows him with his head cocked back, wavy hair receding over a high brow, eyes intense, nose wrinkled, mouth pursed as if to make a quip. The September 29 issue of *Kinematograph Weekly* featured a quarter-page charcoal sketch of the young director, hair parted but somewhat mussed, looking pensive.[75] The brief caption beneath the portrait addressed Hitchcock's recent acclaim and professionalism: "Alfred Hitchcock, who sprang into fame with *The Lodger*, attributes his success to his years of studio experience." It concluded with a reference to the potential for future success of "this 'white hope' among British directors."

Summer and early autumn 1927 saw a flurry of activity on Hitchcock's part, attested in a laudatory article in *Bioscope* titled "Hitchcock's Energy and Keenness."[76] *Easy Virtue* was trade shown at the Hippodrome on August 30, and *The Ring* enjoyed a "semi-public tradeshow" a month later. Simultaneously the press was covering two new Hitchcock projects, citing production plans for *The Farmer's Wife* and casting results for *Champagne*.[77] Hitchcock was frequently mentioned in *Kinematograph Weekly*, where Lionel Collier and P.L. Mannock kept his name before readers through their reviews and news coverage.[78] During this period the hallmark concept of the "Hitchcock touch" became commonplace.[79]

After their trade showings, much discussion of *Easy Virtue* and *The Ring* appeared in industry publications, fueling anticipation for *Downhill*'s upcoming commercial release.

While *Easy Virtue* met with mixed responses, *The Ring* garnered considerable praise from critics.[80] One reviewer called it "significant mainly because Hitchcock himself is significant"; another called it "an artistic . . . triumph, primarily for the young British director"; *The Star* commented "Mr. Hitchcock excels in bringing tension and excitement . . . to the screen"; and *Bioscope* summed it up: "This young director has made a great name for himself."[81] With all this stir, expectations for the commercial success of *Downhill* ran high. In September a blurb in *Kinematograph Weekly* heralding its theatrical run concluded with this phrase: "Cleverly directed by Alfred Hitchcock."[82]

The October issue of *Picturegoer* anticipated *Downhill*'s release with a four-page spread that included photos of scenes from the film and a "narration" of the plot by John Fleming.[83] This summary was intended to pique interest in the movie, as Fleming's synopsis of *The Lodger* in *Picturegoer*'s February 1927 issue had done for that film. Fleming's "narration" was prepared with the express cooperation of Gainsborough Studios, almost certainly in consultation with the film's long-lost screenplay, of which it may be one of the clearest extant reflections. Nevertheless, in its attempt to recount a coherent story in prose and to convey substantial dialogue and analysis of motivation, it differs from the source play, from Montagu's preliminary treatment, and even from the cursory synopses distributed in Gainsborough's press kits.[84] Making explicit what the movie itself could merely suggest in terms of background and dialogue, it also differs from known prints at several points. Moviegoers who expected to see a faithful rendering of the stage play or of Fleming's narration, transposed to the screen, would encounter major divergences, particularly in showings at the Plaza.

Downhill's *Commercial Run*

In the days just prior to the film's general release on October 24, special preview screenings of *Downhill* were arranged at the Plaza Theatre on Regent Street near Piccadilly

Circus. These events featured not only the film, but also Novello in person on stage, performing a scene just prior to the accusation in the headmaster's office. One reporter described the impact of this event:

> The screen projection fades out, a curtain rolls up, and . . . a scene from the play, as it was done on the stage, is actually acted by Mr. Novello and his schoolboy friend. At the close they are summoned to the Head's study, and as the curtain goes down [and projection resumes] the camera shows them walking down the cloisters dejectedly. This is an effective screen device and gives Mr. Novello an opportunity of appearing in the flesh before his admirers.[85]

Several reviewers reported on the striking effect of this experience of film bracketing live action. Although it was hardly unusual for actors to make appearances at premieres of their movies, this experience struck viewers as remarkable: "For the first time in history" rhapsodized a favorably-disposed correspondent, "there is a combination of stage and screen production. Ivor Novello enacts his part . . . without breaking the continuity of the film."[86] That reporter was equally impressed with the after-show party where "about forty congenial souls enjoyed the hospitality of the Plaza directorate." The decision on Novello's part to do this "special" assignment may have been linked to his desire to keep open his options for returning to the stage, should his film career falter as, with the advent of sound, it did.[87]

The performances at the Plaza prompted multiple responses in the *Daily Mail*. It ran a publicity photograph from *Downhill* under the heading "This Week's New Film" in conjunction with an announcement of the special showings at the Plaza.[88] The photo showed Novello and Jeans holding hands, at heart level; he gazes into her eyes as though hypnotized while, clad in a revealing gown, she seems to look right through him. A few pages farther along, nestled among a collection of pictures of current events, was a photo of

Novello in a delirious stupor accompanied by a reminder that in this "new British film . . . the actor will appear personally" during screenings at the Plaza. On the movie review page a photo of Hitchcock, with hair brushed back, accompanied a substantial review of the film. Identifying Hitchcock as "one of the most interesting personalities in the British film-producing industry . . . the most discussed film director in England," the *Daily Mail*'s anonymous correspondent noted how the creativity and aspirations of *Downhill*'s director reflected those of his native country. "His success," the reviewer affirmed, "is the product of tireless work and unbounded enthusiasm." In the eyes of this writer, *"Downhill . . . possessed remarkable properties"* and demonstrated that "films worthy of exhibition throughout the world can be made in this country."

While responding positively to the film's "technical efficiency" and the "inventiveness of the young director," the *Daily Telegraph*'s critic questioned the effectiveness of the combination of "movie" and "speakie" at the Plaza, noting that, at this performance, the experiment met with only mild applause. The *Evening Standard* for October 10 included a caricature by Tom Titt reflecting the artist's reaction to the Plaza screening. The line drawing showed Novello, looking suave, interacting with a perky Benson and a frayed, fearsome Irvine in a compromising situation inspired by the deceptive flashback and the film's poster ads. The *Observer*'s critic observed that Hitchcock's aim was "to enhance the appeal to sight," even if it meant "suppress[ing] the story," and added: "Perhaps we should admire Alfred Hitchcock's moments of pictorial brilliance more if we had not seen his far finer work in *The Ring*."[89]

In late October *Downhill* moved, without the live action segment, to other theaters in London and in the provinces, where it garnered modest attention as viewers ogled the performers and as critics anticipated what Hitchcock would do next for Britain's film industry. The November 5 issue of *Picture Show* included an "art supplement" page titled "A Glimpse of *Downhill*" that showed three scenes from the film, all featuring Novello, and, as an insert, a close-up of his face.

Cinema World gave the film extensive coverage and reproduced Gainsborough's plot synopsis under the rubric "This Month's Screen Classics."[90]

Reevaluating Downhill

Rushed through production at a turbulent time and overshadowed by Hitchcock's subsequent work, *Downhill* sank toward obscurity, silently awaiting rediscovery, reassessment, and (one now hopes) increased visibility that may further illuminate Hitchcock's working methods, approach to unconventional subjects, and cinematic experimentalism. Borne of chaotic production circumstances and evolving, sometimes conflicting combinations of cooperation and compromise, this film was perceived from the start not so much in terms of its intrinsic merits and flaws but rather in terms of what people wanted to see in it: a star vehicle for the starstruck and a reflection of national pride for partisans on both sides of the Channel. François Truffaut, for example, glibly noted that *Downhill* "was not particularly successful . . . [but] there was a very good scene in a Paris cabaret."[91]

Hardly a classic, *Downhill* is nonetheless extremely intriguing, and this product of a crucial phase in Hitchcock's trajectory should be recognized for what it is: a creative experiment for the director and a resilient, enigmatic source of discovery and delight for his aficionados.

Notes

Research for this project was funded by two Faculty Development Endowment Grants from Rhodes College that enabled me to consult documents in London and Paris and to view archival prints at the British Film Institute (BFI) and the Museum of Modern Art (MoMA). My thanks to Kathleen Dickson at the BFI, to Charles Silver at MoMA, and to the staffs at both institutions for facilitating these viewings. Thanks are also due to the British Library, the Bibliothèque du Film, and the Centre Georges Pompidou. I am also grateful to

Sidney Gottlieb for helpful contextualizing suggestions as well as to Darlene Brooks, Roy and Muriel Gibbs, Janet Moat, Kenan Padgett, Sue and David Sevier, William Short, Olwen Terris, and my patient, insightful research associate, Nancy Foltz Vest.

1. Only two of the principal biographers report on selected incidents during production; see John Russell Taylor, *Hitch: The Life and Times of Alfred Hitchcock* (1978; rpt. New York: Da Capo Press, 1996), 85-86, and Patrick McGilligan *Alfred Hitchcock: A Life in Darkness and Light* (New York: HarperCollins, 2003), 91; Donald Spoto's account is sketchier: *The Dark Side of Genius: The Life of Alfred Hitchcock* (1983; rpt. New York: Da Capo Press, 1999), 98-99. Yacowar and Barr are inclined toward interpretation of the finished product rather than the filmmaking process; see, respectively, *Hitchcock's British Films* (Hamden, CT: Archon Books, 1977), 42-53, and *English Hitchcock* (Moffat, Scotland: Cameron & Hollis, 1999), 43-47. Krohn's four-page "Panorama of the British Period" includes two brief but illuminating sections on *Downhill*; see his *Hitchcock at Work* (London: Phaidon, 2000), 20, 22. In *Alfred Hitchcock and the British Cinema* (Urbana: University of Illinois Press, 1986; rpt. New York: Athlone, 1996), Tom Ryall mentions *Downhill* only in passing.

2. Barr, *English Hitchcock*, 46; Taylor, *Hitch*, 84. McGilligan sided with Taylor, citing the film's "imaginative staging, expressive lighting and composition, and unusual camera work" (*Alfred Hitchcock: A Life in Darkness and Light*, 91). Rachael Low found much to praise in *Downhill* (*The History of the British Film: 1918-1929* [London: Allen & Unwin, 1971], 168, 239, 258-259, 279-280), as did Raymond Durgnat (*The Strange Case of Alfred Hitchcock, Or The Plain Man's Hitchcock* [Cambridge: MIT Press, 1974], 77). Hitchcock used the verb "experiment" twice in conjunction with *Downhill* in published conversations with François Truffaut, *Hitchcock*, rev. ed. (New York: Simon and Schuster, 1984), 51; in that interview Hitchcock called the source play "rather poor" and its dialogue "pretty dreadful."

3. Balcon acquired the building and equipment from Famous Players-Lasky "for very little" (Low, *The History of the British Film: 1918-1929*, 143). Information in this paragraph is based on Ray Seaton and Roy Martin, "Gainsborough: The Story of the Celebrated Studio," *Films and Filming*, no. 332 (May 1982): 11; Philip Kemp, "Not for Peckham: Michael Balcon and Gainsborough's International

Trajectory in the 1920s," in Pam Cook, ed., *Gainsborough Pictures* (London: Cassell, 1997), 16; and Duncan Petrie, "Innovation and Economy: The Contribution of the Gainsborough Cinematographer," in Cook, ed., *Gainsborough Pictures*, 120-21. For photographs of the studio's facilities in 1927, see "The Home of Gainsborough Pictures," *Bioscope*, no. 1080 (June 18, 1927): 77. Recently renovated for apartment living, the Poole Street complex now boasts in its central courtyard a gigantic statue of Hitchcock's head.

4. Hitchcock had worked with McDonnell on several previous productions, including *Woman to Woman* (1923), *The White Shadow* (1923), and *The Passionate Adventure* (1924), as assistant director. Hitchcock was back at Gainsborough by "arrangement with British National," the major studio near Elstree, soon to be renamed British International Pictures; see *Bioscope*, no. 1056 (January 6, 1927): 99 and no. 1057 (January 13, 1927): 51, as well as McGilligan, *Alfred Hitchcock: A Life in Darkness and Light*, 88-91.

5. Quotations in this paragraph are from Balcon's "British Film Production: Is the General Conception Too Narrow? A Plea for Wider Vision," *The Film Renter and Moving Picture News* (January 3, 1925): n.p., cited in Kemp, "Not for Peckham," 13. See also *Kinematograph Weekly*, no. 1052 (June 16, 1927): 24, and *Bioscope*, no. 1080 (June 18, 1927): 46.

6. Information in this paragraph is based on Kemp, "Not for Peckham," 22, 27-29.

7. The long-anticipated act was debated in Parliament from March into December 1927. Among the notables who engaged in public discussions were H.G. Wells, George Bernard Shaw, and Thomas Hardy, then in his eighties. For details, see Low, *The History of the British Film: 1918-1929*, 91-102.

8. In a major departure from the source play and the cinematic treatment prepared by Ivor Montagu, two of the principal figures from earlier reels—the protagonist's roommate, Tim Wakeley, and Tim's sister, a potential amatory interest for the protagonist—fail to reappear. It is unclear whether their disappearance is due to scheduling difficulties, artistic preferences, or budgetary constraints. For further discussion of the source materials, see James Vest, "Metamorphoses of *Downhill*: From Stage Play to Cinematic Treatment and Film," *Hitchcock Annual* 13 (2004-05): 65-76.

9. P[atrick] L. Mannock, "British Production News," *Kinematograph Weekly*, no. 1025 (December 9, 1926): 22: "I refuse to believe that Mrs. Hitchcock's interest in studios has ceased, for her years of first-

class work in the cutting room and on the floor contradict such a probability." For additional details of the wedding, the honeymoon, and the impact of both on the Hitchcocks' professional lives, see Taylor, *Hitch*, 80-81; Spoto, *Dark Side of Genius*, 93-95; McGilligan, *Alfred Hitchcock: A Life in Darkness and Light*, 89; and Patricia Hitchcock O'Connell and Laurent Bouzereau, *Alma Hitchcock: The Woman Behind the Man* (New York: Berkley, 2003), 48-49.

10. The play *Down Hill* opened in London at the Queen's Theatre on Shaftsbury Avenue on June 16, 1926, and moved to the Prince's Theatre on July 26, where it ran until September 4, for a total of 93 performances. For additional details about the stage version, see Walter James MacQueen-Pope, *Ivor* (London: W.H. Allen, 1951), 204; Michael Williams, *Ivor Novello: Screen Idol* (London: BFI, 2003), 137-48 and 165; and Vest, "Metamorphoses," 65-69.

11. *Bioscope*, no. 1051 (December 2, 1926): 37, and no. 1053 (December 16, 1926): 27.

12. A news item published December 16 stated that "the director has not yet been decided upon, but a big name is mentioned" and reported that production was to begin January 10 (*Bioscope*, no. 1053: 27). Hitchcock's name was announced in the following issue (*Bioscope*, no. 1054 [December 23, 1926]: 27).

13. Novello was known primarily as the composer of a famous World War I song, "Keep the Homefires Burning," and as a playwright-producer and stage performer. Beginning in 1919, Novello acted in twenty-two films, mostly silent. In 1925 he starred, under the direction of Graham Cutts, in Gainsborough's screen adaptation of another Novello-Collier play, *The Rat*, which enjoyed considerable success as both stage production and film. Novello's three-film contract guaranteed him substantial income and bonuses based on time worked above a specified minimum, plus right of script approval; subsequent contracts would assure him star billing and higher pay. For further discussion of negotiations for film rights and Novello's services to Gainsborough, see MacQueen-Pope, *Ivor*, 202-04 and 217-18. Williams discusses Novello's activities as a composer and how they played into his screen image in *Novello*, 61-67, 76-78, 162-64.

14. All references to the film *Downhill* are based upon multiple viewings of versions preserved in the BFI—one 35mm celluloid and the other a video transfer—and of one 35mm print at MoMA. In July 1999 I saw an exhibition print on loan from the BFI screened at the Pompidou Center in Paris during the Hitchcock centennial festivities;

that version also aired on French television and became the basis for a commercially-available video/DVD copy with French subtitles. I have also seen another, crisper DVD copy from Digital Broadcast. In terms of content, all these versions are generally comparable, with slight variants. The BFI's video transfer (recorded October 11, 1999) contains tinted sequences. The MoMA print, acquired from the BFI in 1978, may be a pre-distribution version: it contains redundant frames (i.e., repeated footage), shows considerable lateral shrinkage, and has framing irregularities in the final reels.

15. Cover letter to C.M. Woolf; BFI's Montagu collection, Item no. 21, catalogued as "DOWNHILL (Hitchcock) 1927: Ivor Montagu's comments on original play and suggested film treatment." For details of distinctive elements of this cinematic treatment, see Vest, "Metamorphoses," 69-76.

16. Stannard's close collaboration with Hitchcock from *The Pleasure Garden* through *Champagne* is chronicled by Charles Barr in *English Hitchcock*, 22-26, and in his "Writing Screen Plays: Stannard and Hitchcock," in Andrew Higson, ed., *Young and Innocent? The Cinema in Britain 1896-1930* (Exeter: University of Exeter Press, 2002), 227-41. In 1920 Stannard wrote that scenarists should be "as intimately acquainted as possible" with the directors with whom they collaborated: "Your joint work should express all that is best in each of you" ("Writing Screen Plays," in *Cinema Practical Course in Cinema Acting in Ten Complete Lessons* [London: Standard Art Book Co., 1920], 24). When *Downhill* was in preproduction, *Bioscope* reported that Stannard was "collaborating with Alfred Hitchcock on the script of *Downhill*" and commented soon thereafter that a "scenario for *Easy Virtue* [was also] being prepared, with the director's cooperation, by Eliot Stannard" (no. 1057 [January 13, 1927]: 51 and no. 1064 [March 3, 1927]: 30). No copy of either screenplay has surfaced. They may have been lost in the devastating fire at Gainsborough, January 18, 1930, that resulted in one fatality and several injuries; see "Gainsborough Studio Blaze," *Kinematograph Weekly*, no. 1188 (January 23, 1930): 31.

17. Hunter would make three films in a row for Hitchcock, returning to play Australian boxing champ Bob Corby in *The Ring*; Farebrother would appear as a juror in *Murder!*; and Jeans would have a minor role as Mrs. Newsham in *Suspicion*.

18. "Shadowland," *The Picturegoer*, no. 74 (February 1927): 52; see also *Kinematograph Weekly*, no. 1031 (January 20, 1927): 62, and Petrie, "Innovation and Economy," 119, 122-3.

19. For Montagu's description of the squabble, involving a high-angle shot (judged by Montagu to be implausible and ridiculous) of a taxi bringing three people back from the theater, see "Working with Hitchcock," *Sight and Sound* 49, no. 3 (1980): 190-91. Montagu remembered the disputed shot in conjunction with *Easy Virtue*; although no such scene appears in that film, two comparable shots do figure in *Downhill*. From Montagu's memoirs it is clear that Montagu served as "editing consultant" on both *Downhill* and *Easy Virtue*, although he did not receive screen credit ("Working with Hitchcock," 190).

20. *Bioscope,* no. 1063 (February 24, 1927): 54; cf. *Kinematograph Weekly,* no. 1036 (February 24, 1927): 54. As described in the industry press, the arrangement with British National would loan Hitchcock to Gainsborough "for one picture" (*Bioscope,* no. 1052 [December 9, 1926]: 43). When that number rose to two, the situation was deemed newsworthy; see *Bioscope,* no. 1064 (March 3, 1927): 30.

21. *Bioscope,* no. 1056 (January 6, 1927): 68.

22. Details in this paragraph are taken from *Bioscope* no. 1058 (January 20, 1927): 54, and from *Kinematograph Weekly,* no. 1031 (January 20, 1927): 62, no. 1033 (February 3): 39, and no. 1036 (February 24, 1927): 54, respectively.

23. Benson's adaptation to life in London after her sojourn in France was reported in *Picture Show,* no. 408 (February 26, 1927): 19; Gott referred to her double role in *Downhill* with pride in the legend accompanying her publicity photograph in *Bioscope,* no. 1080 (June 18, 1927): 114.

24. Quotations in this paragraph are from *Bioscope,* no. 1060 (February 3, 1927): 45; Jennings's name does not appear on cast listings for this film.

25. *Kinematograph Weekly,* no. 1031: 62. The following quotations are from *Bioscope,* no. 1058 (January 20, 1927): 54, and no. 1059 (January 27, 1927): 27, respectively. See also *Bioscope,* no. 1056 (January 6, 1927): 69.

26. *Kinematograph Weekly,* no. 1033 (February 3, 1927): 39. Jesse Lasky admitted that this foggy-bottom property was subject to mists from the adjacent Islington Canal that occasionally plagued filming (cited in Seaton and Martin, "Gainsborough: The Story," 8).

27. Quotations in this paragraph are from *Kinematograph Weekly,* no. 1030 (January 13, 1927): 82, and no. 1033 (February 3, 1927): 58, respectively. Another Hitchcock film, *The Mountain*

Eagle, would debut in late May 1927; see J.L. Kuhns's definitive study, "Hitchcock's *The Mountain Eagle*" *Hitchcock Annual* (1998-99): 31-108.

28. *Kinematograph Weekly*, no. 1033 (February 3, 1927): 39. Seaton and Martin reported that usable space on the upper floor measured 88 x 42 feet whereas the main floor studio space measured 60 x 40 feet, and that the administrative corridor, also on the ground floor, sometimes served for filming as well ("Gainsborough: The Story," 11).

29. *The Picturegoer*, no. 75 (March 1927): 51.

30. *Bioscope*, no. 1064 (March 3, 1927): 30, and no. 1067 (March 24, 1927): 49, respectively.

31. Conversation with Peter Bogdanovich, reprinted in *Who the Devil Made It: Conversations with Legendary Film Directors* (New York: Ballantine, 1997), 491.

32. Quotations in this paragraph are from *Bioscope*, no. 1066 (March 17, 1927): 34.

33. The first two quotations in this paragraph are from *Picture Show*, no. 411 (March 19, 1927): 20, and the others from no. 412 (March 26, 1927): 19. The March 12 issue featured a double-page photo of Novello in profile and three weeks later he was back in a two-page spread heralding his appearance in *The Triumph of the Rat* (*Picture Show*, no. 410: 12-13 and no. 413: 12-13).

34. The publicity photo is found in *Kinematograph Weekly*, no. 1038 (March 10, 1927): 41; the quotation is from *Kinematograph Weekly*, no. 1041 (March 31, 1927): 31.

35. Quotations from Barett in this section are taken from *Picturegoer*, no. 76 (April 1927): 44-48; those in this paragraph are from p. 44.

36. Other reports on the fight scene (e.g., *Bioscope*, no. 1063 [February 24, 1927]: 54) date its filming to mid-February.

37. *Bioscope*, no. 1063 (February 24, 1927): 54.

38. Alfred Hitchcock, "Direction," in *Footnotes to the Film*, ed. Charles Davy (London: Lovat Dickson/Readers' Union, 1938), 3-15; rpt. in *Hitchcock on Hitchcock: Selected Writings and Interviews*, ed. Sidney Gottlieb (Berkeley and Los Angeles: University of California Press 1995), 253-61. Taylor (*Hitch*, 86) presents a slightly different version of this account.

39. *Picture Show*, no. 411 (March 19, 1927): 3.

40. Revised version of Act II; see Vest, "Metamorphoses," 68 and 88, n. 5.

41. Truffaut, *Hitchcock*, 51. As envisioned, this sequence might echo avant-garde and unconventional films of the early 1920s, e.g., F.W. Murnau's *Nosferatu* (1921) and Erich von Stroheim's *Greed* (1924). I am indebted to Sidney Gottlieb for pointing out possible linkages.

42. Sean O'Casey, *Juno and the Paycock* (New York: Macmillan, 1925), 74-77. In both play and film, the spirit of the revelers is boisterous. One woman lets loose with a bawdy song. Then all sing, "If you're Irish, come into the parlour." After a shattering shout by a non-participant, the music of the phonograph stops abruptly, and one hears the solemn chant of a funeral procession outside.

43. Quotations in this paragraph are from *"Downhill* Shot," *Kinematograph Weekly*, no. 1038 (March 10, 1927): 41.

44. Barett's extensive commentary is supplemented by a colorful report in the *Evening Standard* covering the cabaret scenes (March 17, 1927, cited in Krohn 20), where a correspondent who visited that set noted that Hitchcock had 150 dancers tied together with a rope "like a bunch of rhubarb"; the director's commands were simple: 'Now dance!' shouted Mr. Hitchcock, then 'Shoot!'"

45. *Kinematograph Weekly*, no. 1044 (April 28, 1927): 31, and no. 1041 (March 31, 1927): 31.

46. The quotations in this paragraph are from Seaton and Martin, "Gainsborough: The Story," 10-11.

47. *Bioscope*, no. 1068 (March 31, 1927): 40.

48. *Picture Show*, no. 413 (April 2, 1927): 40; no. 414 (April 9, 1927): 9; no. 416 (April 23 1927): 19; no. 417 (April 30, 1927): 19; and no. 420 (May 21, 1927): 5.

49. Quotations from *Picture Show*: "Isabel Jeans' black silky shingled hair," no. 413 (April 2, 1927): 20; "Jeans [was] clad," no. 422 (June 4, 1927): 18; "George Hitchcock," no. 414 (April 9, 1927): 9 and no. 417 (April 30, 1927): 19. The scene between Jeans and Jones is pictured in Ken Mogg, *The Alfred Hitchcock Story* (London: Titan, 1999), 16. Jones had supporting roles in three other Hitchcock films: *Blackmail*, *Murder!*, and *Rich and Strange*.

50. Montagu described his work at Gainsborough during this period as "[overseeing] scripts all day and editing all night" at a salary of "40 pounds a week for both" ("Working with Hitch," 190).

51. McGilligan's filmography credits Montagu rather than Rich for editing *Downhill* (*Alfred Hitchcock: A Life in Darkness and Light*, 757); Barr refers to him as "Script/Editing Associate" (*English*

Hitchcock, 219); Low lists both men as editors (*The History of the British Film: 1918-1929*, 358).

52. Quotation from Montagu "Working with Hitch," 191. Among those who have commented positively on this sequence, McGilligan thought it particularly imaginative (*Alfred Hitchcock: A Life in Darkness and Light*, 91) and Mogg considered it the film's "most brilliant scene" (16). Yacowar applauded Hitchcock's rendering of "a succession of appearances" in this sequence (*Hitchcock's British Films*, 50). Taylor called it "a Chinese box of illusion within an illusion," then added: "At the time *Downhill* was made, no one else was working with this kind of cinematic imagination, telling a film story with this mind-grabbing command of the medium's possibilities" (*Hitch*, 85).

53. Following Yacowar (*Hitchcock's British Films*, 44), Barr posits "an element of 'lying flashback' in the images that accompany Mabel's accusation" (*English Hitchcock*, 47); however, Yacowar's listing of specific visual disparities is inaccurate in several details (45) and neither Yacowar nor Barr pursues the issue in relation to other instances of misrepresentations of prior events in this film or to comparable situations in others.

54. Yacowar's analysis of Mabel's "images of memory" is at odds with extant prints of the film, particularly in his statement that they portray "Roddy taking a pound from her" (*Hitchcock's British Films*, 45). Yacowar's assertion that this particular element is "the only lie in the list" misses the point that other portions of Mabel's flashback involve footage not previously shown. He is justified in connecting this "visual embodiment" of a lie to the flashback in *Stage Fright* (45-46).

55. Low underscored the technical prowess of *Downhill's* "flashy delirium sequence of mixes and dissolves" (*The History of the British Film: 1918-1929*, 168). Durgnat claimed this sequence effected "a visual bewilderment not unworthy of [René Clair's] *Entr'acte*" (*Strange Case*, 77).

56. In her discussion of tinting practices in films of the 1920s, Low commented on *Downhill's* effective use of sepia and green to reflect reality and delirium (*The History of the British Film: 1918-1929*, 279-80). Spoto linked the choice of green to colored stage lights used in theaters to suggest ghostly effects or fantasy (*Dark Side of Genius*, 96). Hitchcock discussed with Truffaut his choice of representational features in these sequences (*Hitchcock*, 51).

57. *Bioscope*, no. 1075 (May 19, 1927): 40.

58. *Kinematograph Weekly,* no. 1047 (May 12, 1927): 43; no. 1049 (May 26, 1927): 49; and no. 1050 (June 2, 1927): 27.

59. *Kinematograph Weekly,* no. 1047 (May 12, 1927): 45, and no. 1048 (May 19, 1927): 33. The poster used for the *Kinematograph Weekly* cover may be seen in Mogg, *Alfred Hitchcock Story,* 16.

60. *Bioscope,* no. 1074 (May 12, 1927): 23.

61. *Kinematograph Weekly,* no. 1038 (March 10, 1927): 41 and no. 1049 (May 26, 1927): 43.

62. *Kinematograph Weekly,* no. 1049 (May 26, 1927): 42; all subsequent quotations in this paragraph are from this article, p. 43.

63. Quotations in this paragraph are from *Bioscope,* no. 1076 (May 26, 1927): 43.

64. The film ends with a brief sequence showing a disheveled Roddy returning, like Odysseus, to be recognized by the old servant and to be reconciled with his family. This was a departure from the stage version, where his parents were dead. For additional details, see Vest, "Metamorphoses," 69, 75.

65. Cf. Montagu's comment: "If you made yourself publicly known as a director—and this you could only do by getting mention in the press *in connection with your directing*—this would be the only way you became free to do what you wanted. If your name were known to the public you would not be the prisoner of where you happened to be working—you could move on" ("Working with Hitch," 190, italics in original).

66. *Cinema World,* no. 1 (May 1927): 28; directors were often called "producers" in Great Britain.

67. Spoto reports the opening date for *The Mountain Eagle* as May 23, 1927 (*Dark Side of Genius,*97); *Kinematograph Year Book* and *Bioscope,* as May 25. In either case that would place its opening within one day of the trade showing of *Downhill.* For further details, see Kuhns, "Hitchcock's *Mountain Eagle,*" 93, 96-100. Concerning Hitchcock's move to BIP and his relationship with its predecessor, British National Pictures, see McGilligan, *Alfred Hitchcock: A Life in Darkness and Light,* 88-89, 93-94.

68. Quotations concerning *The Ring* are from reports in *Kinematograph Weekly,* no. 1043 (April 14, 1927): 27, and *Bioscope,* no. 1070 (April 14, 1927): 23; see also *Bioscope,* no. 1074 (May 12, 1927): 23, and no. 1077 (June 2, 1927): 24. For details of the luncheon program at the Grosvenor Restaurant in Glasgow on May 25, 1927, see *Kinematograph Weekly,* no. 1050 (June 2, 1927): 41.

69. *Bioscope,* no. 1080 (June 18, 1927): 88.

70. "Creative Artists and their Methods," *Bioscope,* no. 1080 (June 18, 1927): 99.

71. "Have We the Talent?" *Picturegoer,* no. 78 (June 1927): 8-10. The other directors surveyed were Maurice Elvey, T.A. Welsh, Sinclair Hill, and Manning Haynes; the article included photographs of all six.

72. Angus MacPhail, "Testing the Public Pulse: Bernstein Questionnaire," *Kinematograph Weekly,* no. 1060 (August 11, 1927): 36-37. The number of responses represented in this sample is not stated. MacPhail became a frequent Hitchcock collaborator in both Britain and America, and Bernstein would finance Transatlantic Pictures, Hitchcock's venture into independent production in the late 1940s, which enabled him to make *Rope* and *Under Capricorn.*

73. *Bioscope,* no. 1089 (August 18, 1927): 36; *Kinematograph Weekly,* no. 1062 (August 25, 1927): 47.

74. *Bioscope,* no. 1080 (June 18, 1927): 102; in the *Evening Standard* the drawing was attributed to "Tom Titt."

75. *Kinematograph Weekly,* no. 1067 (September 29, 1927): 48; the sketch is signed Ginsbury.

76. *Bioscope,* no. 1089 (August 18, 1927): 36.

77. *Daily News,* October 5, 1927: 4, and October 15, 1927: 5, respectively; see also *Bioscope,* no. 1087 (August 4, 1927): 23, and *Kinematograph Weekly,* no. 1064 (September 8, 1927): 67, and no. 1067 (September 29, 1927): 54.

78. *Kinematograph Weekly's* comments ranged from the pointed— "Alfred Hitchcock, now making an intensive study of ringside modes will shortly begin *The Ring* for British International"—to the indirect: "Mrs. Alfred Hitchcock (Alma Reville) was injured in a car smash last Saturday, but not seriously" (no. 1050 [June 2, 1927]: 35, and no. 1058 [July 28, 1927]: 27).

79. Although the first use of the phrase "Hitchcock touch" has yet to be identified, it (or an analogous variant), is attested at least twice by summer 1927; see, for example, a review of *Easy Virtue* in *Bioscope,* no. 1090 (August 25, 1927): 51, citing an unnamed source.

80. For a sample of responses to *Easy Virtue,* see *Kinematograph Weekly,* no. 1063 (September 1, 1927): 67, and *Bioscope,* no. 1091 (September 1, 1927): 67). The highly-touted trade showing of *The Ring* on September 30 at the Capitol Theatre in Haymarket created quite a stir. The film critic for the *Daily Chronicle* called that event "one of the most notable occasions in the history of British films" (cited in an advertisement for the picture in *Kinematograph Weekly,*

no. 1068 [October 6, 1927]: 18), and several critics pointed to this film's ability to compete with the best products from abroad (e.g., *Daily Mail, Daily Telegraph, Daily News, Evening News, Reynolds's,* all cited in that same ad).

81. Respectively, *Sunday Express* 457 (October 2, 1927): 4; *Daily Mail* and *The Star* (cited in an ad for the picture in *Kinematograph Weekly,* no. 1068 [October 6, 1927]: 18); and *Bioscope,* no. 1095 (September 29, 1927): 66. See also *Kinematograph Weekly,* no. 1067 (September 29, 1927): 56.

82. "Putting Over the Coming Releases," *Kinematograph Weekly,* no. 1067 (September 29, 1927): 84.

83. "Downhill," *The Picturegoer,* no. 82 (October 1927): 39-42. Relationships between Fleming's digest "narration" and the source play, preliminary cinematic treatment, and screenplay of *Downhill* are discussed in Vest, "Metamorphoses," 76-81.

84. For example, the 800-word synopsis for *Downhill* issued by Gainsborough (reprinted in *Cinema World,* no. 6 [October 1927]: 21-22) that offered a brief plot summary sprinkled with bits of dialogue taken directly from the film's intertitles.

85. Sydney Tremayne, from an article in *Eve* (October 19, 1927), cited in Barr, *English Hitchcock,* 220. The *Sunday Express* for October 16 commented on the frequency and length of these appearances: "*Downhill* continues at the Plaza with Ivor Novello in 10-minute stage appearance twice daily" (4). A pre-release in the West End was not an unusual event and was anticipated for *The Ring* (see *Daily News* [October 1, 1927]: 5); however, the live appearance of a principal actor, melded into the action of the film, was newsworthy. In press coverage of this event the second actor remained unnamed. Barr claims it was indeed Robin Irvine (*English Hitchcock,* 18).

86. *Kinematograph Weekly,* no. 1069 (October 13, 1927): 40; cf. *Daily Telegraph* (October 11, 1927): 6, and *Daily Mail* (October 10, 1927): 17. Christine Gledhill discusses this and other instances of combined live and filmed performances in Britain in the 1920s in *Reframing British Cinema 1918-28: Between Restraint and Passion* (London: BFI, 2003), 11-16. Mike Budd documents a framing Prologue and Epilogue enacted at select screenings of *Caligari* as early as 1921 (*The Cabinet of Dr. Caligari: Texts, Contexts, Histories* [New Brunswick: Rutgers Univ. Press, 1990], 64-68). With *Downhill* the novelty resided in the fact that the live performance interrupted the film at a key moment in its unfolding narrative rather than coming before, after, or at the interval.

87. See Williams, *Novello*, 159-66; MacQueen-Pope, whose interest lay in Novello's stage career, viewed the actor's films as minor ventures.

88. *Daily Mail* (October 10, 1927): 8.

89. *Daily Telegraph* (October 11, 1927): 6; *Evening Standard* (October 10, 1927): 4; M.W.D., "Plaza (This Week): *Downhill,*" *[Sunday] Observer* (October 16, 1927): 15.

90. References are, respectively, to *Picture Show,* no. 444 (November 5, 1927): 11, and *Cinema World,* no. 6 (October 1927): 5, 19, 21-22.

91. Truffaut, *Hitchcock,* 51.

Michael Walker

"A Hitchcock Compendium": Narrative Strategies in Torn Curtain

The screenwriter of *Torn Curtain*, Brian Moore, has said of the film: "Apart from . . . three ideas, the film is little else than a Hitchcock compendium. I told him that . . . the credits should read 'Screenplay by Alfred Hitchcock, assisted by Brian Moore,' but he said he never took writing credit."[1] This article looks at *Torn Curtain* from the point of view of its "borrowings" from earlier Hitchcock films. We would of course expect any Hitchcock film to have connections to his other works. The reasons for this have been well-rehearsed: his complete control over his films extended to working with the writer in structuring the narrative, and then with all his other collaborators to ensure that, so far as possible, the film was exactly the way that he wanted. But Brian Moore, who had viewed Hitchcock's previous films as part of his "homework" whilst working with the director,[2] evidently felt that *Torn Curtain* went further than the usual auteurist links. It is this I would like to explore.

There are two main threads to my argument. The first is relatively straightforward: I merely point out some of scenes and incidents in *Torn Curtain* that support Moore's observation. The second, which will form the core of this essay, is more contentious. I will argue that, so far as the film's narrative is concerned, *Torn Curtain* is in fact a heavily skewed Hitchcock compendium, since most of its "derivative" Hitchcock material is from one film, *Psycho* (1960). It's as if the earlier film provided a skeletal narrative framework, which was then fleshed out with the necessary

trappings of a very different sort of story. I will suggest
possible reasons for Hitchcock's adoption of this strategy
later. First, I will look at the details of the connections
between the two films. Elements from other earlier films—
together with the three ideas that Moore modestly lays claim
to—will be considered as they arise. In order to highlight the
narrative links between the two works, I will discuss the two
films together, act by act, following the model proposed by
Kristin Thompson which I applied in my article on *Topaz* in
Hitchcock Annual 13.[3] The first three acts of each film may be
paralleled with some precision; only the fourth act occurs at
a different structural point in each work. Accordingly, Act IV
is cited twice: at the point where it begins first in *Psycho*, then
in *Torn Curtain*.

Act I

In comparing and contrasting *Psycho* and *Torn Curtain*, I
shall assume that the plot of *Psycho* is well-known; I will only
refer to it in order to draw the connections. Each film
introduces its hero and heroine in a bed scene, in which it is
implied—within the censorship conventions of the time—that
they have just had sex. In *Psycho*, they are in a Phoenix hotel
and the first comment Sam Loomis (John Gavin) makes to
Marion Crane (Janet Leigh) is that she has not eaten her lunch.
In *Torn Curtain*, they are on a ship in a Norwegian fjord and
the first comment Michael Armstrong (Paul Newman) makes
to Sarah Sherman (Julie Andrews) is also about lunch. As each
couple's dialogue continues, it becomes apparent that,
whereas the heroine is anxious to marry, the hero is reluctant.
Sam explains his reluctance: his dead father's debts; his ex-
wife's alimony. Michael, a nuclear physicist, is evasive: it only
emerges later that he has made plans—a fake defection to the
communist East Germany in order to steal a nuclear secret—
which do not include Sarah, even though she is both his
assistant and his fiancée.

Each film thus begins with the heroine experiencing a
blockage in her relationship with the hero that creates a sense

of insecurity. He is not as committed to the relationship as she would like. What happens, in effect, is that the hero leaves the heroine but she follows, without his knowledge, as her way of dealing with this problem. Sam merely flies home to Fairvale, California. However, Marion is then tempted by $40,000 cash waved in front of her by Cassidy (Frank Albertson), a client of her boss; she steals the money and sets out to drive to Fairvale. Her behavior is irrational: the money is presumably meant to solve Sam's financial problems and thereby enable them to marry, but it will be obvious to everyone that she stole it.

In *Torn Curtain*, time elapses before Michael makes his equivalent, but more sinister, plane flight from Copenhagen to East Berlin in order to present himself to the East German authorities as a defector. During this period, in place of the scene with Marion in her office, is Sarah's visit to a Copenhagen bookshop to obtain a book for Michael, a book which—as befits the spy genre—includes a message in code, read in secret by Michael, about an organization called "pi." Sarah then learns that Michael is postponing their wedding indefinitely: he tells her that he is going to Stockholm, but she discovers that he is in fact flying to East Berlin. To his horror, she follows him on the same plane. Here it is Michael's failure to trust Sarah that prompts her pursuit, which is motivated, like Marion's, to be with the man she loves, but without Marion's irrationality.

Structurally, the message in the book is the spy movie equivalent of the $40,000: each becomes a guilty secret carried into what Robin Wood calls the chaos world: the world of danger and disorder into which Hitchcock's protagonists are typically plunged.[4] In each film, we enter this world at the beginning of the second act: Marion arrives at the Bates Motel; Michael and Sarah arrive in East Berlin. By this stage the "guilty secret" is carefully hidden: Marion has concealed the stolen money in her purse; Michael has memorized the message, which is encapsulated in the mathematical symbol pi. That in *Psycho* it is Marion who carries the guilty secret and in *Torn Curtain* Michael is a feature of the shifting points of identification in the later movie, an issue I shall discuss later. The dominant point of view in the film is still Sarah's, but the scene in which Michael first reads about pi is set in a men's toilet. In another link with *Psycho*, the one scene in which Marion takes out the stolen money in order to spend some of it occurs in a woman's toilet (at the garage where she changes cars).[5]

While Michael and Sarah are in Copenhagen, there is a short scene that derives from a Hitchcock film other than *Psycho*. As Michael is having a shower, Sarah takes a phone message from the bookshop and, because he is resisting her suggestion that they do something together, announces that she will go and pick up the book. Michael fails to exit from the shower in time to stop her. The material here is a reworking of a far more complex scene in *North by Northwest* (1959) between Eve (Eva Marie Saint) and Roger (Cary Grant) in her hotel room in Chicago, where the equivalent phone message is for her, and where he only pretends to take a shower because he is suspicious of her wish to get rid of him. Whereas Roger handles the situation expertly, even decoding Eve's destination from the trace of its imprint on the note-pad, Michael is simply clumsy, with the result that Sarah goes off to do something that might have been dangerous. The sense of possible danger is enhanced in that she is accompanied to the bookshop by Professor Karl Manfred (Günter Strack), who has been showing an unusual interest in the couple's activities.

During her drive, Marion is observed, on a number of occasions, by men to whom her behavior seems suspicious: her boss as she leaves Phoenix; a highway patrolman and a car salesman en route. Karl creates a similar sense of suspicious observation in the early scenes in *Torn Curtain*. In fact, Karl will eventually turn out to be an essentially sympathetic figure whom Michael is using in order to carry out his fake defection. But, at this stage, Michael's duplicity means that Karl is quite properly suspicious: why hasn't Michael involved Sarah in his plans?

Psycho is more focused here: our point of view stays with Marion and we share her anxiety about characters looking at her with suspicion. *Torn Curtain* is more complicated. In the early scenes, Karl is the suspicious figure. But as soon as Sarah has given Michael the book, he begins to behave in a manner which *she* finds suspicious: he obtains some tickets from a travel agent; he disappears into the men's room with the book (he said he was going to leave it with the concierge). This relates *Torn Curtain* to a number of 1940s Hitchcock films in which the heroine becomes worried about the behavior of the man she loves: *Rebecca* (1940), *Suspicion* (1941), and *Shadow of a Doubt* (1943). The common ingredient is that the man either cannot or will not be honest with the heroine about his actions. But whereas the earlier heroines for the most part suffer in silence, Sarah confronts Michael with her suspicions and, when he still won't come clean with her, actively sets out to do something about it. She follows him on the plane to East Berlin.

The scene on the plane is another that echoes a similar scene in an earlier Hitchcock movie. In *Notorious* (1946), Devlin (Cary Grant) and Alicia (Ingrid Berman) fly from Florida to Rio de Janeiro in order to spy on a cell of Nazis. Behind them, towards the back of the plane, sits Prescott (Louis Calhern), Devlin's boss. The spatial positioning of the characters on the plane is very similar in *Torn Curtain*: Michael and Karl, the former a would-be spy, sit at the front of the plane, Sarah at the back. Although this in itself is of minor interest, next to Sarah on the plane sits a ballerina (Tamara Toumanova) who will later play an important role in seeking to expose Michael to the East German authorities. Her heartless indifference to the fate of the hero and heroine is not dissimilar to Prescott's indifference to that of Alicia. Like Prescott, she puts ideology before humanity. In both films, the figure at the back of the plane, silently watching, is one who will turn out to have the real power.

Act II

When the protagonist(s) arrive in the chaos world, two new key characters are introduced: in *Psycho*, Norman Bates (Anthony Perkins) and, in the background, his "mother" (in quotes to emphasize that she has an animated presence only in Norman's psychotic version of her); in *Torn Curtain*, Gerhard (Hansjoerg Felmy), head of state security, and Gromek (Wolfgang Kieling), the secret service agent appointed to keep an eye on Michael.

"Mrs. Bates" and Gerhard may be seen as the superego figures who "watch over" the chaos world, with Norman and Gromek as their agents. The former function as superego figures in the sense that they act to censor and control those who enter their world. The psychological power structure of *Psycho* ("Mrs. Bates" as a split-off part of Norman that tyrannizes him) is thus reworked in *Torn Curtain* in political terms. The two superego figures "instruct" their agents quite differently—Norman is berated for wanting to consort with Marion; Gromek is expected to shadow Michael—but the underlying position is the same: the intruder (Marion; Michael) is viewed with great suspicion.

The key structural difference between the two movies is encapsulated in the contrasting nature of the superego figures. In *Psycho*, the core of the film is psychological; in *Torn Curtain*, it is political, and each film's concerns are modulated accordingly. Thus, to the superego figures, the harmony of their world is potentially threatened by the arrival of the intruder, but Marion represents a sexual threat, Michael a political one. However, it is a measure of the superiority of *Psycho* that "Mrs. Bates" may be related, psychically, to Marion as well as to Norman,[6] whereas Gerhard is an external superego figure, without a dynamic relationship to either the hero or the heroine.

At the airport in *Torn Curtain*, Michael reads a statement to the assembled dignitaries and journalists stating that he is defecting to East Germany in order to share his knowledge with their scientists about an anti-missile missile project "and thereby abolish the terror of nuclear warfare." The East German vice minister smiles cynically at this: he does not see Michael's defection that way. But the very fact that Michael is really intending to do the opposite—and steal the communist scientists' knowledge—precisely aligns him with the vice minister: he is just as cynical. It is here that we have a beginnings of a typically Hitchcockian critique of the opportunism of the hero. It may be somewhat buried, but it is at least implicit.

Relevant to the Hitchcock compendium, however, is that here Michael becomes—in the eyes of Sarah and the western world—a "falsely accused man," one of Hitchcock's most familiar plot structures.[7] Although we do not yet *know* that he is "falsely accused," we may well suspect it, and it is not very long before it is confirmed, i.e., we learn that he is not in fact intending to defect. But there is an important difference between *Torn Curtain* and other Hitchcock films with this plot. In all the other examples, either the heroine "knows" that the hero is innocent or he protests his innocence. In some of these cases, she refuses to believe him, but at least he is able to speak on the matter. *Torn Curtain* is the only Hitchcock film in which the falsely accused hero feels that he *cannot* tell the heroine of his "innocence" because the knowledge could jeopardize his mission and endanger her. This means that the character in earlier Hitchcock who most closely mirrors Michael in this respect is not a hero at all, but Eve in *North by Northwest*.

In *Hitchcock and Homosexuality*, Theodore Price suggests that Michael's "defection" is a coded reference to his homosexuality, and that the film contains a number of details which support such a reading.[8] Unfortunately, Price misses the crucial point here: that Michael is only *pretending* to defect. It is true that it looks from Sarah's point of view as if Michael and Karl have "run off together": the plane scene, and the way—like Devlin and Alicia before them—they are the couple at the front, is a good example. But Michael is really like Eve: someone who seems to be involved in a "suspect" liaison, but who is in fact using this liaison to pursue a secret mission. Just as Eve cannot tell Roger "the truth" about her relationship with Vandamm (James Mason), so Michael cannot tell Sarah "the truth" about his relationship with Karl and, beyond that, the communist régime.

A further point in common at this stage between *Psycho* and *Torn Curtain* is each heroine's more considered reaction to her pursuit of the hero. After her conversation with Norman in his parlor, Marion is sufficiently moved by his story (his version of his relationship with his "mother") that she now regrets what she's done: she wants to go back to Phoenix and return the money. Sarah also wants to go home, but only if Michael will take her: she wants to put a stop to what she sees as his defection. When he declines, she decides to stay.

The difference here arises from each heroine's awareness of her relationship to "the law": Marion has broken it, and now seeks to rectify this; Sarah sees Michael as the person who has broken it, and stays—we assume—to continue her project of convincing him that he's wrong. Just as, in *Psycho*, we see nothing of the reactions of those from whom Marion has stolen (we have, instead, her thoughts imagining their reactions), in *Torn Curtain*, apart from a few barbed comments from the western journalists during Michael's airport press conference, we see nothing of the reaction of American public opinion to his apparent defection. From one point of view, Sarah represents this public opinion. Were Michael a genuine defector, she would represent his conscience; as it is, she is now sidelined as the narrative shifts to follow him.

This begins the following day, when Michael sets out to shake Gromek from his tail. To do this, he visits the Berlin National Gallery, walks through it very rapidly and slips out a back exit. This scene is a typical example of Hitchcock's introduction of famous tourist sites into his narratives: there are echoes here of the use of the British Museum for a chase in *Blackmail* (1929) and the Palace of the Legion of Honor for the revelation of a plot detail in *Vertigo* (1958). But to note these earlier instances is to draw attention to the rushed super-ficiality of this sequence in *Torn Curtain*. The repetition—from *The Man Who Knew Too Much* (1955)—of the eerie effect of echoing footsteps is slightly more effective: even as Michael keeps tabs on Gromek's pursuit by listening for his footsteps, he is unable to muffle his own giveaway steps.

Having (temporarily) eluded Gromek, Michael takes a taxi to a local farm to make contact with a member of pi. It is at this point that he is revealed to be a false defector, with pi as the organization which will help him escape from East Germany once he has completed his mission. The latter, we learn, involves tricking a German scientist into revealing a secret formula which he, unlike Michael, has managed to work out. The formula is the film's MacGuffin: the object of the quest in a Hitchcock spy movie.[9]

The farm in *Torn Curtain* is in one crucial respect the equivalent of the Bates Motel and house in *Psycho*: it is the out-of-town site where the film's famous and horrific murder takes place. It is this feature of the Bates Motel and house that has led Carol J. Clover to refer to them as the seminal example of the "terrible place" of the modern horror film.[10] But if we see the whole of East Germany as the chaos world, i.e., the equivalent of the motel and house, then at least one additional parallel may be drawn. Immediately outside the motel is the swamp, where Norman buries his victims in their cars. In the background shots of East Berlin in *Torn Curtain* are bombed buildings, presumably a relic of the war. In both films, the more recent structures (we learn that the motel was relatively recently built) have been constructed alongside emblems of decay and destruction that still remain. The latter signify "the repressed" of the chaos world: a feature that is either hidden (*Psycho*) or ignored (*Torn Curtain*).

When Gromek succeeds in finding his way to the farm, he identifies Michael as an American spy through the shape of pi Michael had earlier traced on the ground. This is the equivalent of the assumed name, Marie Samuels, that Marion used to sign the motel register, which likewise reveals to Norman—after the conversation in the parlor—that she is an "impostor." Immediately after this discovery, Norman spies on Marion as she undresses. Then the famous shower murder occurs: Marion is brutally killed by Norman in an amnesiac fugue as his "mother." Norman's voyeuristic spying on an unwitting Marion is again translated, in *Torn Curtain*, into its political equivalent: Gromek identifies Michael himself as a spy. A violent struggle ensues, in which Michael and an unnamed farmer's wife (Carolyn Conwell) finally manage to kill Gromek.

The messiness of the murder here—the sheer difficulty of killing a strong man who is fighting for his life—is one of the three ideas Brian Moore lays claim to, and that aspect of the murder is undoubtedly very powerful. Equally, however, the murder scene occurs at the same point as in *Psycho*: in the second half of the second act, forty-seven minutes (*Psycho*) and forty-eight minutes (*Torn Curtain*) into the film. The links between the scenes are strengthened by the participation of the farmer's wife, whom Michael introduces to Gromek as a relative of his mother. Just as Marion's murder is carried out by Norman and his "mother" acting as one, so Gromek's murder is carried out by Michael and a woman who is structurally a mother figure.

Although I do not wish to do a detailed comparison of the two murder scenes, a few points may be made. The contrast between them illustrates the familiar Hitchcock distinction between surprise and suspense. Marion's murder—short, shattering, its impact heightened by rapid editing, the slashing knife, Marion's naked vulnerability and Bernard Herrmann's shrieking violins—is a brilliant example of surprise, or, more accurately in this case, shock. Gromek's murder—prolonged, painful, its impact heightened by the way in which, whatever damage is done to his body, Gromek fights grimly on—is by contrast a rather grisly example of Hitchcockian suspense. In this case, there is no music, and the tension is enhanced by the need for the killers to keep the murder as silent as possible: the taxi driver is still waiting outside. At the beginning of the struggle, Gromek, confident of his ability to handle these two amateurs, is actually cracking jokes. But as the fight continues, with Gromek first stabbed by the farmer's wife and then beaten to the floor by her with a shovel, the tone changes—we begin to empathize with his suffering. At the very end, as the two finally succeed in killing Gromek by gassing him, his fingers release their hold on Michael's neck and flutter. Marion's dying gesture, too, is focused on her hands: she reaches out to grasp the shower curtain before collapsing over the bath. Both gestures, in their helplessness at the moment of death, seem similarly poignant.[11]

As Robin Wood points out, a crucial feature of this scene in *Torn Curtain* is that we *want* Michael and the farmer's wife to kill Gromek. We are implicated in the murder.[12] At the same time, we cannot help but feel for Gromek in the way he is subjected to such pain. This sympathy is enhanced by Wolfgang Kieling's quite brilliant performance, and the sense, as Robin Wood points out, that at some level Gromek wants to die. Overall, this is one of Hitchcock's most disturbing sequences, an excellent illustration of the fruitful collaboration between the director and his co-workers.

After the murder, Michael is so traumatized that he cannot function properly: it is the farmer's wife who takes off his bloodied coat and then leads him to the sink to wash his bloody hands—exactly as if he were a child. In the aftermath of *Psycho*'s murder there is a similar moment when Norman goes to the sink to wash his bloody hands. At the end of the murder sequence, the victim and her/his vehicle are buried together: Marion in the trunk of her car in the swamp; Gromek and his motorcycle on the farmland. And, just as the remainder of the $40,000 goes with Marion into the swamp, so the giveaway symbol of the "guilty secret" in *Torn Curtain* is also, in effect, buried. The sequence at the farmhouse ends with the farmer's wife erasing the sign for pi Michael had traced in the ground.

Although the victims are structural opposites, the sense that both murders are prompted by voyeurism strengthens the links between the two scenes. "Mother's" murder of Marion may be seen as both an attempt to repress the sexual allure of her nakedness—what she aroused in Norman when he spied through his peep-hole—and to punish Norman for his voyeurism. On the familiar analogy that can be drawn between voyeurism and espionage,[13] Michael is a would-be voyeur, and Gromek is the agent of the state whose job it is to prevent him. Accordingly, Gromek is murdered in order to avoid the consequences for both the killers of Michael's political voyeurism being exposed. Here the punishment for voyeurism is brutally warded off.

By now it is clear that the narrative of *Torn Curtain* is motivated less by the heroine's desire than by the hero's wish to advance his career. Because of the failure of Michael's anti-missile missile project ("Gamma 5"), he has been demoted from Washington research to university teaching, and this has emasculated him: his self-esteem is so reduced, he is even reluctant to marry his fiancée. Michael's pursuit of the MacGuffin is thus symbolically the pursuit of the phallus: the secret formula that will make his anti-missile missile work. In *Psycho*, the $40,000 has the same intended function as the nuclear secret: Marion wants to give it to Sam so that they can marry, i.e., she seeks to make him "potent." In other words, the $40,000, too, may be seen symbolically as the phallus.

As with a number of the links between the two films, however, what happens in *Psycho* is more radical. It is Marion who steals the money: a basic transgression of gender norms. Marion is fully aware of her transgression: during her car drive, she imagines Cassidy wanting to punish her: "If any of it's missing, I'll replace it with her fine, soft flesh." As V.F. Perkins has noted, shortly after this moment there are crucial pre-echoes of the shower murder: the rain on the windscreen prefigures the shower water, the windscreen wipers themselves the stabbing knife blade. Perkins uses these pre-echoes to suggest that, in the murder itself, it's as if "[Marion] is destroyed by an explosion of forces existing within her own personality."[14] But in *Torn Curtain*, where it is the hero who is in quest of "the phallus," and where the heroine is not transgressive of gender norms, a similar narrative path can be followed without the traumatic disturbance brought about by Marion's violation of such norms.

The contrast between the murder victims necessarily creates different narrative imperatives. In *Psycho*, the heroine has been killed, and the film needs to unravel the mystery of her murder. In *Torn Curtain*, the hero has killed a "villain," and the film needs to extricate him from this predicament. In addition, Michael still has to obtain the MacGuffin, which means that he has to gain the confidence of the scientist who knows the secret formula, Professor Lindt.

Act III

Despite the contrasting narrative trajectories, structural links between the films continue. In each, we now have a shift of location, followed by the introduction of two further characters: the film's "helpers." In *Psycho*, the narrative moves to Sam's hardware store in Fairvale: Lila (Vera Miles), Marion's sister, and then Arbogast (Martin Balsam), a private detective, arrive, each independently looking for Marion. In *Torn Curtain*, the action shifts to Leipzig, where Michael is contacted by Dr. Koska (Gisela Fischer), who will arrange his escape out of East Germany. He then meets Professor Lindt (Ludwig Donath), who is destined to become an involuntary helper, providing Michael with the nuclear secret despite himself.

In both films, the female helper offers her services without preconditions. Lila is simply concerned to find Marion; Dr. Koska is a politically motivated activist. The male helper, by contrast, is suspicious, and instigates an investigation of sorts into the integrity of the hero. This extends the suspiciousness of the primary superego figures to another character (Arbogast thinks Sam is in league with Marion), or another area (Lindt thinks Michael is not as clever as he pretends). Arbogast is wrong, but his suspicion—that Marion is hiding out somewhere locally—eventually takes him to the Bates Motel. Lindt is right, but his curiosity about Michael's nuclear program is aroused. However, at this stage in each film, the investigating helper is blocked by a lie. Questioned by Arbogast, Norman says that Marion did come to the motel, but stayed the night and left the next morning. As Lindt and other scientists question Michael about his research program, the session is interrupted by the arrival of Haupt, Gromek's replacement, who asks Michael about his visit to the farm: Michael admits going there, but denies that he saw Gromek. Each lie is prompted by anxiety that the murder will be discovered. And, although neither lie is believed, it produces a blockage: Norman won't let Arbogast talk to his mother; the other scientists are now forbidden to speak to Michael. As Arbogast and Michael seek to find ways round this blockage, two strikingly different results occur. Arbogast's return to the house to talk to Mrs. Bates results in his murder; Michael's decision to take Sarah into his confidence (so that she can act in his place) leads to a renewal of their relationship.

The scene in which Michael "confesses" to Sarah is another that belongs in the Hitchcock compendium. It takes place at the top of an obviously studio-bound hill, as Karl and Haupt watch from below: the first part of the scene is shown from their point of view, so that we cannot hear what Michael is saying. The image of the couple on the hill top evokes other such scenes in Hitchcock, notably those in *Suspicion* and *The Birds* (1963). The connotations of this are the subject of an excellent article by Alain Bergala on the Genesis imagery in Hitchcock.[15] In terms of structure, however, the scene may be seen as a reworking of the one in *Strangers on a Train* (1951) when Guy (Farley Granger) confesses to Anne (Ruth Roman)—whilst his police minder Hennessy (Robert Gist) looks on from across the road—his knowledge of his wife Miriam (Laura Elliot)'s murder. Again the comparison shows the superiority of the original scene. In *Strangers on a Train* the scene is beautifully worked out: we stay with Guy and Anne as he tries desperately to explain the highly improbable situation he is in, and Hennessy, watching his performance with a keen eye, is immediately suspicious. In *Torn Curtain*, not only do Karl and Haupt have no equivalent suspicions, but Michael—who, unlike Guy, is genuinely guilty of murder—is let off the hook by his fiancée: it is Sarah's overwhelming joy and relief at his story that is communicated. This points to a characteristic weakness of the film: its failure to confront—except obliquely—the implicit nastiness of the hero.

Even though *Psycho* and *Torn Curtain* have contrasting events at this stage, they continue to have parallel scenes. Baffled by Arbogast's failure to return from the motel, Sam goes there to look for him. He arrives and calls for him while Norman is out in the swamp sinking his car and body. The next scene in *Torn Curtain* is Gerhard searching the now empty farm. In other words, both films at this point show a fruitless search of the terrible place, looking for a character who has mysteriously disappeared, and who we know has been murdered. In effect, the two murders of *Psycho* are collapsed into one in *Torn Curtain*. Just as, with Marion's murder, it is the murderer (Norman as "mother") who parallels those (Michael and the farmer's wife) in *Torn Curtain*, so, with Arbogast's murder, it is the victim. Gromek and Arbogast are similar in key respects: each is an officially licensed snooper, who threatens to expose the unnatural nature of the relationship between the man and the woman in the terrible place. Again, psychological deviance (*Psycho*) has been replaced by what is, from the communist point of view, political deviance (*Torn Curtain*).

Later that night, Gerhard's men dig up Gromek's motorcycle: they've found his body. Up to this point, Michael has been linked structurally with a series of characters in *Psycho*: Sam, then Marion, then Norman. These shifting associations seem appropriate to the slipperiness of Michael's character. However, now that he has told Sarah the truth about his motives, and the discovery of Gromek's body has placed him in jeopardy, his identity as "hero" is stabilized. He and Sarah are now working together as a couple. This, in turn, relates back to the next stage of *Psycho*, in which Sam and Lila now act as a couple.

Act IV (Psycho)

The last act of *Psycho* begins with Sam and Lila learning that Sheriff Chambers (John McIntire) has already visited the Bates motel and has failed to find anything untoward. Accordingly, the resolution of the mystery falls to them. The sequence in which they visit the motel posing as a married couple, and Sam keeps Norman busy while Lila searches the house for Mrs Bates, is structurally the equivalent of Michael teasing the secret formula out of Lindt, while Sarah waits anxiously elsewhere in the university building. In *Psycho*, both Lila and Sam are actively involved; in *Torn Curtain*, only Michael, but there are crucial links in the confrontations between the two men. First, the men are shown as in some sense like doubles of one another. Second, the hero is finally tackling the other man (Norman, Lindt) over the very object which, it was hoped, would in some sense restore his potency (the $40,000; the secret formula). But, whereas in *Torn Curtain* the secret formula is the only mystery to be solved, *Psycho* leads to a deeper mystery: the nature of the horrors in the terrible place.

In *Psycho*, as Robin Wood has noted, Sam and Norman in the office are filmed *visually* like mirror images.[16] But I would read this "doubling" more to Sam's detriment than Wood does. Sam is trying to get Norman to tell him what he, Sam, thinks lies behind Marion's disappearance: that Norman killed her for the $40,000. In other words, Sam is pressuring Norman to agree to his own (petit bourgeois) version of Norman's secret: murder prompted by greed. In addition, Sam resents the thought that Norman (he assumes) has the $40,000, as if it gives the latter a potency that Sam feels should be his. When he says to Norman "I think if you saw a chance to get out from under, you'd unload this place," he's projecting his own wishes onto Norman. But Norman is far more pathetic than Sam realizes. He possesses neither the $40,000 nor the phallus: the former went into the swamp with Marion, and other symbolizations of the latter, such as the knife "mother" wields so lethally, merely serve to emphasize Norman's lack.

In the confrontation in *Torn Curtain*, the men are not matched visually, but they are professionally equivalent figures. Here Michael knows that Lindt possesses "the secret of the phallus," and so he's more subtle in his approach than Sam. But he is also more ruthless than Sam: by the end of the scene, he has tricked Lindt into giving up the formula. At the beginning of the scene, confident of his superior knowledge, Lindt lights an enormous cigar. But at the moment Michael irritates him to the point where, in exasperation, he is goaded into revealing his secret, he hurls the cigar to one side—an act Hitchcock emphasizes through a shot of it bouncing off the blackboard frame. This play with the cigar is a typical example of Hitchcock's sometimes humorous use of Freudian symbols.

A final link is that, just as the scene here ends with the revelation of the secret inside Lindt's head, so the sequence in *Psycho* culminates with the revelation of the secret (repressed) inside Norman's head: Mrs. Bates's skeleton. In *Torn Curtain*, the secret is an unseen mathematical formula written on the blackboard. Because it's the MacGuffin, it can remain unseen: it doesn't matter what the formula says. But in *Psycho* the enigma posed by the materialization of Mrs. Bates as a skeleton and of Norman dressed in her clothes is so puzzling that a psychiatrist (Simon Oakland) is wheeled in to explain to us what has been going on. The secret in Norman's head is far more interesting to us than that in Lindt's.

The idea of having the MacGuffin as a secret formula that needed to be tricked out of a physics professor was, according to Spoto, the second of Moore's original contributions to the script. Hitchcock had of course used the idea of the MacGuffin hidden inside a character's head before: the state secrets memorized by Mr. Memory (Wylie Watson) in *The 39 Steps* (1935); the treaty clause known to Van Meer (Albert Basserman) in *Foreign Correspondent* (1940). Nevertheless, *Torn Curtain* elaborates the idea more successfully: considering that, so far as the audience is concerned, Michael and Lindt are writing mathematical gibberish, the "blackboard duel" is remarkably exciting. Again, Moore has come up with an idea that is quintessential Hitchcock, but has also found a way of dramatically improving it.

During the blackboard duel, there are announcements over the ubiquitous loudspeakers concerning Michael and Sarah, announcements which finally alert Lindt to the fact that Michael is now a wanted man. This "voice of God" effect is an extension of Gerhard's power, and it could perhaps be related to the first manifestation of "Mrs. Bates," her voice booming out from the Bates house across to Marion's cabin. There is no doubt that this effect in *Psycho* could only be achieved with the aid of a loudspeaker, but we accept its implausibility as an aspect of the film's stylization. However, it is striking that Hitchcock has given each superego figure a similar trope of power in her/his authority over the chaos world.

Act IV (Torn Curtain)

In *Psycho*, there are only two more scenes after the psychiatrist's "explanation": Norman as "mother" alone in a cell, with "her" thoughts in voiceover, and the brief closing shot of Marion's car being hauled out of the swamp. In *Torn Curtain*, the equivalent of this last shot is Gromek's motor cycle being disinterred, which is at a much earlier stage in the narrative. After Michael has scribbled down the MacGuffin, *Torn Curtain* has some way to go: Michael and Sarah are still deep inside East Germany, and an elaborate escape plan is put into action to get them out. It is their escape that constitutes the fourth act in this film. Their journey on an unscheduled bus from Leipzig to East Berlin has echoes of Marion's car journey in the first act of *Psycho*: at one point they are threatened with a policeman's suspicious scrutiny; the scheduled bus behind them creates the same sort of suspense as the patrolman's car following Marion. But, for the most part, *Torn Curtain* has no equivalents in *Psycho* for the various sequences during their escape.

It is perhaps significant that, in these sequences, *Torn Curtain* notably loses its tension and drama. The bus journey has its moments, but is too long. The episode with the Countess (Lila Kedrova) in East Berlin (Moore's third contribution) I find almost unwatchable because of the actress's overindulgent performance. Only one scene in this act has the density of Hitchcock's best work: that set in a theatre during a ballet performance of *Francesca da Rimini*. As I note later, critics have drawn allusive parallels between the events on stage and the plight of the protagonists. At the same time, this is another sequence which belongs in the Hitchcock compendium. Making her second appearance in the movie, the ballerina notices Michael in the audience, and summons Gerhard and his police. Realizing that he is surrounded, Michael leaps up and shouts "Fire!," creating a very similar audience stampede as in equivalent "public disturbances" in *The 39 Steps* and *Saboteur* (1942).[17] This enables Sarah and him to escape.

The first two-thirds of *Torn Curtain* seems to me to sustain interest despite some weak scenes but, in the last third—with the notable exception of the theater scene—Hitchcock's inspiration seems to have largely deserted him. Even though Hitchcock and Moore were unlikely to have consciously modeled the narrative of the film on that of *Psycho*, it's as if their intuitive use of the earlier film was a lifeline. When it was no longer possible, the film became (by Hitchcock's standards) routine.

The very end of *Torn Curtain* then reintroduces, in a displaced form, material from the last two scenes of *Psycho*, but in reverse order. In the final shot of *Psycho* what we are seeing is Marion's coffin: the car trunk. In the penultimate scene of *Torn Curtain*, Hitchcock plays with the idea of a similar fate for Michael and Sarah, but then saves them for a happy ending. In order to escape from East Germany, they have hidden in two costume baskets on a ship bound for Sweden. As the ship docks and the baskets are lifted ashore, the ballerina (who has traveled on the same ship) deduces that "amerikanische Spione" are in them, and prompts an East German naval officer to machine-gun them. But, as the baskets fall back on the deck, only costumes spill out; Hitchcock then pans to show two different baskets, now empty of Michael and Sarah, who are busy swimming ashore. Rather than the baskets becoming their coffins, the imagery is of rebirth.

In the penultimate scene of *Psycho*, the camera tracks in to Norman as "mother," wrapped in a blanket, imagining that there are people out there watching her. In the last scene of *Torn Curtain*, Michael and Sarah, having shed their wet clothes, are each wrapped in a blanket. As a man signals through a transom that he would like to take their photograph, Michael hides both of them behind his blanket. In the final shot, the camera tracks in to the blanket. But the tone is again radically different in each film: whereas Norman's insanity is deeply disturbing, Sarah's appreciative "Oh, Michael" tells us that romantic relations have been resumed between them.

Before concluding, a brief comment on the relationship of *Torn Curtain* to Hitchcock's earlier spy narratives is in order. *The 39 Steps, Saboteur,* and *North by Northwest* all have very similar narrative structures, but they are quite different from that of *Torn Curtain*. Peter Wollen's Proppian analysis of *North by Northwest* suggests an explanation: that the narratives of these films conform to an older, archetypal pattern.[18] Obviously this pattern is inflected by Hitchcock in certain specifically auteurist ways, but if we take the Propp structure as a generic feature, then what we have in these films is the sort of authorship and genre mix familiar in classical cinema.

Torn Curtain does not really work this way. Although there are elements that evoke the Propp functions—lack, departure, pursuit, journey between "two kingdoms," interrogation, the roles of the helpers—these are intermittent. They do not account for the film's basic narrative structure, which, as I have argued, comes from that of *Psycho*. One could hypothesize why this should be so: having problems during the scripting of *Torn Curtain* with the direction its plot should take, and not wishing to follow *The 39 Steps/North by Northwest* format again, Hitchcock (albeit unconsciously?) fell back on another structure that had already worked. But *Psycho* seems a curious choice. Raymond Bellour has argued that its narrative structure is in fact highly untypical, both of Hitchcock and of the classical cinema in general.[19] The narrative of *Torn Curtain*, by contrast, seems far from untypical. The film has the characteristic features of Hitchcock's spy movies: the hero's two parallel quests (to prove that he is "falsely accused" and to obtain the MacGuffin); the heroine's ambivalent response to his quests; Oedipally charged confrontations with hostile father figures; the constant fear of being exposed/caught/ murdered by the rival agents. In addition, *Torn Curtain* conforms to (and *Psycho* violates) one of Bellour's key features of classical cinema: "the end must reply to the beginning."[20] In *Torn Curtain* the couple behind the blankets at the end "answers" the couple under the blankets at the beginning, with the hero presumably now no longer having difficulty with his relationship with his fiancée.

One reason why the narrative of *Psycho* provided such a useful template for *Torn Curtain* is implicit in the transformations: the ease with which a psychosexual element in the former could be translated into a political one in the latter. An explanation for this would seem to lie in the Freudian nature of Hitchcock's narratives: specifically here the focus on voyeurism and its political equivalent, spying. Norman's sexual voyeurism—the last and most eroticized of the male gazes directed at Marion—provokes psychotic murder; Michael's political voyeurism, when exposed, provokes defensive murder. In addition, both films are motivated, from the heroine's perspective, by frustration of sexual desire. In *Psycho*, this is annihilated in the central murder, but in *Torn Curtain*, an equivalent narrative trajectory is followed in order to find a way of getting past this murder and satisfying desire. Viewed thus, *Torn Curtain* functions as a retracing of the path of *Psycho* so as to provide the couple with a happy ending. Both films also include more general auteurist features: guilt and the sense of being watched; transgression linked to entry into the chaos world; the translation, in the chaos world, of sex into murder; the reverberations of this murder across the film's subsequent narrative. Although this by no means accounts for all the links between the two films, it at least suggests that the narratives have a certain compatibility.

At the same time, some of the transformations—$40,000 into a hidden message in a book on mathematics; a false name in a register into a mathematical symbol in the earth; a woman's skeleton into a mathematical formula on a blackboard—suggest a fundamental impoverishment of the material. The transformations are ingenious, but they lack the resonances of the originals, resonances that even extend to Marion's false name (see below). *Psycho* is dealing with far more challenging material than *Torn Curtain*, and there is a general sense, in the transformations, that the radical aspects are lost.

The Central Murders

I would like to conclude by looking at one feature common to *Psycho* and *Torn Curtain* that seems to have resonances beyond the structural links: the central murder. In the conclusion to his original chapter on *Psycho*, first published in 1965, Robin Wood refers to the Nazi death camps, mentioning that, at the end of the war, Hitchcock was involved in the compilation of a documentary on the camps.[21] This story has since been researched in detail.[22] Wood makes no specific links between the camps and anything in *Psycho*, but in a lecture in the late 1960s, Kevin Gough-Yates pointed out a number of connections that could be made between the circumstances of Marion's murder and events in the concentration camps:

1) The Bates Motel, located a short way outside town, is a place where terrible things have been going on over the years, but no-one has really investigated them, as if a collective blind eye has been turned.

2) Marion is brutally murdered in a shower, and this is followed by (a) an extensive sequence in which all signs of the crime are removed and (b) the disposal of her body in what could well turn out to be a "mass grave" of Norman's victims (the swamp).

3) Samuels is a Jewish surname.

4) The words Marion imputes to an irate Cassidy during her car drive clearly evoke Shylock's "pound of flesh" in Shakespeare's *The Merchant of Venice*, another Jewish reference.

5) A customer in Sam's shop muses about mass extermination: "They tell you . . . it's guaranteed to exterminate every insect in the world, but they do not tell you whether or not it's painless. I say, insect or man, death should always be painless."[23]

Although each of these features in isolation seems unremarkable enough, collectively they are very suggestive. The documentary Hitchcock helped structure was not shown for over forty years, but he was still one of the first to see the terrible footage of the camps. It's as if the traumatic material of *Psycho* released echoes of this, albeit only in the subtext. A further factor is the horrific material in the case history that first prompted Robert Bloch to write the novel of *Psycho*: the activities of a notorious serial killer, Ed Gein. In his book on the making of *Psycho*, Stephen Rebello actually quotes Bloch as saying of Gein: "the gentleman was also given to perversions in the time-honored tradition of the Nazi death camps."[24] Although, for obvious reasons, none of Gein's specific depravities could be shown in a Hollywood film of 1960, they suggest another reason why the film might include death camp overtones—as a trace of these original "perversions."

In *Psycho*, intimations of such horrific practices could only be registered in the subtext. But as the Hollywood serial killer film has, in recent years, pushed further and further into the sickness and evil of the killer, the links between what the killer gets up to and Nazi death camp atrocities have become steadily more pointed. In *Se7en* (David Fincher, 1995), for example, such links are almost explicit—in, for example, the meticulously documented sadistic "experiments" by John Doe (Kevin Spacey) on live victims. And, to complete the associations that began with *Psycho*, Doe's torture of the Jewish lawyer, Gould (the figure punished for "Greed") is to force him, literally, to cut a pound of flesh out of himself.

In *Torn Curtain*, the murder in the isolated farm house lacks these associations, but includes two further features: the German setting itself and the use of the gas oven. Although these features alone are hardly sufficient, the way in which they supplement those in *Psycho* suggests that the echoes of the camps have not subsided. If we see the film as a reworking of the material in *Psycho*, then *Psycho*'s version of the slaughter—Marion as a metaphorical Jewish victim—is answered by this version, in which, symbolically, the "victims" turn on a "guard" and murder him. In fantasy, *Torn Curtain* returns to the terrible place of *Psycho* and enacts a different version of the slaughter, in which the protagonist is able to kill rather than be killed. At the end of the film, not only do Michael and Sarah look like refugees, but they are addressed as such by the Swedish authorities who have taken them in. They have survived the trauma which is symbolized by the murder in the terrible place, and escaped, like refugees, with only the clothes on their backs.

Over the years—the earliest reference I have found is in an interview with Bryan Forbes at the National Film Theatre, London in October 1969—Hitchcock himself has occasionally

mentioned the death camps in reference to the killing of
Gromek. In a recent biography, he indicates that the
connection was in fact first made by the critics: "It has been
suggested that the killing of Gromek by putting his head into
a gas oven was a reference to the Holocaust. Who knows? I
was deeply affected by film footage of the prison camps I saw
at the end of the war."[25] I would argue, however, that the
shower-bath murder in *Psycho* had already alluded to this
material and, implicitly, its psychic importance to Hitchcock.
And it is that version, in which the heroine is killed, that is by
far the darker of the two.

Both *Psycho* and *Torn Curtain* are "descent films," in which
we are taken from a world of order into a metaphorical
underworld. In *Psycho* this underworld deals with
psychological horrors, horrors that may be related, if only
obliquely, to one of the greatest atrocities of the age. *Torn
Curtain* would seem to pale beside such a powerful work, but
if it is seen on its own terms, it has much to offer. Robin Wood
mentions that the "souls in torment" credit sequence is picked
up in the symbolism of the ballet performance of *Francesca da
Rimini* on stage.[26] Peter Conrad develops this line of analysis,
noting the relevance of the stage imagery of Dante's Inferno to
the protagonists' passage through the "underworld" of
communist East Germany.[27] Peter Wollen has suggested that
Michael "combines the figures of Peeping Tom and Faust," so
that, during the theatre performance, Gerhard is like
Mephistopheles coming to claim him.[28] That all of these
allegorical readings have resonances with the events in the
film would suggest that, although *Torn Curtain* does suffer
from comparison with the best of Hitchcock's earlier works, it
is by no means a negligible achievement.

Notes

Thanks to Sid Gottlieb and Richard Allen for extremely constructive
feedback during the drafting of this article. The essay will appear in
Unexplored Hitchcock, forthcoming from Cameron and Hollis.

1. Donald Spoto, *The Dark Side of Genius: The Life of Alfred Hitchcock* (London: Frederick Muller, 1988), 489.

2. Spoto, *Dark Side*, 488.

3. Michael Walker, "Topaz and Cold War Politics," *Hitchcock Annual* 13 (2004-05): 149-51; Kristin Thompson, *Story Telling in the New Hollywood: Understanding Classical Narrative Technique* (Cambridge: Harvard University Press, 1999), 22-44.

4. Robin Wood, *Hitchcock's Films Revisited* (New York: Columbia University Press, 1989), 145, 198.

5. I discuss Hitchcock's fondness for setting scenes in toilets and bathrooms in *Hitchcock's Motifs* (Amsterdam: Amsterdam University Press, 2005), 112-14.

6. I discuss this in *Hitchcock's Motifs*, 280-82.

7. See Wood, *Hitchcock's Films Revisited*, 241-45.

8. Theodore Price, *Hitchcock and Homosexuality* (Metuchen, NJ: Scarecrow Press, 1992), 367-80. I discuss the muddle Price gets himself into in *Hitchcock's Motifs*, 255.

9. See Walker, *Hitchcock's Motifs*, 296-306 for a discussion of the MacGuffin in Hitchcock's work.

10. Carol J. Clover, *Men, Women, and Chainsaws* (London: British Film Institute, 1992), 30.

11. I discuss the difference between male and female gestures under "Hands" in *Hitchcock's Motifs*, 220-37. I argue that Gromek's dying gesture is coded as "female," thus contributing to our sympathy for the character, 223-24.

12. Wood, *Hitchcock's Films Revisited*, 202.

13. See Peter Wollen: "Hitchcock's Vision," *Cinema* (UK) 3, (June 1969): 2. I discuss this aspect of Hitchcock's films in *Hitchcock's Motifs*, 171-73, 255-57.

14. V.F. Perkins, *Film as Film* (Harmondsworth: Penguin, 1972), 113.

15. Alain Bergala, "Alfred, Adam and Eve," in Dominique Païni and Guy Cogeval, eds., *Hitchcock and Art: Fatal Coincidences* (Montreal: The Montreal Museum of Fine Arts, 2001), 111-25.

16. Wood, *Hitchcock's Films Revisited*, 147.

17. I discuss this under "Public Disturbances" in *Hitchcock's Motifs*, 335-43.

18. Peter Wollen, "*North by Northwest*: A Morphological Analysis," *Film Form* 1, no. 1 (1976); reprinted in Wollen, *Readings and Writings: Semiotic Counter-Strategies* (London: Verso, 1982), 18-33.

19. Raymond Bellour, "Psychosis, Neurosis, Perversion," *Camera Obscura* 3/4 (1979): 105-32; reprinted in Bellour, *The Analysis of Film* (Bloomington: Indiana University Press, 2000), 238-61.

20. Bellour, "Psychosis, Neurosis, Perversion," in *The Analysis of Film*, 238.

21. Wood, *Hitchcock's Films Revisited*, 150.

22. See Elizabeth Sussex "The Fate of F 3080," *Sight and Sound* (spring 1984): 92-97.

23. I don't think Kevin Gough-Yates has ever published this material. In an article that alludes to some of its elements, "Private Madness and Public Lunacy," *Films and Filming* (February 1972): 27-30, he is much more circumspect. He adds a further point—that the shower flattens Marion's hair so she looks as though her head has been shaved—but merely comments: "The shower sequence relates to the whole social guilt of mass murder and the propensity to pretend it does not exist" (30).

24. Stephen Rebello, *Alfred Hitchcock and the Making of* Psycho (New York: HarperCollins, 1991), 13.

25. Charlotte Chandler, *It's Only a Movie: Alfred Hitchcock: A Personal Biography* (London: Pocket Books, 2006), 286.

26. Wood, *Hitchcock's Films Revisited*, 199.

27. Peter Conrad, *The Hitchcock Murders* (London: Faber and Faber, 2000), 275-79.

28. Wollen, "Hitchcock's Vision," 2-3.

JACQUELINE TONG

Hong Kong Rear Window:
Backyard Adventures *(1955)*

In 1955, Alfred Hitchcock's Technicolor film *Rear Window* (1954) was remade into a Cantonese dialect black-and-white film in Hong Kong (color film was not common in Hong Kong until the 1960s). Entitled *Backyard Adventures (Houchuang)*, the film was produced by Liang You Film Company (Liangyou Yingye Gongsi), founded by the Cantonese actor Zhang Ying.[1] It was directed by Chen Pi, Zhu Ji, and Wu Hui. The film was produced in commemoration of the death of a famous leftist Cantonese comedian, Yi Qiushui (1904-55). The production crew and cast of Cantonese opera and screen stars participated voluntarily in the production so that the revenue could be used to help the destitute family left behind by Yi Qiushui, who contributed all the money earned from his film career to charitable and patriotic causes.[2]

The term "leftist" here describes those filmmakers in Hong Kong who are sympathetic to the Communist cause and set up film collectives to realize their political ideals. The majority of performers from the cast of *Backyard Adventures* were of Cantonese origin, born in mainland China, and who had taken up residence in Hong Kong. Many performed on stage in either plays or Cantonese operas. In Hong Kong, interpersonal networks were formed in drama societies and other contexts among cultural workers with a shared sympathy for progressive and patriotic goals. Personal contacts in social and professional activities provided expedient contexts for these associations and collaboration in cinematic ventures. Many of these filmmakers had no official

Chinese Communist Party affiliation or extensive knowledge of Marxism.[3] They brought with them, however, a strong commitment to the fate of the modern Chinese nation and a focus on educational films with a social consciousness to raise patriotic and moral awareness among the public.[4] Since the establishment of the Peoples Republic of China (PRC) in 1949, prominent Hong Kong-based leftist film companies such as The Union Film Enterprise Limited, Xinlian Film Company, and Hualian Film Enterprise Limited, although not directly funded by the PRC, were granted distribution rights in the Mainland despite China strict censorship of other Hong Kong films.[5] Leftist filmmakers in 1950s Hong Kong were influenced by Hollywood films and it was common for them to adapt Hollywood films and foreign literature.[6] These films and literary works that were not banned in the British colony Hong Kong (as they were on the Mainland) were frequently remade with a local flavor.

The popularity of Hitchcock in Hong Kong encouraged the remaking of Hitchcock films.[7] At the time when both *Rear Window* and *Backyard Adventures* were made, the portrayal of life in tenement buildings was an already established genre in Hong Kong leftist cinema. *Rear Window* had interesting points of contact with the tenement building genre. Although social realism is not the main theme in *Rear Window*, it nevertheless displays American life in the tenement buildings in Greenwich village in postwar America. *Backyard Adventures* borrowed Hitchcock choice of tenement buildings and the courtyard as narrative locales, while adapting the plot to suit Hong Kong leftist filmmakers commitment to postwar social realism. It therefore exemplifies how non-Hollywood filmmakers' manipulate Hollywood material for their own very different purposes. Presenting people's lives in tenement buildings enabled filmmakers to exhibit disparities of fortune and aspirations among citizens from different social strata realistically, and to highlight conflict and cooperation in a group setting. A tenement building can be read as a collective microcosm where it is necessary for people of different backgrounds and aspirations to live together. Hong Kong tenement building films like *In the Face of Demolition* (1953) emphasize interdependence.[8] Each tenant has to follow an unspoken code of conduct in his or her private space, the apartment, and respect the other tenants, in order to preserve a sort of order and avoid conflicts. Those who do not conform end up isolated and become helpless in crises. As an expression of social realism, filmmakers used tenement building films to convey strong moral messages, addressing social themes in strongly materialistic terms.

Backyard Adventures is about a photojournalist, Yu Wangyuan (Zhang Ying), the counterpart of L.B. Jefferies (James Stewart) in *Rear Window*. Like Jeff, he is wheelchair-bound and lives in an apartment. He broke his leg while taking pictures with some sailors on an ocean liner traveling back home. As a result of his immobility, he lives in the apartment of his fiancée, Minhua (Zhou Kun-ling), who plays the remake's version of Lisa Fremont (Grace Kelly). To alleviate Wangyuan's boredom, Minhua has recommended that he looks out of the apartment at the people in the opposite buildings. He sees a variety of people, including: a *gandie* wanting to marry his *gannuer*,[9] but who falls in love with his son; a divorcée, neglecting his young son, going out with the landlady, a widow who has inherited her husband wealth; a hoodlum living off his girlfriend's money, earned from prostitution; a married couple, who are an actor and an actress, rehearsing their scenes at home; a gym trainer and the landlady quarreling because his dog has bitten her cat; a sly Chinese fortune teller fraudulently making money; a newlywed couple always closing their curtains; people working out in a gym; and Cantonese opera performers practicing in a Cantonese opera school out on a balcony. Wangyuan has been very entertained until he suspects the divorcée of having murdered his ex-wife, the prostitute, who is also the hoodlum's girlfriend. After a series of attempts to solve the crime, it turns out that the man has not killed his ex-wife, but the trainer's dog.

According to film veteran and Cantonese opera actor Ruan Zhaohui, a lot of film workers pleaded to take part in this charity production.[10] A film veteran, Xue Hou, who was affiliated with the Hong Kong leftist film circle in 1950s, recalled that *Rear Window* was chosen to be adapted because it could be remade into a script with many subplots to accommodate a lot of actors.[11] Because each window or apartment can accommodate a subplot, it allows performers who usually act in different genres to appear in distinct stories and distinct styles, unified by Wangyuan's main plot. For example, a Cantonese opera school scene is added for actors who usually appeared in Cantonese opera films.[12] This combination of diverse genre performers into a cinematic showcase can be seen as a strategy to create diverse audience appeal, in order to maximize revenue. The film rights were sold to distributors in North and South America.[13]

Backyard Adventures marks an important chapter in Hong Kong film history. First, it was made for Yi on an impressive scale of production with the support of many important Hong Kong film personalities. Three three-storied building blocks were built for *Backyard Adventures* at a discounted price of 2,000 Hong Kong dollars offered by the Feng Shengquan Scaffolding Company.[14] This set was built outdoors. Second, Yi was an extremely important actor, as he was a Cantonese opera actor for more than ten years and had appeared in nearly 400 films.[15] Many magazines and newspapers in 1955 emphasized that this was the first time in Cantonese film history that this many prominent performers were gathered together in the same film. A majority of the cast and crew involved were affiliated with the most important Hong Kong leftist film production companies. The filming lasted from July until November in 1955.[16] It was shown for three days in twenty cinemas and was popular with audiences.[17] The film raised 1.8 million Hong Kong dollars and Yi's family used the money to purchase a building and rent it out.[18]

Various aspects of *Backyard Adventures* recall *Rear Window*. As my description above of the narrative indicates, there are many similar characters in both films: a photojournalist (the main character in each), a salesman (in *Rear Window*, Lars Thorwald is a salesman; the equivalent character in *Backyard Adventures* is a failed businessman, although his business is not specified in the film), newlywed couple, artists (there are singers and opera and screen performers in *Backyard Adventures*, and a sculptress and a composer in *Rear Window*), and a white-collar worker. The layout of the apartment in *Backyard Adventures* is similar to that of Jeff's apartment, including the location of the telephone, the stairs just beyond the door, and the windows. The placement of the tenants' apartments, the tenement buildings, and the courtyard also recalls specific details in *Rear Window*. The suspense plots, other than their different endings, also evolve in similar ways: in the middle of a night, Wangyuan vaguely sees what looks like a person being pushed by another person out of the third floor into the courtyard, with a distinct loud sound in the background (Jeff hears a woman screaming in the middle of the night), but his vision has been blurred because he has taken sleeping pills (Jeff has fallen asleep while he observes Lars Thorwald). Wangyuan has earlier seen the divorcée, Mok (Lu Dun), and his ex-wife, Lily (Zi Luolian), fighting on the stairwell (Jeff sees the Thorwalds quarreling frequently).

Lily's subsequent failure to appear in public reinforces Wangyuan's suspicions that Mok has murdered her (Jeff suspects Lars Thorwald of having murdered his wife; the blinds are down in their bedroom and he does not see her after they are opened again). Moreover, in both films the inferences made by the protagonists and the way they seek to trap the criminal are similar: they see the hand saws and large luggage, and therefore believe that the victim has been chopped up and removed; they call on the aid of a detective; and they call the suspect and send a note to him. In both films the suspect goes to the protagonist's apartment, although Wangyuan does not use any flashbulbs to protect himself. Both protagonists are thrown out of the window by their respective suspects and eventually end up with both legs broken. Finally, both Jeff and Wangyuan sleep peacefully at the end of the two films. But despite these similarities, many plot points in *Backyard Adventures* were altered in a manner that reflects the different production circumstances and intentions of the films.

The filming of *Backyard Adventures* was not as pre-planned as *Rear Window*, and its control was not as centralized. Some decisions concerning the plots in *Backyard Adventures* were made on location. *Rear Window* was solely directed by Hitchcock, whereas *Backyard Adventures* was shot by three directors. It is well known that Hitchcock scrupulously pre-planned his films and would typically shoot according to what he had already envisioned, scripted, and often story-boarded.[19] But during shooting, the directors of *Backyard Adventures* adjusted to their performers' abilities and preferences. For example, there is a scene with two blind singers, played by prominent Cantonese opera and screen actresses Ren Jianhui and Hong Xiannu. According to Ruan, these roles were added so Ren and Hong could sing in the scenes.[20] Some decisions concerning a Cantonese opera scene were made on location. There is a scene in which Wangyuan is casually looking out of his window and sees on the opera school balcony a group of performers rehearsing a scene from a Cantonese opera called *Blood-Stained Armor Dyed Red as Rouge* (*Yanzhi Xueran Zhanpao Hong*).[21] The scene is about a general requesting more soldiers from a princess. According to Ruan, this opera was chosen because it was what the actors Mai Bingrong, Chen Jintang, and Chen Yannong were most famous for, and they just decided to do that scene right before it was filmed.[22] During the rehearsal, the performers are wearing Cantonese opera costumes, and the opera director stands on the side of the balcony to supervise them. He yells out from time to time when he is dissatisfied, which is intended to show that it was a rehearsal in a school instead of a real performance. The narrative structure of *Backyward Adventures* was thus more loosely constructed and impro-vised than in the Hitchcock film.

Furthermore, *Rear Window* establishes a close connection between the main romantic plot and the various sub-plots in the courtyard that is absent from *Backyard Adventures*. In *Rear Window*, the relationship between Jeff and Lisa is unstable and changing, and the neighbors' actions may all be considered to reflect different phases and aspects of it. The audience's perception of the social space of the courtyard is thus subordinated to the main plot of the romantic relationship. All the narratives in the courtyard focus on the vicissitudes of romance and marriage, which the audience is cued to connect with the state of Jeff and Lisa's relationship throughout the commentary the characters give on what they see and hear. In addition, the relationship between Jeff and Lisa changes through the film as they respond to events across the courtyard. At first, the relationship is volatile and difficult, but when Lisa joins Jeff in his investigation and proves herself adventurous and brave, his attitude to Lisa begins to shift from resistance to empathy.[23]

However, in *Backyard Adventures*, Wangyuan's relationship with Minhua is stable, harmonious, and full of hope. From the beginning of the film, Wangyuan has decided to give up his job as a photojournalist to become a civil engineer in order to have a stable life with Minhua. He is recovering from his broken leg in Minhua's apartment, whereas Jeff in *Rear Window* lives alone. He does not have a nurse to take care of him like Jeff. Rather than acting in the manner of Jeff, who resists Lisa taking care of him, he is very happy to be under Minhua's attentive care. (Minhua works the night-shift so she could attend to Wangyuan in the daytime; her exact occupation, however, is not mentioned in the film.) While in *Rear Window* the conflicted romance takes center-stage and the rest of the action revolves around it, in *Backyard Adventures*, the focus is shifted from the now-harmonious relationship of the protagonists to the social interactions of the various members of the tenement community that surround them, and of which they form a part. In *Backyard Adventures*, the courtyard is a collective social microcosm. Even if there are issues in romance and marriage, they are not related to Wangyuan's relationship with Minhua.

In comparison with *Rear Window*, the narrative of *Backyard Adventures* appears highly decentered. Scenes were added to accommodate diverse performers, without a unifying theme. The Hitchcock plot, which is highly unified around crime and romance, is relatively dispersed in *Backyard Adventures* due to the fact that the various stories that take place in the courtyard can no longer be viewed as reflections of the states or stages of the central romance. Yet the social ideologies of the Hong Kong filmmakers do, to some extent, re-unify the plot around the idea of collective social portrayal, of which the main relationship forms a part.

Rear Window emphasizes the subjectivity of the film protagonist, Jeff, and his relationship with Lisa, while *Backyard Adventures* does not put as much emphasis on Wangyuan's subjectivity. Using eyeline matches and point-of-view editing, Hitchcock gives the impression that shots of the tenants' activities are mainly drawn from Jeff viewpoint.[24] The film moves between omniscient and restrictive narration, and Hitchcock rarely lets his audience look at things that Jeff would not be able to see. On the whole, perceptual subjectivity is emphasized. Masks surround the visible frame from Jeff's point of view as he looks through the long lens of his camera or through his binoculars. What Jeff can see is always limited. Physically small objects in the apartments across the courtyard are blurred or not visible from Jeff's position. Jeff is restricted in his ability to see, while the audience is analogously restricted by the camera placement. For example, Jeff cannot see if Lars Thorwald has pulled out a wedding ring from his wife's handbag. He cannot see the Thorwalds' physical interaction behind the wall between their windows. Most of the tenants' dialogue is not decipherable or audible from Jeff's physical distance. Jeff can only hear muffled noises and piano music, not the conversations going on in the songwriter's apartment during his party. He cannot clearly make out what the Thorwalds are arguing about either. The use of sound thus on the whole strengthens the impression that the audience's access to narrative information is mainly mediated through Jeff's perception or from his space.

The presentation of the tenants' stories in *Backyard Adventures,* on the other hand, is not mainly based on Wangyuan's point of view. There are shots of places that are impossible to be seen from Wangyuan's apartment, such as a scene of Minhua at the harbor after she has left work and a long take of Minhua running to Mok apartment. Furthermore, Wangyuan is often shot from outside his window, as if the tenants opposite are also observing him. The implication that Wangyuan is being observed strengthens the effect of a collective portrayal: people are actually observing one another, and the right to observe is not merely limited to Wangyuan. In this way, social realism is embedded in the cinematic style of the film. Wangyuan, like Jeff, uses binoculars to read the tenants' stories. Indeed, Wangyuan uses his binoculars to observe the tenants from the beginning until the end of *Backyard Adventures*, whereas Jeff does not start using his until the suspense plot starts in the middle of *Rear Window*. The binoculars function as a pretext for the audience to become involved in the lives of these characters.

Framing and editing are executed differently in *Backyard Adventures* than in *Rear Window*, in order to emphasize a collective portrayal. In *Rear Window*, there are always black masks that indicate portions that are out of the range of Jeff's binoculars or telephoto lens, and therefore not visible to him. In *Backyard Adventures*, no mask is applied when Wangyuan looks through his binoculars and his long lens. There are shots of Wangyuan looking through his binoculars, followed by a cut to medium to long shots of the tenants' activities and their immediate surroundings occupying the whole frame without masks. The audience thus gains access to more visual information about every tenant's life in *Backyard Adventures* than in *Rear Window*. We see events independently and fully, not from Wangyuan's restricted point of view. Since what we see in the film is not primarily a projection of Wangyuan's romantic relationship and individual concerns, a stronger sense of a shared social space is created. The visual style of the film thus helps give equal weight and autonomous status to the stories of characters other than the main protagonist.

The sound design in *Backyard Adventure* also reinforces the impression that our access to narrative information is not mediated through one individual perception. Many conversations between the tenants are clearly decipherable to the audience. The sound would not be audible if we were confined to the protagonist's point of view. One of the tenant's stories is about a well-off middle-aged *gandie* (He Zecang) who wants to be romantically involved with his *gannuer* (Fang Yanfen). The *gannuer* is much younger than him and is in love with his son. He prevents them from getting married, but the *gannuer* and the son trick the *gandie* into sponsoring them to get married. This sequence criticizes the bourgeoisie in using wealth to suppress individual freedom and demand obedience from the underprivileged. In a stationary low-angle medium shot of the *gandie* and the *gannuer*, the sound of the *gandie* clicking the cigarette lighter is clearly audible to the audience. The characters speak in a moderate volume that is compatible with the lighter clicking sound. The audience hears conversations taking place very far from Wangyuan, but the film cuts to Wangyuan reacting to the tenants' conversation, although it would be physically impossible for him to have heard them. Wangyuan starts to find the other tenants' conversations inaudible only when they are related to the suspense plot of the film. *Backyard Adventures* sacrifices verisimilitude for the sake of omniscience, which reflects the filmmakers' intention to focus on the collective space of the building and on the various stories.

Although rear-window ethics is a major theme in *Backyard Adventures*, the sexual dimension of voyeurism is eliminated and the emphasis is simply on spying. The film has removed the sexual objects as the focus of the male gaze and the male urge to peep. In *Rear Window*, Miss Torso and Lisa are thebjects of sexual desire or fantasies for Jeff and Doyle, implied by their instant attention to Miss Torso and Lisa's night gown. Jeff has given Miss Torso that name because he objectifies her body. Jeff is attracted by how Lisa looks when she wears her night gown, and Doyle is curious when he sees the night gown in the suitcase. Voyeurism is a way for Jeff and Doyle to fulfill their sexual curiosity and fantasies. In *Backyard Adventures*, no women dress as skimpily as Miss Torso, and Wangyuan has neither sexual curiosity nor fantasies about his neighbors. Wangyuan and Minhua's actions are not suggestive of sex. Minhua has never tried to please him with revealing clothing and we don't see them kissing, in contrast to *Rear Window*, where there are dramatic shots of Jeff and Lisa kissing and several instances of her on display for him.[25]

Voyeurism in *Rear Window* plays a significant role both in its plot and in the development of character. Voyeurism enables Jeff to uncover a crime and gives him the chance to develop a better understanding and loving relationship with Lisa, despite also giving him another broken leg. Jeff is educated to become a more compassionate person through peeping and investigating Thorwald's crime. In *Backyard Adventures*, spying does not help Wangyuan solve a crime other than the death of a dog, and there is no indication that Wangyuan's attitude has changed toward the people around him at all as a result of these activities. Wangyuan lacks Jeff's cynical edge. He is compassionate, warm, and friendly to people around him throughout the film. For example, he is always smiling to other people and is kind to his cousin who comes to visit him. Because his legs have become broken as a result of having mistakenly suspected someone as a murderer, Wangyuan says he will not spy anymore, but overall Wangyuan changes less drastically and is perhaps less in need of personal change than Jeff.

The morality of spying is a central concern of *Rear Window* and the film arrives at a rather ambiguous conclusion. While the film overtly critiques voyeurism, this criticism is to some extent undercut by the fact that Jeff's peeping actually leads him to infer correctly that a crime has taken place and brings a murderer to justice. Although Jeff, Lisa, and Doyle express their concern that voyeurism might be unethical because it invades others' privacy, Jeff's discovery of a murder has redeemed him from being simply an immoral voyeur. In contrast, the morality of spying is not central to *Backyard Adventures,* for the main function of the spy story is to provide a pretext to portray social life in the courtyard. Wangyuan mistakenly concludes from what he sees across the courtyard that a person has been killed, when in fact the only crime that occurs is the killing of a dog. This allows the film to end on a light, comical note. In *Rear Window*, both a dog and a person are killed, and both of these events are grim and serious mysteries, although ultimately resolved or at least brought to light as a result of Jeff's compulsive curiosity.

Unlike *Rear Window*, *Backyard Adventures* focuses on cultural conflicts between the older and younger generations, which respectively embody traditional Chinese values and modern Chinese values with Western influences. The *gandie*, wanting to marry his *gannuer*, represents a paternal mindset based on traditional Chinese feudal order, in which young women were often forced because of their traditional financial dependence on men into a marriage with a much older man whom they do not love. The younger generation, the *gandie's* son and the *gannuer*, think independently and go against their father's wishes, showing their aspiration for individualism and equal opportunities, which is different from the traditional Chinese belief that individuals have to be bound by societal order. In another scene, a father (Ma Shizeng), who is in his traditional Chinese costume, criticizes his daughter (Rong Xiaoyi) for wearing an off-the-shoulder shirt and mini shorts. He insists on her wearing a traditional loose Chinese *qipao* of his deceased wife, or else he would not give her the money to see a movie with her friends. The daughter then wears the *qipao* over her initial outfit to deceive her father and get the money away. Right after she gets out of his sight, she takes off the *qipao* and puts it into her handbag.

The fact that Minhua works the night shift while Wangyuan stays at home also shows the switch of traditional gender roles in this relationship. The fact that it does not cause any disagreement between the lovers shows their liberation from traditional norms. The relationship between Wangyuan and Minhua demonstrates the leftist filmmakers aspirations for equality between genders. *Rear Window* also focuses on the struggle for equality and harmony between the sexes and dramatizes the switching of gender roles, but the tensions and disruptions caused by the attempted linking of an independent, assertive, working woman and a feminized, domesticated man are by no means completely resolved.

Backyard Adventures presents an analysis and critique of people's suffering and their disregard for others' interests in society. The subplot mentioned above shows how freedom is threatened and suppressed by the wealthy class and feudal conventions. *Backyard Adventures* also emphasizes the contrasts between the rich and the poor. There is a scene in which Wangyuan looks out of his window from his spacious and well-furnished apartment. Two blind women and two musicians are holding onto one another's shoulders in a line, walking between Wangyuan's tenement building and the building opposite. There is a long take dedicated to the group pausing at the corner of the opposite backyard to sing a song. (It was common that blind people sang on the streets for a living in 1950s Hong Kong.) The song is a *nanyin* about desperation, self-pity, loneliness, and the tiresomeness of life.[26] They leave after failing to get the tenants' attention. Wangyuan looks out the window sympathetically. Even if Wangyuan wants to help by attending their performance, he is confined to his apartment. The scene reveals the segregation between the rich and the poor, and people disregard for others in society. Another example that exhibits people's selfishness and disregard for others is the relationship between the landlady and the divorcée, who is a failed businessman. The divorcée spends his time dating the landlady, frequently leaving his young son alone in the apartment crying, and eventually killing the gym trainer's dog because it has bitten the landlady's cat. The inclusion of a landowner in a film is common in 1950s Hong Kong cinema, representing a repressive authority figure who abuses and exploits the poor. The divorcée can be interpreted as a person who deliberately disregards familial or social responsibilities for his own materialistic concerns.

As we have seen, the central concern in *Backyard Adventures* is with the establishment of community in the modern urban environment, rather than with the ups and downs of the protagonist's relationship. But *Rear Window* also dramatizes a concern with social relationships and the establishment of community. Jeff's romantic relationship with

Lisa is actually strengthened via the empathic social bonds he develops with his neighbors. While the focus remains on the romance, the film is also about the establishment of community in an urban environment, which involves overcoming the boundaries of rear-window separation. In *Rear Window* the suspense plot is the central way in which the lives of the central couple are linked to the wider community. In *Backyard Adventures*, however, the suspense plot functions more as a pretext to stage the main concerns of the film in an entertaining way that self-consciously draws on the appeal of a highly successful Hitchcock thriller.

Comparing *Backyard Adventures* to *Rear Window* adds an interesting footnote to the study of Hitchcock's far-reaching influence, but also serves a broader purpose. There has been much research in general on the relationship of Hong Kong and Hollywood films, but the detailed investigation of foreign influences on postwar Hong Kong films in the 1950s is still in the beginning stage. Material from primary sources is scanty and often difficult to access, but well worth pursuing, as I hope my essay demonstrates. The making of *Backyard Adventures* illustrates how Hong Kong leftist intellectuals were open to Western influences to help them create new forms of cinematic expression in postwar Hong Kong to propagate their ideals, a subject that deserves and, I hope, will attract more attention from researchers.

Notes

I would like to thank Héctor Rodríguez, Richard Allen, Sidney Gottlieb, Renata Jackson, and Christina Chu for their support and suggestions during the writing of this paper. Special thanks to Hung Hing and Ainling Wong from the Hong Kong Film Archive (HKFA) for their precious time and effort in helping me out with gaining access to sources. Thank you to Li Lam, Elsa Li, and Sally Ng for their kind support. Thank you to Ms. Pinky Tam (HKFA), Ruan Zhaohui, and Paul Fonoroff for their invaluable information concerning *Backyard Adventures*, and You Tingfang, Lu Li, and Chen Wen for referring me to various people for information.

1. All the Chinese names in this article, including citations, are in pinyin. People's names are spelled out according to the Chinese practice of having the last name come before the first name.

2. For Hong Kong actors' biographies (1940-1969), see *Chinese Movie Database* (in Chinese), at www.dianying.com/b5/topics/hkstars/hkstar1.html.

3. The association of these compatriots could be defined as what Héctor Rodríguez referred to as "associational public spheres." These loose groupings often had "members who would join and leave depending on the evolution of their academic interests, political commitments, and personal relations"; see "Organizational Hegemony in the Hong Kong Cinema," *Post Script* 19, no. 1 (1999): 109.

4. Rodríguez, "Organizational Hegemony in the Hong Kong Cinema," 110; Ian Jarvie, *Window on Hong Kong: A Sociological Study of the Hong Kong Film Industry and Its Audience* (Hong Kong: Centre for East Asian Studies, 1977), 29.

5. Jarvie, *Window on Hong Kong*, 110.

6. Some examples from this period are Wu Hui's *The Matchmaker* (*Yuanyang Pu*) in 1955, a remake of Billy Wilder's *Sabrina* (*1954*); Zhou Shilu's *Snow White and the Seven Fellows* (*Xuegu Qiyou*) in 1954, an adaptation of the Brothers Grimm fairy tale, *Snow White*; and Zuo Ji's *The Sorrowful Lute* (*Pipa Yuan*) in 1957, a remake of Charles Vidor's *Love Me or Leave Me* (1955).

7. Hitchcock visited Hong Kong for four days from December 8 to 11, 1955, while *Backyard Adventures* was shown in cinemas from December 7 to 9, 1955. He attended a press conference to greet Hong Kong reporters on December 9, and a lot of prominent Chinese and English newspapers reported his arrival. There was no mention of whether Hitchcock has seen the Hong Kong remake, but it can almost be certain that he did not, and probably did not know of it, as Cantonese films were not dubbed or subtitled in Hong Kong back then. There are also other Hong Kong leftist remakes of Hitchcock films, such as Huang Keng *Black Cat, the Cat Burglar* (*Feizei Heimao*) in 1956, a remake of *To Catch a Thief* (1955), and Zhang Ying *The Night of Spirit Returns* (*Huiyunye*) in 1962, a remake of *Vertigo* (1958).

8. Tenement buildings used as backdrops in unfolding human stories in Shanghai films such as *Crows and Sparrows* (1949) also influenced a whole genre of Hong Kong melodrama.

9. A *gandie* is a man whose position is roughly equivalent to a foster father and godfather in Western countries without religious or

legal implications. I referred to *Dr. eye i-dictionary* (in Chinese) for this definition, at www.dreye.com:8080/axis/ddict.jsp?w=&dod= 0102&ver=big5. A *gannuer* is a girl or a woman whose position is roughly equivalent to a foster daughter and goddaughter in Western countries, also without religious or legal implications.

10. Ruan Zhaohui (b. 1945). Ruan was ten years old when he took part in *Backyard Adventures*, acting as a practitioner in a Cantonese opera school. I spoke with Ruan on the phone on May 10, 2006 about the film.

11. Xue Hou. *The Golden Age of Hong Kong Cinema* [*Xianggang Dianying de Huangjin Shidai*] (Hong Kong: Holdery Publishing Enterprise Limited, 2000), 84.

12. The actors who acted in Cantonese opera films at that time were all Cantonese opera performers on stage. Cantonese opera film was an indispensable genre in 1950s Hong Kong.

13. "An Announcement Concerning the Income from Backyard Adventures [*Houchuang* Shozhi Koushi Gongbu]," *Shangbao*, April 13, 1956.

14. It initially cost 3,500 Hong Kong dollars to build the set. The Feng Brothers, the owners of the Feng Shengquan Scaffolding Company, knowing that the film was a charity production for Yi Qiushui's family, reduced the price to 2,000 Hong Kong dollars. See "A Story behind *Backyard Adventures*: Scaffolding Workers Touched by Yi Qiu-shui [*Houchuang* Paishe de Gushi zhi Yi: Qiushui Gandong Dapeng Jishi]," *Shangbao*, June 25, 2006. There is no written record concerning who actually paid for building the set. Ruan and Paul Fonoroff, whom I spoke with on the phone on May 8, 2006, think Huada Film Studio probably sponsored it.

15. Li Muchang, "Film Talk: *Backyard Adventures* and Yi Qiushui [Yingtan: *Houchuang* yu Yi Qiushui]," *Dagongbao*, December 11, 1955. According to the Hong Kong Film Archive (HKFA), the exact number of films that Yi took part in is unknown, but it has a collection of 373 films in which he appeared.

16. Muchang, *Film Talk*. There was conflicting information concerning how long it took to film *Backyard Adventures*. According to Ruan, the film was shot in less than seven days. Because it was a charity production and they did not have much funding, the filming had to be done as quickly as possible. According to a magazine, *Backyard Adventures*, published especially for the film by Wenguang Printing House (Wenguang Yinwu Chengyin) in 1955, the production was a very slow process because there were too many actors.

17. "Relieve Yi Qiu-shui's family: *Backyard Adventure* was shown in twenty theaters in Hong Kong and Kowloon [Jiuji Yi Qiushui Yishu: Gangjiu Yajia Yingyuan Zuo Fangying Huochuang]," *Wenhuibao*, December 8, 1955.

18. Lin Jiang, *Backyard Adventures* [*Houchuang*], *Xinwanbao*, December 14, 1955; and Yu Muyun, *Anecdotes of Hong Kong Cinema, Volume 3, Part 2 of 1950s, 1955 to 1959* [*Xianggang Dianying Shihua, Juan 5, Wushi Niandai, Xia, 1955 to 1999*] (Hong Kong: Sub-Culture Ltd., 2001), 18.

19. For more information about the production details of *Rear Window*, see *Rear Window Ethics: Remembering and Restoring a Hitchcock Classic*, directed and written by Laurent Bouzereau, on the DVD of *Rear Window* (Universal Studios, 2000). See also Scott Curtis, "The Making of *Rear Window*," in *Alfred Hitchcock's* Rear Window, ed. John Belton (New York: Cambridge University Press, 1999), 21-56; and Steven DeRosa *Writing with Hitchcock: The Collaboration of Alfred Hitchcock and John Michael Hayes* (London: Faber and Faber, 2001), 5-51.

20. Phone conversation with Ruan Zhaohui on May 10, 2006.

21. The story is about Prince Sui Yangguang (569-618), the second son of Emperor Wen (541-604), of the Sui Dynasty (581-618). He has been involved in a forbidden liaison with a courtesan, Xianghong. Emperor Wen is enraged, and relocates Prince Yangguang from the capital to Lintong. Prince Yangguang is vengeful, and collaborates with the Princess who is in charge of Junhengshan in Danyang to make himself emperor. After Emperor Wen passes away, Yangguang changes Emperor Wen will, making himself the successor to the throne. Fights arise among the nobles and the princess.

22. Phone conversation with Ruan Zhaohui on May 10, 2006.

23. For a more in-depth analysis of the transformation of Jeff's attitude toward his investigation of Thorwald's crime, see Paula Marantz Cohen, "James, Hitchcock and the Fate of Character," in *Alfred Hitchcock: Centenary Essays*, ed. Richard Allen and S. Ishii-Gonzalés (London: British Film Institute, 1999), 15-28.

24. David Bordwell, *Narration in Fiction Film* (New York: Routledge, 1985), 42.

25. There is a scene in which Minhua and Wangyuan are about to kiss each other, but do not. Minhua sits on Wangyuan's lap after he has arrived in his home and she is about to kiss him. Wangyuan suddenly moans painfully and Minhua jumps up to see if he is hurt.

It turns out that Wangyuan is merely making fun of her. His suffering face turns into a smile and he says that he is hungry. Minhua then rushes to the kitchen to cook for him.

26. *Nanyin* (also called *nanguan*) is a traditional musical genre originating in the Fujian province of China. It has ancient roots believed to trace back to the Tang Dynasty (AD 618-907). It is most popular in Fujian and in Taiwan. The instruments used in this scene in addition to the two voices include a three-string banjo (*yueqin*), and a two-string fiddle (*erhu*). For a definition of *nanyin*, see en.wikipedia.org/wiki/Nanguan.

Figuring Hitchcock

George Toles, *A House Made of Light: Essays on the Art of Film.*
Detroit: Wayne State University Press, 2001. $44.95 cloth;
$22.95 paper.

A House Made of Light: Essays on the Art of Film is a
wonderfully literate and complex book about our inhabitation
of, and by, cinema. A hint of that complexity is on view in the
introductory chapter, where George Toles observes that "the
first condition" of his entry into the "House Made of Light" is
that *he* is "the one in the dark" (13). I want to situate that
darkness by citing two additional passages, one from Peter
Wollen's *Paris Hollywood: Writings on Film*, one from *A House
Made of Light* itself.

In Wollen's "Alphabet of Cinema" the letter C "is for
Cinephilia." By "cinephilia" Wollen means

an obsessive infatuation with film, to the point of
letting it dominate your life. To Serge Daney, looking
back, cinephilia seemed a "sickness," a malady which
became a duty, almost a religious duty, a form of
clandestine self-immolation in the darkness, a
voluntary exclusion from social life. At the same time,
a sickness that brought immense pleasure, moments
which, much later, you recognized had changed your
life. I see it differently, not as a sickness, but as the
symptom of a desire to remain within the child's view
of the world, always outside, always fascinated by a
mysterious parental drama, always seeking to master

one's anxiety by compulsive repetition. Much more than just another leisure activity. (5)

It should come as no surprise that H, in Wollen's Symbolic Order, stands for Hitchcock. In Toles, by contrast, H stands for Hitchcock's gender-indefinite other. At the heart of "Mother Calls the Shots: Hitchcock's Female Gaze," the third of three chapters Toles devotes to Hitchcock, is a "seer" who knows (too much of) something. Toles devotes four paragraphs to a "composite portrait of H" (201), from which I'll extract the following as representative and telling:

> H is well aware that the obsession with control is a problem, a personal weakness. Too much of "her" is stifled, there is not enough occasion for openness and for genuine (as opposed to ironic) self-expression. In the stories "he" is drawn to, control — and with it, safety — are continually taken away from those who need it and have come to rely on it. Those who manage to retain control in these stories are almost always certain to abuse it. . . . H longs for the release of *vulnerability* and enters, through the art of storytelling, into secret complicity with those who are openly, even abjectly, emotional and who do not hide their misery behind an iron mask. . . . When vulnerability is most intensely avowed, there is an immediate, strong counterpressure (call it paranoia) to bring betrayal into the picture. The two modes of expression — intimate sympathy and extreme, fearful suspicion — have a Siamese twin kinship for H. (200)

I'd say these passages from Wollen and Toles also betray a form of kinship. Each pictures cinema — either from the viewer's or maker's perspective — as a site of excessive emotion or devotion that entails a burden of moral anxiety as well as of illicit or utopian fantasy. Indeed, though Wollen's professed difference from Serge Daney does not quite escape the medical metaphor and its imputation of debility, his Toles-like evocation of a child's view of the world is tellingly gender-neutral and also Wordsworthian (or Freudian) in using vulnerability as an ethical measure. We are all children in the cinematic dark. Is cinema a trustworthy parent or not? Is our love of film, as if literally, "misplaced"?

The answer Toles gives to the latter question is a vigorous if carefully qualified "No," uttered as an explicit rejoinder to those for whom the "Classical Narrative Cinema" and the "Art Film" reading protocols often applied to it are equally suspect, for trafficking too readily in the coin of pleasure and sentimentality and transparency, for which the antidote is an "optics of suspicion" (160). Per Toles, on the contrary, "a condition of healthy psychic dependence on the work itself" is "the central element" (13) of the experience of filmic significance, on the assumption that "Movies are arguably one of the last refuges of the sublime in a culture progressively deprived of ways to express longings for awe, nobility, beauty, terror" (19). "Film satisfies and awakens us most fully," he avows, "when it outwits the conventions it employs, finding means to go beyond what conventions can be said to 'know' and what we know in our settled relation to them" (21).

Perhaps the clearest expression of Toles's antipathy to the hermeneutics of suspicion in *A House Made of Light* is developed in chapter three, "Thinking About Movie Sentiment: Toward a Reading of *Random Harvest*." The obvious background set is the whole "subject position" scenario, here associated chiefly with Mary Ann Doane's work on melodrama but more generally with the "Brechtian" strain of Lacan-inspired feminist film theory famously initiated in Laura Mulvey's call for "passionate detachment" in the face of mainstream cinema's voyeuristic and narcissistic appeals to disavowal and identification. Part of the force of Toles's argument in this chapter involves its vaguely Hegelian demonstration that the "subject position" argument is self-refuting, to the extent that the advocacy of "distance" from the affective appeal and power of film replicates the voyeuristic distance, in the service of objectification and control, that is often attributed to the "male" subject position in the Mulvey scenario. But the most persuasive and critically pertinent claim of "Thinking About Movie Sentiment" involves the epistemological consequences of privileging critical "detachment" over sentimental "immersion."

The risk of separating feeling from knowledge is allegorized, according to Toles, in Mervyn Le Roy's *Random Harvest*, where a "recovery" from war-induced amnesia leaves the Ronald Colman character deprived both of knowledge (of his life as "John Smith," of his Oedipally-tinged marriage to Greer Garson's Paula) and of affect, as if a lack of feeling were itself a barrier to knowledge, especially to the revelation necessary to the task of putting his two lives, his two selves, together. (Toles reads *Vertigo* as a nightmare version of this "second chance" scenario.) The film-critical version of this epistemological dilemma leads Toles to ask if it is possible "to separate the emotional content of film scenes from other ways of knowing what the narrative is 'saying' through them? In making such a division do we not lose those aspects of film reality which only emotion can reveal?" (79). And against the view that "sentiment depends for its effects on obviousness" and on a rhetoric "overwhelmingly committed to an almost primitive transparency"—which sets sentiment *against* knowledge—he adduces Chaplin's *City Lights* and Dreyer's *Ordet* as instancing that "the unexpected force of one's engagement and emotional release is what awakens us to the presence of something not at all transparent" (80).

Indeed, he goes on to assert that "tears themselves have their foundation in something real," and the "something real" is inevitably the (newly) self-conscious viewer. "Tears," writes Toles, "are inherently self-reflexive; we cannot forget that it is *we* who are crying," and the "unsettling lack of knowledge about *where* the tears are coming from" effectively "brings the viewer back to himself, by its sudden rupture of the state of passive or rapt concentration" (88). Hence blanket dismissals of our affective investments in film leave us quite literally incapable of understanding film's power to unsettle our habitual viewing routines.

A similar effort to demystify film-critical orthodoxy on behalf of "the art of film" is on view in Toles's chapter six, "*Rear Window* as Critical Allegory." I take "Critical Allegory" as a reference to Fredric Jameson's "Allegorizing Hitchcock" chapter from *Signatures of the Visible,* which seems apt because Marxism is the first of three critical frameworks Toles adduces (along with deconstruction and feminism) as explicitly contesting his own willingness to respect the objective authority of the text—to the extent that each of the three reading strategies in question challenges "the self-sufficiency and completeness of the work as it can be imagined under Hitchcock's control," thus "shifting responsibility for the making of the film's meaning to the *necessarily* insubordinate interpreter" (161). (The logic by which Toles's unnamed Marxist reads "murder" as *Rear Window*'s symptomatic antidote to urban capitalism's mass-culture practices of fragmentation and nominalization, as the generic supplement to the fact that real social connections "must be sought," murder-mystery fashion, "behind the screen of the visible" [162], further confirms the Jameson allusion.)

But Toles critiques these avowedly partial construals of *Rear Window* by adopting an "If you can't beat 'em, join 'em" strategy. Partly this involves (again) the contention that his Marxist, feminist, and deconstructive colleagues, in their suspicion of Jefferies's "rear window" ethics, risk becoming what they decry, to the extent that Jefferies, "in addition to being a voyeur and a prototype of the moviegoer, is also a critic of sorts," one whose "expectations too strongly and too readily structure" (169) what he sees, whose practice is thus self-confirming in ways that discourage self-critique, as Jefferies refuses to answer his doppelganger's "What do you want from me?" question and retreats behind a screen of blinding lights. Then again, it is only by provisionally "identifying" with the critical positions under study that Toles earns the right to offer critique, indeed a self-critique. As he puts it, "The critic characters I was choosing to play had to be located somehow within me before I could speak for them, or allow them to speak *through* me" (171-72). (So selfhood is inevitably multiple or split, as much for critics of films as for characters within them.) And the purloined punchline, in all this, involves the degree to which, in terms explicitly evoking Paul de Man's contention, in *Blindness and Insight*, that literature's rhetorical mode is always already deconstructive, Toles concludes his critique of Marxist, deconstructive, and feminist criticism by going them all one better—not so much by claiming that Hitchcock got there first as by suggesting that determining whose irony is whose is more difficult than is known in some philosophies.

Toles thus observes that his Marxist, deconstructive, and feminist interpretations tend to underplay the ambiguity of the film's reflexive "commentary on the process of viewing and making a film" (172) by folding the latter too readily into the textual unconscious—as symptom of absence rather than irony. Toles ascribes an allegorical dimension to the film, one announced in its opening shot, in which Hitchcock's mobile and self-conscious camera is decisively opposed to the perspective of the static and slumbering Jimmy Stewart character, as if exploring the space of dream, picturing the invisible. But the "allegorical" dimension, he allows, is less insistent in *Rear Window* than in *Blow Up*. Where Antonioni turns reality irretrievably into allegory, Hitchcock never so overtly renounces the "conventional murder mystery" aspect of the plot; his allegory of film viewing can go quite unnoticed.

Indeed, to the extent that the resolution of the murder mystery is taken to ameliorate doubts about the probity of Jefferies's suspicions, precluding any questioning of the fantasies that spur them, we are justified in seeing the film as "dissolving" in its second half the ethical qualms expressed by Lisa and Stella in its first half. But if, inspired by the allegorical distance asserted between Jefferies's point of view and the camera's, we try to ask the "What do you want from me?" question of *Rear Window,* we find that Hitchcock, like Jefferies, draws a blank, can give us nothing but special effects and fast motion photography, as if thereby to acknowledge "the drastic limits of the *camera's* power to image truth" (179). As Toles goes on to say, "The only depth that the camera makes visible, as its own response to Thorwald's *demand* for depth, is transparently a conjurer's trick" (180).

This is an odd defense of Hitchcock, to say the least, or of the "objective" authority of the Hitchcockian text. Perhaps oddity just *is* the point. Against the claims of a skeptical Marxism or feminism that would seek to recuperate *Rear Window* for criticism by asserting its own ironic authority, Toles wonders whether narrative films are "ever, in any meaningful sense, *against* the inclinations that they arouse and satisfy" (177)—as if critical attributions of irony were just so much more cover story, that many more Platonic shadows on the wall. And even when the irony of Hitchcock's allegorical distance from Jefferies is fully in play, viewers can still be in the dark as to their own motives and values, however clear their suspicion of Jefferies's suspicions. "Whether we are comfortably contained in the mirror of Jefferies's gaze or remain steadfastly outside it," writes Toles, "the difficulty of ascertaining where we are, really, as watchers of this film— and why—is formidable" (181).

I have thus far done my best, by way of summary, to speak on Toles's behalf, to let him speak through me. But in doing so I have emphasized those chapters of *A House Made of Light* where theoretical arguments are most explicitly advanced, by way of keeping his introductory promise to defend "the lost cause of art" (17) against the claims of a triumphalist film theory. But if it is logically cogent to assess theories of ideological closure for their blindness to the prospect of affective or interpretive rupture or freedom—even when rupture and freedom are the goals, as they are alike for Mulvey and Toles—reading *A House Made of Light* chiefly as an argument to that effect is finally not very satisfying. Such an account barely suffices to indicate the underlying story of the book, whole chapters of which barely adduce the theoretical topics that are central to the two chapters thus far discussed.

Toles himself offers at least two other ways to organize one's reading of *A House Made of Light*. His table of contents groups the book's eleven chapters into three parts, each bearing a loosely topical heading: 1) Sentiments of Peace and War (four chapters, including essays on Capra's *It's a Wonderful Life*, Le Roy's *Random Harvest*, and De Sica's *The Children Are Watching Us*); 2) Three Faces of Hitchcock (chapters on *Psycho* and *Rear Window*, plus "Mother Calls the Shots"); and 3) Cruel Pleasures and the Limits of Irony (a chapter on "The Art of Humiliation in Film," followed by chapters on the Coen brothers' *Fargo*, Jean-Claude Lauzon's *Léolo*, and on Toles's work as a screenwriter for Guy Maddin).

Given the astonishing density of Toles's prose style—rarely does a page turn without some strikingly apt allusion to literature or philosophy (Rilke, Kafka, Nietzsche, von Hofmannsthal, Shelley, Wordsworth, Barthelme, Borges, Diderot, etc.)—it would be foolish to ignore the instruction implicit in these headings. Though the "war" text might seem mostly a matter of background in the essay on Capra, for example, its juxtaposition with the chapter on De Sica and Neorealism clarifies the extent to which "war" for Capra and De Sica alike is one of those moments for Toles where the ordinary and fantastic are only an untaken breath apart. Then again, Toles is eager to point out how different each of his three Hitchcock chapters is from the others. For all of Hitchcock's efforts to assert control, as Toles observes, the "enormously diverse critical commentary" his films have inspired indicates "that spectators have found remarkable freedom of maneuver . . . within his tight, 'mechanical' designs" (22). As it is quite beyond the scope of even an extended review to trace how each of these three sections works on its own, much less how they work in concert, I will take Toles up on his offer of another method of organizing an understanding of *A House Made of Light*, which involves the title metaphor itself.

Toles concludes his "Introduction: A House Made of Light" by reference to Henry James's preface to *The Portrait of a Lady,* where he describes the "'house of fiction' as a dwelling with countless 'possible windows' to accommodate a host of dissimilar artists and their widely divergent points of view on the 'human scene' " (23). Precisely because of the ambiguity in James, as between the watchers and the watched, and given the fact that houses of various sorts are "compulsively attend[ed] to" in nearly every chapter—"from the cottage in *Random Harvest,* to the homes of Marge Gunderson, Boo Radley, and Norman Bates"—Toles proposes "a modified Jamesean metaphor for the House of Film" (23). It is "a frame we long to enter in the spirit of homecoming, but that we cannot possess any more securely than the lost home of our beginnings. . . . What the house of film withholds from us is exactly congruent with what it so effortlessly and profusely yields, as we caress its particulars: what we know and what we desire" (23-24). Not surprisingly, given the emphasis here on longing and desire and homecoming, Toles evokes Freud in declaring this home "both uncannily familiar and estranged" (23).

The instruction I derive from this Jamesean and Freudian tutorial is that *A House Made of Light* must be read figuratively, in terms of its compulsively repeated settings and characters, which gain their power as much from their obscurity as their explicitness. The chapter of *A House Made of Light* where the tactics of figuration are most emphatically on display is Toles's chapter five, "*Psycho* and the Art of Infection." Here the topic of metaphor is introduced, as it were, generically: *Psycho* is compared to Poe's "Berenice" and Bataille's *Histoire de l'oeil* as a way of foregrounding the "eye" figure as "the principle locus of metaphoric transformation and exchange" (138). In all three cases, the eye-as-object both epitomizes vulnerability and blocks it—a tactic taken to extremes, perhaps, in Bataille, where the eye, as pure object divorced from personality or body, is more alive than the "copulating phantoms" (139) that assault it, and for whom it expresses a complete indifference; no matter how horribly attacked or abused, "it is perfectly restored in an instant" (140). For Toles, Hitchcock's famous "wit" is the functional equivalent of

Bataille's "indifference," and no more so than in the concluding voice-over of *Psycho,* where Hitchcock's "mode of joking seems to merge with the awareness of a figure within the film's world" (141). Except that "Mrs. Bates's" assertion of "innocence"—punctuated by a lap dissolve wherein gaze and eyeless skull seem literally to fuse with and cancel one another in our last look at Norman/Mother—communicates by "infection," evincing a blindness as much to the internal as to the external world.

Or so Toles concludes in his extended analysis of the shower murder sequence where Hitchcock's graphic matches of eye to shower head to drain pipe have the effect (contra V.F. Perkins) of displacing the moral and emotional situation from the center of attention. As Toles puts it, "Hitchcock's decision to link the 'eye' throughout the shower sequence with as many other ovals as possible derives from his conviction that any painful subject can be stabilized if one locates a point of concentration apart from the 'thing itself' " (146). And in this there is little to choose between the Norman who looks away while "Mother" commits murder and the Hitchcock who looks at dead eyes rather than ponder (I twist Toles only slightly) "what it is those alien, impenetrable eyes might know about him" (149). Toles associates mimicry with trauma here: like Poe's eye, Hitchcock and Norman each "must turn into the thing [he] dreads in order to be spared the sight of it" (139). Accordingly, "the world of *Psycho* is traumatically fixated; it has no capacity for enlargement" (152). In this respect, indeed, *Psycho* represents a culmination of an emphasis on interiority in Hitchcock that begins for Toles with *Rear Window* and continues in *Vertigo* (where the swirling "eye" motif is announced in the credit sequence and is allegorized in Scottie's traumatic and traumatizing effort to recreate Madeleine) and in *The Birds* (where "Nature" as senseless cruelty literally invades the home, threatening catatonia and blindness—in the case of Dan Fawcett, blindness unto death).

To be sure, not all the domiciles on view in *A House Made of Light* are as ceaselessly dark as the Bates house in *Psycho,* though certain of its architectural features, most of them signs of the transitory—windows, doors, mirrors, curtains, stairs—are discussed across a considerable range of cinematic dwellings, including the farm house at the end of *Grand Illusion*, George and Mary's house in *It's a Wonderful Life*, the apartment flats in De Sica's *Umberto D.* and Polanski's *The Tenant*, the Gunderson and Lundegaard homes in *Fargo*, coming to a gruesome crescendo, as it were, in the "fearsome house of childhood" (298) occupied by Léolo in Jean-Claude Lauzon's film of the same name. As Toles promised, this image cluster extends across all three sections of *A House Made of Light*.

As the instance of *Léolo* attests, moreover, this emphasis on houses is often accompanied by an emphasis on children: Ana in Victor Erice's *Spirit of the Beehive*; Scout and Jem in *To Kill a Mockingbird*; the young George and Mary in the Gower drugstore episode of *It's a Wonderful Life*, and Zuzu and Jane in the film's Christmas Eve climax; the father and son, both named John Smith, in *Random Harvest*; Prico in De Sica's *The Children Are Watching Us*; Bruno in *Bicycle Thieves*; Douglas Bridge in *Mr. and Mrs. Bridge*; Scotty Lundegaard in *Fargo*, the child Marge is carrying in the same film; the orphaned children in Andrew Birkin's *The Cement Garden*; Geza in Guy Maddin's *Archangel*, or Franz in Maddin's *Careful*. Obviously enough, the title metaphor of Toles's book asserts an analogy of screen and home, and of viewer and child, to which compound trope I will return in closing.

One last figure deserves comment here, the one I began with—"H." He/she appears in "Mother Calls the Shots: Hitchcock's Female Gaze," the third essay under the gender-ambiguous "Three Faces of Hitchcock" heading, which has the effect, via the *Three Faces of Eve* intertext, of casting H in the Eve role, except that it is "gaze theory" *à la* Mulvey that has cast Hitchcock as the original cinematic sinner—not the first male director to objectify women as figures of sexual spectacle, to be sure, but the "ideal transmitter of an infection that has always been latent in the visual process of cinema" (185). Toles plays on the "original sin" notion by taking literally the idea that Mother comes first, that the camera's "power" is "'borrowed' from the Mother" so that its exercise threatens to "unman" (187) its male borrowers—Hitchcock, perhaps, among them.

As Toles's "composite portrait of H" attests, however, "point of view" in Hitchcock is not exclusively male, though it is often fearful or guilty—nor is it exclusively visual, to the extent that shots are "called," are often accompanied by voices, which may inflect (or infect) the gaze, sometimes undoing its purported mastery, as in the case of Norman Bates. According to Toles, indeed, the "gaze" is most controlling in Hitchcock "when the imagined 'eye' is female" (199)—of which Mrs. Bates in *Psycho* and Rebecca in *Rebecca* are exemplary instances, though each exists, like Hitchcock, as a ghostly presence, represented by surrogate selves or signature devices. Of course, the "composite H" is likewise a metaphor, as avowedly a construction as Mrs. Bates or Rebecca de Winter; perhaps assigning "power" to the "female" gaze is only another male cover story, especially when women—e.g., Marion, the second Mrs. de Winter—are depicted as victims. (If there's a feminist payoff here, perhaps it's in Toles's brief discussion of *Shadow of a Doubt*, where the real struggle of the film is understood as matriarchal, between Emma and Charlie Newton.) But the figural *tour de force* in "Mother Calls the Shots" is Toles's discussion of *Rope*, which he describes as a contest of vantage points: revolver versus rope.

The "revolver" or "male" perspective is associated chiefly with Brandon, whose bravado gesture of using a dinner party both to conceal *and* reveal a murder is akin to Hitchcock's *tour de force* gesture of shooting the film in extended long takes, as if to deny yet thereby to highlight the technology of film authorship; Brandon's gun eventually winds up in Rupert's hands, where its signal discharge punctuates his desperately rationalistic denial of any association with the students who have, on his view, twisted his teachings. By contrast, the rope lives on metaphorically or fetishistically even after its lethal potential is realized in the strangulation of David Kentley that begins the film. Like Hitchcock's women, the rope plays multiple roles, undergoes multiple transformations, and is in that sense excessive and dangerous. Even in its absence the female gaze "haunts" the cinematic proceedings—staining or coloring them in ways beyond the (conscious) knowledge of the film's characters. Hence, in Toles's account, the "rope" in *Rope* connotes female excess because the title word "Rope" in the film's credits is written in red, which matches the dress of Janet (the deceased David's fiancée), which color finally suffuses (anticipating the red suffusions in *Marnie*) the whole apartment as the evening sun sets outside the penthouse windows—which subsequently allows Toles to suggest a link of "rope" and "coiled" female hair, and of both with the self-motivated camera movements, as it were, that sinuously bind together the spaces and characters of the movie.

Though brief to the point of parody, my summary of "Mother Calls the Shots" is coherent enough to indicate the way Toles employs figuration to tell his story, and not in this chapter alone. The story he has to tell is nearly always one of emotional revelation or recollection. As he puts it in his concluding chapter, paraphrasing Guy Maddin, a story that rings true is "an amnesia story" (331), and the characters he is drawn to—both as screenwriter and as critic—are typically, like those in folklore or fairy tale, in "the renewable condition of being lost" (330). Hence the frequency with which characters in the films under study in *A House Made of Light* are described as haunted by memory, or its absence—inspired by a vision of home, or benumbed by ignorance of how to get there. This is most obviously and movingly the case in *Random Harvest*, where the clues that would bring Charles's life with Paula back to mind are all about him, though they are effectively (affectively) invisible until they achieve the proper sequencing and distance—and much the same can be said about George Bailey in *It's a Wonderful Life*, where the "spectral city" that is Pottersville "ultimately defines itself as George's anguished memory of a lost reality he still firmly possesses" (73). The traumatic converse is under examination in *Psycho*, where Norman's "uncontrollable repetition" is enacted as murder because "Killing is, paradoxically, the deepest place of forgetting" (154).

To the extent that cinema is "a house made of light," then, watching and thinking about films has the potential to bring us home to ourselves. And crucial to this process, for Toles, is our momentary adoption of a child's eye view of the world. He repeatedly invokes his own childhood—by way of reporting his traumatic 1960 encounter with *Psycho* ("For the first time I was caught, if you like, watching myself watching" [190]), and explaining the emotional resonance of a corporal punishment scene he wrote for Guy Maddin's *Archangel*. But the basic logic here is the logic of dreamwork, which Toles explicitly associates with childhood. A "memorable movie experience," writes Toles, "is a partial story that completes itself through a productive confusion with genuine psychic needs. It either triumphantly confirms or disturbingly disrupts the feeling/dreaming part of ourselves that we have surrendered to the film, in a condition closely resembling early childhood dependence" (41). Later, Toles will liken this experience to the experience of therapy, where the recovery of experience takes priority over explanation of it, where premature explanation prevents rather than advances the task of discovery: "Part of what sentiment [in] movies can accomplish is to restore access to our own buried feelings, in however early or infantile a form" (91-92). Hence the power of the cinematic sublime involves the "not altogether unwelcome recognition that we are made smaller by what we behold" (19).

Like art work, as Toles understands it, dreamwork expresses by repression. Putting self and film together is therefore akin to the experience of Charles in *Random Harvest* or George Bailey in *It's a Wonderful Life*, where one's "other" life seems like a movie which tells, in a displaced/disguised fashion, the story of your own life, however difficult or traumatic may be the task of putting them together, of "awakening" one to the other (and vice versa), pictured in each case as a matter of homecoming. Again, *Psycho* provides the negative image of this process, there being so little to choose, in Norman's case, between imprisonment in the cruel space of his traumatic childhood, under the dead eyes of mummified birds, and imprisonment in the empty courthouse cell, under the equally ineffectual gaze of the film viewer. More benignly, in movies "Memories we can hardly bear are transfigured for us. . . . They have become objects of vision, for our sake, and wait to reenter us until we step forward to meet them" (42).

I began by reference to the darkness of cinematic projection and to the question of cinephilia: Is film a "trustworthy parent," one descrving of filial devotion? In chapter one, "Being Well Lost in Film," Toles poses a related question: "What is it we hope to secure from fictions that we often yield to with far more conviction and commitment than the beckoning realities of our own lives?" Toles answers indirectly, metaphorically, by invoking the concluding scene of *To Kill a Mockingbird,* where the contrast between the Finch residence and the Radley house presents "a ceaseless dialectic between open and closed environments" (47). We can also read the "two houses" figure as an instance of the dream/art logic that Toles repeatedly relies upon. The open, well-lighted house of Atticus Finch derives its human and moral value from the containment implied by the shades-drawn darkness and isolation of the Radley dwelling. If we see the latter as the home of memories we cannot face directly, but which have the power to save us even in their absence and mystery, then we have no choice but to trust the film before us, to venture, like Scout, into its precincts. As Toles makes the point, paraphrasing Cynthia Ozick, "Perhaps we might say of film viewers that if they are not at risk, they are not viewing" (86). To refuse the risk of darkness is thus to refuse cinema altogether.

I am keenly aware, in closing, how simplistic this cut-and-paste account of *A House Made of Light* must seem; for all my elaboration of Toles's figurative procedures, I have left much in the dark. Nor have I devoted sufficient attention—beyond passing references to Jameson, Doane, and Mulvey—

to the larger critical discourse wherein *A House Made of Light* should find a home. Of recent Hitchcock books, the two that seem closest to *A House Made of Light* are Robert Samuels's *Hitchcock's Bi-Textuality: Lacan, Feminisms, and Queer Theory* and Christopher Morris's *The Hanging Figure: On Suspense and the Films of Alfred Hitchcock*. Both writers, like Toles, are openly figural in their analytical procedures, and Toles shares with Samuels a sustained interest in the gender-ambiguities on view in Hitchcock, though Toles's preference for Freud over Lacan confirms his avowed commitment to a Romantic view of art and of criticism that both Samuels and Morris would likely find retrograde. But I want to conclude by reference to an earlier book, one somewhat at the periphery of recent Hitchcock studies, Gaylyn Studlar's *In the Realm of Pleasure: Von Sternberg, Dietrich, and the Masochistic Aesthetic*.

Like Toles, Studlar privileges the similarity of cinematic experience and childhood dependence. "The realm of pleasure" that is film inevitably recalls, for Studlar, the "symbiotic wish" (184) of the pre-Oedipal infant to retain the "'sense of oneness' with the mother" (190) characteristic of the oral stage. The cinema, she writes, "offers a psychic reparation that may pleasurably restore archaic identifications and replay significant object relations as it provides an opportunity for a creative imaginary repetition of these early stages" (190). Where Toles parts company with Studlar—despite the many passages where their analyses of the psychic and spiritual expansiveness (and ambivalence) of cinematic experience are echoes of each other—is in his reluctance to extend the analogy by reference to "perversion," specifically to "masochism." Ever the Bazinian Romantic, Toles sees film as "art"; though it may evoke the state of childhood, may appeal to the child within us, it has for him a higher calling than the "masochism" label allows for. As Toles puts it—the only passage in his book that even hints of an awareness of Studlar's—"we can become this wayward and helpless child [of art] without instantly punishing him with the too knowing labels of 'regression' and 'masochism'" (20).

Though an ally of Toles in her critique of "gaze theory," Studlar goes largely unacknowledged in *A House Made of Light*. I bring her into the conversation at the last instant because her assertion that the "dream screen" of cinema involves a "primary identification" with the pre-Oedipal mother confirms a second way of understanding the home/screen analogy that is so central to Toles's defense of film as art. As Toles himself observes in his discussion of *Random Harvest*—citing Freud to the effect that the maternal body is the only place "of which one can say with so much certainty that one has already been there" (107)—it is possible to see "Mother" as the "home" toward which all "homecomings" are directed. Indeed, though Toles registers dissatisfaction with the mother/home equation—because it does not account for enough of *Random Harvest*'s complexities—it looms large across his entire book. His first chapter begins with Garbo's Queen Christina memorizing the room she has shared with John Gilbert; among the objects she touches for memory's sake is a painting of a Madonna. The penultimate example of a cinematic mother on view in *A House Made of Light* is of a maternal ghost, in Maddin's *Careful*, who consoles a dying son, her expression of "unconditional love" coincident with his icy demise.

If the psycho-logic of the dreamwork/art work equation requires a childlike vulnerability if the benefit of cinema is to be realized, the equation of "Mother" and "home" offers even sterner evidence of the necessity for a trusting dependency on the film before us. If the screen is a mother, and the viewer her infant child, then dependency of an extreme sort is an unavoidable "first condition" of film, which may be why the only time we see the author in *A House Made of Light*, on the last page of the last chapter, he is literally pictured as a mother, "The mother of Count Knotkerss (George Toles) lying in her coffin in *Careful*" (334), as the caption has it. It is a joke-like evocation of a classic Hitchcock cameo, to be sure, but the implication that merger risks death is unavoidable and chilling and dark. Yet darkness is also a "first condition" of our potentially enlivening encounter with the sublimities of the "House Made of Light" that is cinema. To judge by *A House Made of Light,* few writers are as capable of describing the richness and intricacy of that encounter as George Toles, for whom Hitchcock is (quite literally) a central figure. Indeed, it is in the "Three Faces of Hitchcock" section of his book that Toles, in confronting Hitchcock, most clearly confronts the limits of film, and of his own methodology as well. Hitchcock scholars have many good reasons for reading this book.

ANGELO RESTIVO

Hitchcock in Pieces

Tom Cohen, *Hitchcock's Cryptonymies*. Volume 1: *Secret Agents*. xx + 284 pp. Volume 2: *War Machines*. xvi + 300 pp. Minneapolis: University of Minnesota Press, 2005. $25.00 each volume, paper.

Over the past decade and a half, one can discern a move within some of the best Hitchcock scholarship away from the analysis of the films as self-contained textual systems, and toward a reading practice which "tracks" key elements of the Hitchcockian system across his entire *oeuvre*. We can see this procedural shift in, for example, Slavoj Žižek's elaborations of disruptions of the system of the "gaze" across Hitchcock's work; or in Fredric Jameson's uncovery of the link between the genre of the thriller and a narrative movement toward the episodic—which then authorizes a reading practice in which narrative "gestures" can be tracked from film to film. Nowhere, however, is this procedure so thorough-going than in this new, two-volume study by Tom Cohen. Among other things, these volumes present an exhaustive inventory of wordplay, recurring series of letters and numbers, citations, graphic and auditory marks, and "tele-technic" relays that range across the entire body of Hitchcock's work—so exhaustive, indeed, that this review will necessarily have to focus on only a small subset of these topics, as they occur in a limited group of films. In selecting the films to discuss below, I will take my cues from Cohen's volumes themselves, which tend to foreground for the closest scrutiny those that are (relatively) less discussed in the literature—*Sabotage*, for example, or *To Catch a Thief*.

Cohen refers to these cryptonymies, phonemic scraps, and prefigural markings that are so prevalent in Hitchcock's work as "secret agents," playing on the fascination that Hitchcock himself had for secret agents, espionage, and the like. And just as the figure of the secret agent as a narrative actant works to disrupt the machine of state power (and always, in Hitchcock's films, in the name of only the vaguest "foreign" power), so too, Cohen argues, do these other "secret agents" work to undermine completely our most fundamental presuppositions about the cinema itself, as a machine for the mimetic representation of the world—and so undermine, by extension, the entire Western metaphysics of presence, of model and copy, of the "human" as gendered subject. In Hitchcock, Cohen wryly notes, the cinema has become a "weapon of mass de(con)struction" (II, xv). Yes, the argument is that far-reaching, and radical. Thus, it would be useful to begin by articulating some of the foundations of Cohen's argument, which, it should be noted at the outset, mobilizes the highest of "high theory," drawing as it does upon grammatology and deconstruction, a de Manian inflected reading of Walter Benjamin, and key ideas from the later Nietzsche.

First, Hitchcock's work must be seen as bearing a fundamental relationship to modernity. This is an idea that has gained currency of late: after all, more than any other director, Hitchcock is associated with "the cinematic," marking him with a profound affinity to this technology of modernity. Further, his films exhibit a fascination with the modes of transport and communication we associate with the quintessentially modern. Cohen uses Hitchcock's initial cameo in *The Lodger* to illustrate this: here Hitchcock sits, back turned to the camera, as if commanding the giant machinic nerve-center of informatics, as telephones, printing presses, delivery trucks, and so on, disseminate information on the strangler. Secondly, the delight Hitchcock took in shocking audiences is well known. For Hitchcock, the cinema was potentially profoundly destructive: in *Sabotage*, for example, the most harrowing bomb blast comes from the one connected with the cans of movie reels. Of course, the connection between the experience of "shock" and the experience of modernity was first elaborated theoretically by Walter Benjamin, and following this connection will bring us to the heart of Cohen's argument.

As we know not just from Benjamin but from Eisenstein, the cinematic shock (via montage effect) could be seen as having great political effect. Cohen writes, "The cinematic image is politicized at its advent: either it will appear to ensure the mimetic real or it will suspend what could be called this statist epistemology, expose the mnemonic machines as prosthetic" (I, 66). Cohen takes from Benjamin's canonical essay "The Work of Art in the Age of Mechanical Reproduction" the idea that the cinema's political potential lay precisely in the fact that, as mechanical reproduction, the cinema presents us with an art stripped of "aura": it is a "de-auratic" art form, as Cohen continually reminds us. And it is this fact more than anything else that Hitchcock understood, as his elaborate systems of cryptonymies, graphic markings, and "traces" collude to block the auratic potential of the image, if only we allow them to do their work. (While it might seem here that I am instating—"through the back door," so to speak—an ideology of authorship which is counter to Cohen's fundamental position, I do this intentionally, as it seems to me that this entire problematic of authorship takes on the quality of an aporia that runs through the two volumes.) For Cohen, film studies has never really followed Benjamin's observation to its conclusion; rather, it tends to reaffirm "aura" in the form of authorship, mimetic realism, "identity," and a host of other normalizing operations. Cohen, instead, opts for a much more deconstructive reading practice, the assumption being that, before being a mimetic copy of a familiar world, the cinematic image is a system of tracings and pre-signifying inscriptions.

Consider, for example, the "bar series"—the purely graphic "/ / / /"—that William Rothman uncovered as one of the most pervasive "signature effects" in Hitchcock. Cohen argues that to see these marks as the signs of authorship is to take refuge in the security of "aura," when in fact these marks are first and foremost inscriptions that estrange us from the image as a representation of the world. Indeed, Cohen criticizes Rothman for returning to these marks of pure difference an "aura," via interpretations that press them back into service for the sake of narrative or thematic coherence (e.g., the theme of imprisonment). Cohen, on the other hand, wants to hold these marks open, in the name of putting into "suspense" the experience of the image as immediately representational of the world.

What is at stake here is very much, in the first place, the practice of reading itself. For Cohen, state power and ideology are held in place by an archive whose reading practices demand a suppression of the sheer materiality of inscription; and thus, by an archivally generated historicism ("the birth of a nation," the story of a subject, and so on). Again borrowing from Benjamin—this time from the "Theses on the Philosophy of History"—Cohen argues for a "materialist historiography" to counter this historicism. For Benjamin, history is (re)written when, in a "state of emergency," one suddenly apprehends an image-constellation that shatters the teleology of the archival narratives, and thus allows for the emergence of new possibilities for understanding the past and virtual alternatives for the future. One could then say that, in the "state of emergency" which was Hitchcock's—and our—century, "Hitchcock's cryptonymies" are precisely those Benjaminian image-constellations that might allow us to blast away the historical continuum, and its concomitant modes of apprehension, which the twentieth-century media had anyway already put into crisis.

The above is a necessarily truncated summary of the complex foundation for Cohen's argument; it should be noted that this "foundation"—perhaps inevitably, given its complexity and its departure from current modes of thinking in film studies—is not presented to the reader in one "place," but rather unfolds over the course of the introduction and the first four chapters of Volume 1. (Here, a complaint must be raised. While the two volumes contain extensive endnotes, there is no bibliography, and the index includes only

Hitchcock's film titles. Thus, if one wants to track a particular concept through the books, there is no ready mechanism provided to do so; and if one wants to go to a source, one has to wade through pages of notes. Given the complexity of the argument, the highly theoretical vocabulary, and no systematic structure laying out the conceptual framework, these books make for extremely difficult reading: *caveat lector*.)

One of these opening four chapters, "The Avenging Fog of Media," sets out a provocative new reading of *The Lodger*, a reading that sets forth many of the key ideas that will be tracked through the two volumes. Cohen makes great use of the film's epigraph—"A story of the London Fog"—to assert that the film is making claims both about the conditions of visibility itself ("fog") and visibility's relationship to the apparatus of the state ("London"). The fact that this "story" pertains to what is essentially non-narratable ("fog") announces in advance the centrality of "de-auratic" markings (like the triangle on the Avenger's calling card) to the cinematic apparatus; similarly, one can say that fog— suspended particles that refract in varying intensities the light that hits it—figures the "digital" precondition for the representational image, which latter then becomes meaningful (or "mimetic," to use Cohen's vocabulary) only via our pre-programmed memory systems. (In relation to this argument, a problem arises which I will address more fully toward the end of this review. Cohen describes the fog as "suspended water particles refracting shadow and light" [I, 22]. Technically speaking, however, only light is refracted: how is it possible for "shadow" to be refracted? The error may seem minor; but it points to a larger problem with how perception can be theorized from the deconstructive position.) In other words, both perception and reference are grounded, not by a Platonic model of original and copy, but rather via performative repetitions "managed," if you will, by the bureaucratic state.

Such a notion of the performativity of writing is familiar to those versed in deconstruction, and Cohen mobilizes this notion to argue for the deconstructive role that the cameo plays, both here in its inaugural appearance(s), and in the rest of Hitchcock. First of all, in *The Lodger*, the film in which this Hitchcock signature effect is first performed, it is in fact performed not once, but twice (at least for many commentators, who claim to see him again, after the first back-turned-to-audience cameo as director of the media and information machine, as a figure in the crowd near film's end). Thus, at the purported "origin" of a signature effect, what we have instead is the announcement of its iterability: the signature is always already a citation whose originary moment is unrecoverable. Following the logic of deconstruction, we could then say that language (and the mimetic image, Cohen would add) is predicated on this logic of citation. We see this, for example, in the way Hitchcock inscribes performance as citation within the films themselves—not just via espionage, which is inherently performative; not just in *Vertigo*, where Judy is at the outset performing Madeleine and then "grows into" her second performance; or the moment in *North by Northwest* when Cary Grant slips from his role as Roger Thornhill and into his star persona (when the woman in the hospital bed says "Stop! . . . Stop!); but even, more originally, in *Rope*, where the cocktail-party chit-chat regarding the screen performances of "what's his name" and "what's her name" (alluding to Grant and Bergman in *Notorious*) can make the audience aware that Jimmy Stewart is yet another "what's his name" in the pecking order of Hollywood's star system. This perpetual folding of the film's outside into the inside shows just how the mimetic realism of image, character, or event is always produced in relation to an already-existing archive. Thus, in the neon "S T R" that appears atop the warehouse as night falls on the set of *Rope*, the letters might be part of the word "storage" (which Peter Conrad has already argued), thus alluding to the archive in the very film (I would add) in which Hitchcock is attempting a simulation of a recording without "gaps"! But the letters could also, Cohen suggests in a neologism, allude to "starage"—playing on the astronomical fact that the stars, by giving off light, themselves iterate the sun, and thus undermine the solar logic which, beginning with Plato's cave, forges the authorizing link between appearance and concept, copy and original.

But probably the most useful (and certainly the most extended) textual analyses in Volume 1 are of *Sabotage* and the second *Man Who Knew Too Much*. Cohen notes of *Sabotage* that "in no other work does the . . . Benjaminian 'shock' as the cinematic 'dematerializing' of the world. . . get such direct analysis" (I, 145). In this film, the cinema theater is a front for saboteurs, the bomb is carried by the boy inside film cans, the initial act of sabotage (the blowing up of the electric plant, which leads to a retraction of light) interrupts the spectatorship of the moviehouse patrons, and so on. Thus, sabotage against the state is here clearly connected to a "de-auratic" (i.e., interrupted) cinema. But what's really clever here is the way Cohen handles the fact—acknowledged by Hitchcock himself in the Truffaut interview—that the bus bombing was a "mistake," a violation of the rules of suspense he would soon become master of. Suspense, of course, is all about timing—in the case of cinema, about the orchestration of the temporal sequencing. If Hitchcock here "blew it" with his time bomb—and as Cohen notes, the bomb goes off one minute later than it was supposed to—then what this means is that the very logic of temporal succession, of before and after, has been sabotaged.

Thus, at the film's end, we can recall that, crucial to Mrs. Verloc's getting away with her revenge murder, is the detective not being able to recall whether she said her husband was dead *before* or *after* the apartment blast occurred. But, Cohen argues, the most radical move *Sabotage* makes is ultimately the displacement of the human itself. The film presents us with what we might call an "animal series"—the aquarium, the pet shop, the bird—which culminates in the animated cartoon whose characters are all singing "Who Killed Cock Robin?" while Mrs. Verloc looks on, just before she goes up and murders her husband. This series thus constructs a "non-anthropomorphic vista," a crossing between the human and nonhuman at the point of "this knife of technicity"—"cuts" that we will later see in the animated wings cutting the images in *The Birds* (I, 161). The political stakes in this move toward the deanthropomorphic are articulated thusly by Cohen: "'Terrorism' may be the name for whatever can be anthropomorphized to distract from the deanthropomorphized cataclysms that cannot enter the mimetic political networks (dying oceans, global warming, disappearing species, supergerms, and so on). The cinematic shares more with a generalized nonanthropomorphic domain of visual practices by other life forms, since the camera itself is not human . . . . *Seeing* has to do, Hitchcock finds, with eating, with teeth, much as it does with the consumption programmed by advertising" (I, 75).

In a chapter at the end of Volume 1 entitled "Extraterritoriality," the notion of being "out of time" is connected to that of being "out of place" in Cohen's analysis of the second version of *The Man Who Knew Too Much*. That the film is connected to a certain notion of futurity is announced—loudly—by Doris Day's belting out of the song *"Que será será"*: however, Cohen astutely connects this to the film's insistent concerns with "legacy," the handing down of traditions from one generation to the next. (Here it is worth noting that Cohen finds even in the earlier *Sabotage* a Verloc "family" that, besides being desexualized, is also generationally "out of sync.") This concern with generations is most obviously evident in the disruption produced by the kidnapping of the son, but one might say it is echoed in the political intrigue, where the assassination of the prime minister will throw into crisis a "proper" mode of political succession. But this is only a prelude to a bravura reading of an offhand bit of dialogue early on in the film—when, after Dr. McKenna explains to his wife that their trip is being paid for by all the patients' body parts he has excised (which he lists), she glimpses a Moroccan mother carrying a baby in a native sling, and pops *"the* question" (as Ben McKenna calls it): when are they going to have another child? Then Hank, the son, points to a row of Moroccan women sitting before modern sewing machines in a kind of canopied, outdoor sweatshop, and says "It looks like a television commercial." Thus, in these quick brushstrokes, the question of reproduction gets shifted to the question of mechanical reproduction, in which an emergent globalized division of labor is connected to the television as mediatic relay in the system.

But more familiar to the viewer of *The Man Who Knew Too Much* is its centerpiece, the Albert Hall concert in which the assassination plot will unfold. This entire set piece is a "natural" for the kind of reading Cohen is doing. The musical score, which we see in close-ups, is itself a set of inscriptions (or a bar-series) within the archive that governs the production of aesthetic meaning (the performance of the work, an act of "technicity"); while the event that would sabotage state power, the assassination, must occur at a precisely (pre-)scripted moment—at the moment when the cymbals crash. Technologies of reproduction, in the form of musical recordings, must be used to rehearse the timing of the historical intervention. Of course, the scream of Doris Day is what derails the event: and it seems to me that here is where Cohen's argument falls short, and where a certain kind of psychoanalytic reading might not. For it seems that it is the eruption of the biological—of the voice as object—that intervenes to disrupt the automatism of archival logics. The scream is a kind of "extraterritorial" (non-)inscription, just as the Embassy of "Ao—" is a little piece of non-England lodged in the heart of London.

The last section of Volume 2, entitled "The Black Sun" and comprised of four chapters running a full hundred pages, is largely devoted to a reading of one "minor" film, *To Catch a Thief*. Yet again, I have to begin with the caveat that here I can only sketch out some key elements of the argument. However, I think it necessary to deal with this last section not only because of the length accorded it in the books, and not only because the film is so little discussed anyway, but because it brings to the table certain questions of history that have been motifs "waiting in the wings" to be developed. First, we can note that even as early as the analysis of *The Man Who Knew*

Too Much at the end of Volume one Cohen seems to be proferring a periodization in Hitchcock that is pretty much consonant with the commonly held notion of a historical break that occurs some time in the aftermath of World War II. Early Hitchcock might be said to be "modern" insofar as, for example, the theme of espionage situates itself within the context of the "home state" and "the mass"; and in postwar Hitchcock we see this theme take a back seat to more domestic or "touristic" ("extraterritorial") narratives, in keeping with an emergent, globalized regime of production and consumption managed by television. But second, in *To Catch a Thief* history is something very much in play, or even—I think Cohen would approve of my phrase here—"up for grabs." The memory of the Resistance is the backstory of the plot (a backstory which comes to the fore at film's end); the climactic sequence is a costume ball which cites the ancien regime; and the Mediterranean setting—played with in so many ways cinematographically in this film—resonates with antiquity and the origins of logos. (And, one might add, with the first moment of its deconstruction, if we recall that Nietzsche composed part of *Thus Spoke Zarathustra* while residing in Nice.)

In Cohen's analysis of *To Catch a Thief*, the film is seen as fundamentally concerned with the simulacrum, the copy of the copy: most obviously in the premise, where Cary Grant is the ex-jewel thief nicknamed "the cat," whose modus operandi is being copied by a "copycat," forcing Grant to copy the copycat in order to catch the thief. Thus, for the first time, we see the work of Jean Baudrillard coming into play in the analysis of the film. Cohen writes: "In the postwar or posthistorial world of the French Riviera—one of *faux* Baudrillardian seduction without production, of copies without originals, of obscene gendered performance without sex—signs do not have referents, or rather, their definition as signs does not efface them toward any assured signifieds" (II, 184). The film begins with the travel advertisement, and the postwar French Riviera is called "travel folder heaven," suggesting a collapse of the real into its photograph, and "one is in an economy entirely of service industries: insurance, restaurants, catering, gambling, hotels, police, that is, all theft and circulation *without production*" (II, 209). And the band of former Resistance fighters—which in earlier Hitchcock might have been connected to the sabotage of the home state—now instead has become an underground criminal network of thieves. But the unhinging of sign to referent goes way beyond these examples, and Cohen tracks the general unravelling of linguistic reference through the entire film.

One example should suffice: Francie's mother (played by Jessie Royce Landis, who will later play Cary Grant's mother in *North by Northwest*) asks for bourbon throughout the film; but the most telling occasion is at the costume ball, since the ball presents us with a simulacrum of the *Bourbon* court. In this way, the signified of "bourbon" shifts to an American commodity, erasing its own genealogy. One could connect this as well—although it is if anything only between the lines here in Cohen—with a postwar globalization effected partly through advertising. But what I was surprised Cohen didn't connect all this to, given the *North by Northwest* connection he does indeed note, is the bit in the latter film in which the bottles of bourbon have become books (and Landis gets the great line "Bourbon! I remember when it used to come in bottles!")

But what of the portentously metaphysical "black sun," the rubric under which this entire analysis is unfolding? It should be noted that Cohen identifies this motif early in the first volume: and in this review, the motif was alluded to (without being "named") in the discussions of the revocation of light in *Sabotage*, and in the notion that the "star" exposes and disseminates the "solar logic" that subtends logos (the light of truth). Significantly, Robert Burks's cinematography of travel-photo heaven garnered an Oscar; but as Cohen notes, the aerial photography of the Riviera landscape makes it seem strangely barren, folded in on itself, and primal. The light of the Mediterranean is thus more blinding than it is luminous, and Cohen spots in one of these aerial shots the (black) shadow of the plane carrying the cinematic apparatus—redoubled later when the black helicopter mars the sky as it pursues Grant and his copycat in the speedboat. We can then note that at the film's opening, the Mediterranean light is immediately retracted, in the theft montage ("black on black") in which the black cat is less a material body than a shadowy form (the "trace" of a body) that traverses the shots. Theft thus becomes a trope that moves beyond the nominal plot: theft is "preoriginary," so that before the Platonic light of logos that fixes identity (and by extension, the proprietary), there is the trace that shows it all up as "theft," as citation.

Thus, the famous fireworks scene needs to be read in an entirely different way: not as the achievement of metaphor (e.g., fireworks equals ejaculation), but as metaphor's utter collapse, the sun become pyrotechnics in the night. In this "light," it isn't surprising that both language and the sexual relation lie in rubble in this scene. Even earlier, when Grace Kelly invites Grant to her room, he tries to decline with the words, "I can't come." Then, in the scene itself, Grace Kelly piles double-entendre upon double-entendre to the point where referentiality falls into an abyss, all the while taunting Grant with the jewels that she knows he knows to be fake. We can then begin to note along with Cohen the many ways in which the film subverts Cary Grant's sexual identity: his copycat is a tomboy, on the beach he's framed between the legs of a cabana boy, he goes to the costume ball as a eunuch in blackface, and so on.

It is for all these reasons that Cohen concludes that "the heliocentric 'West'. . . appears with its lights knocked out . . . . The 'war' is not over, it has been totalized; it is the teletechnic empire and everything that the cinematic services. . . . Hitchcock is questing for a postwar enemy state of things, . . . and he finds it totalized, 'global'" (II, 244).

One can sense from the foregoing discussion just how complex and intricate Cohen's argument is; and indeed there are entire strands of argument that I have not taken on here. One in particular deserves mention before moving on to an assessment of the larger theoretical implications of the work.

It is the elaborate numerology and "alphabetology" Cohen tracks through Hitchcock's work. To be honest, this piece of the argument left me largely unconvinced. I understand, of course, that this minute fragmentation of the "weave" of Hitchcock's images and sounds is in keeping with the Benjaminian project of the work, and I'll even grant that it is somewhat more convincing when the fragments are phonemes—like the "mar" series (Marion, Marnie, Mark, and so on) that runs through Hitchcock's work and can be linked to marking, machine, the sea (*mare*) and "Mother" (*mère*). But in addition, numbers and letters are ruthlessly tracked: with A" and "C" corresponding to "1" and "3," "M" with the number 13 (as M is the thirteenth letter in the English alphabet). But then, when A and C occur in proximity, they point to the magic "13, even though 13 is only graphically a one and a three, not mathematically. The figure pi gets somehow linked to the equilateral triangle, when of course it is fundamentally about the circle. To me the problem is the arbitrariness of it all: if one jumps through enough hoops, one could connect any letter with any number.

But enough of this. One of the values of a work as challenging a work as Cohen's is that it forces the reader to reconsider the most fundamental presumptions of (film) theory. I see a work such as this not so much an argument demanding assent or disagreement as much as it is a provocation to think deeply about these issues. With that in mind, I'd like to end by identifying what for me are the most interesting of these. To begin with, one might ask whether the procedure of fragmentation—with its roots in the Frankfurt school's valorization of montage—can in any way be compatible with the notion of a "textual system." The issue here is not necessarily to reinstate coherence to the single film: the problem arises rather because of the fact that, as much as Hitchcock's effects are de-auratic, Hitchcock clearly mobilizes "aura" as well. If one then looked at the Hitchcockian text as a compromise formation balancing the auratic and the de-auratic, then one might be able to articulate with more specificity the way that particular ideological clusters (around such concepts as "family," "nature," and so on, with all their accompanying aura) are working. Cohen may believe that this post-1968 project of ideological demystification is over and done with; for him, the critical discourses of film theory (and their underlying philosophical assumptions) have anyway been too complicit in trying to salvage some form of "aura." But I think the following sentence, taken from the introduction to the first volume, contains a telling symptom:

> But if Hitchcock's practice assumes a *graphematics* that precedes the perceptual and mnemonic effect, an entire series of epistemological prejudices goes into *partial* default. (I, 5: second italics added)

It is the "partial" here that is so telling, because then the critical question becomes, which is the part that doesn't go into default?

One could say, indeed, that it is precisely over the issue of "what goes into default" that deconstruction and psychoanalysis have been at loggerheads. Deconstruction argues that psychoanalysis always ultimately returns to "aura" via some sort of conceptual totalization (phallus, gaze, *sinthome*, and so on), while psychoanalysis argues that the abyss opened up by deconstruction should be seen as a symptom. One of the values of Cohen's reading practice is that it puts to the lie the cliché that deconstruction is only vaguely political and blissfully unconcerned with historical specificity. But just how the political is to be conceived here remains—necessarily, I think—vague: the books are an initial contribution to a "politics to come." But the same technicity that has potentiated this "politics to come" is the very technicity that has given us the triumph of the simulacrum, under the direction of globalized capital. Thus, it seems to me that the theoretical race toward the "post-human" is at least as likely to play into the hands of an ever-increasing control society as it is to bring forth "the community to come," to borrow a phrase from Giorgio Agamben.

Take, for instance, the notion of the Oedipal scenario–whether viewed simply as the triangulation of desire in the family, or more complexly as the mechanism by which one is integrated into the social system—which has been so central to Hitchcock criticism and which Cohen labels, not without some humor, "Freud's cultural MacGuffin" (II, 86). What psychoanalytic criticism of Hitchcock has allowed us to see is just how the Oedipal is a kind of machine of social reproduction: as such, it potentially allows us to articulate the very connection between power and resistance that is seemingly occluded in Cohen's argument. In any case, Cohen calls it a MacGuffin without seeming to get the full implication of this: for the MacGuffin may be a "nothing," but it is a nothing that is essential for constructing the plot. Cohen claims that in *The Birds*, when Annie Hayworth dismisses the Oedipal as an explanation of Mitch's attachment to his mother ("with all due respect to Oedipus, . . ."), she is refusing the Oedipal as "pre-packaged" explanation; but in the context of the plot of the film, how could anyone take Annie's explanation seriously, when she herself is practically a walking advertisement for the Oedipal (in the perverse triangle she constructs with Mitch and his little sister)?

Of course, there is something in *The Birds* operating beyond the Oedipal: psychoanalysis names this the death drive, which has the status of the "Real," the radical outside of the logic of representation. This indeed is how Lacan was able to conceptualize that very stumbling block Freud came up against in *Civilization and Its Discontents*, and it remains one of psychoanalysis's most radical concepts. Over the past fifteen years or so, there has been increasing theoretical interest in the death drive, and important new work on Hitchcock coming out of this. The general argument is that, in an ongoing process of postmodernization, such characteristics of its culture as multiplicity, the simulacrum, seduction without desire, and so on, have the status of symptoms: they announce the eruption of the death drive into a social field in which the social fantasy is no longer enough to achieve consensus; and a film such as *The Birds* is an announcement of this development. Now, curiously, as the reader moves through the two volumes of *Hitchcock's Cryptonymies*, encountering over and over again the same phonemic scraps, graphic marks, number series, and other secret agents, one might easily feel that one has become enthralled by a demonic compulsion to repeat. One encounters this repetition too often to keep account of in these volumes: a certain "take" on *The Lodger*, for example, will come up again and again, every time repeating the take with only minor variations in the vocabulary. It is almost as if, once the "law" governing the assignment of reference has been suspended, only the blind repetition of the death drive is left, and Cohen is demonstrating the validity of the psychoanalytic in spite of himself.

Slavoj Žižek has been the theorist most associated with this new interest in the Real, and his Lacanian readings of Hitchcock are particularly singled out for criticism by Cohen, who argues that they always end up reinstating the aura of authorship, representation, and so on. But at least in the case of authorship, Cohen is misreading Žižek. Žižek's conception of authorship is derived from the psychoanalytic notion of the transference: "Hitchcock" is *positioned* as "the subject supposed to know," and it is this transference effect that allows new knowledge to be produced. This, it seems to me, would be one way to get around the contradiction over authorship that comes up in Cohen's work, insofar as he has to posit a Hitchcock who "knows too much," and yet can't possibly know *that* much.

Finally, one needs to ask whether deconstruction—when turned upon the *image* rather than upon the word—needs a more fully elaborated theory of perception. The entire argument is predicated on the notion that the visual field, before presenting us with a "world," is actually a series of graphic, non-signifying markings. In order to "ground" this notion, deconstructive critics have to resort to a kind of "pointillism" of the visual field, arguing that light itself is a phenomenon of photons, and therefore discrete units of presence-absence. But the question of how we get from this to the perception of objects in the world—let alone memories—remains open. (We might note here that both psychoanalytic theory and Deleuze's film books are grounded in fully developed theories of perception—in the first case, via "the gaze" coming out of a close reading of Merleau-Ponty's *Le Visible e l'invisible;* in the second, via Bergson's *Matter and Memory.*) As it stands, the "pointillism" of the visual field seems merely an analogy coming out of the current technologies of the digital. Thus, for example, the London fog dematerializes the image through the droplets that "refract light and shadow"—notwithstanding the fact that a shadow does not refract, and thus is not equivalent to the "zero" of a binary, digital logic.

Still, it is rare when a book comes along that so fundamentally challenges so many of the assumptions that are taken for granted in film studies. There is something of considerable import going on in the pages of these two volumes, as I hope my summary of the books' argument makes clear. Cohen's work may present difficulties for those not well versed in theory, but his readings of the films are often dazzling, and the overall argument certainly opens up for inquiry a number of important questions.

KENNETH SWEENEY

Hitchcock on DVD: The Universal Titles

The Alfred Hitchcock Masterpiece DVD Collection. 15 Discs. Universal Studios Home Entertainment, 2005. $119.98.

Since the Digital Video Disc (DVD) format release in the late 1990s, home video consumers have seen a staggering drop in VHS videocassette programming and distribution and the annihilation of the laserdisc format. In the short history of the currently preferred American home video device, consumers are noticing hundreds of previously existing DVD titles being repackaged as newer, special editions that often boast superior transfers of image and sound. While there is no question that a more recently produced DVD can offer an improved image and sound transfer simply because film-to-digital technology has advanced since the first DVDs were created, there is no guarantee that the newer product is always a better version. Even with advancements in technology, image and sound transfers are only as good as the judgment exercised in rendering the theatrical film presentation to DVD.

When an existing DVD is replaced by a newer version, consumers should be looking for printed evidence of "remastering" on the new DVD's packaging. Remastering a particular title usually begins with digitally processing the best available analog source material (the original film elements) and using computer software to remove numerous instances of dirt and scratches that may be noticeable. This is, of course, particularly the case with older titles. Also, the rate of compression used when authoring the DVD plays a factor: using a higher "bit rate" when transferring means that the image will have a more detailed appearance in playback, as there is more video information on the DVD. Also, the phrase "anamorphically enhanced for 16 x 9 widescreen televisions" describes a process that has become the norm for films in wide aspect ratios whereby the image will appear "letterboxed" with black bars on the top and bottom of the screen, preserving its correct aspect ratio on standard 4 x 3 televisions, but is also anamorphically processed to "stretch" and fill a 16 x 9 television screen with added density. This additional density makes a tremendous difference in clarity on 16 x 9 widescreen sets, making films shot in wide aspect ratios look sensational.

Audio tracks which may have age-related defects or hiss are now easily cleared and filtered. Digital Dolby 1.0 or 2.0 monaural tracks are being produced that, in many cases, can make a very old film sound remarkably clean. Some DVD production companies, when given the necessary budget to remaster the audio, can offer a more enveloping soundscape by generating a new 5.1 Digital Dolby or DTS track even if the original theatrical presentation was not in stereo.

Enter Universal Studios Home Entertainment. In the spring of 2000, twelve of the fourteen Alfred Hitchcock feature film titles licensed for distribution by Universal debuted on DVD along with DVD reissues of *Vertigo* and *Psycho* (two titles previously released on DVD in 1998), as the "Alfred Hitchcock Signature Collector's Editions." They were sold primarily as single units but also bunched together in convenient box-sets by the studio for the serious collector. While these twelve debuting titles had solid image transfers and those in wide aspect ratios were properly enhanced for 16 x 9 screens, some collectors rightfully complained that *Vertigo* and *Psycho* were mere repackagings of the existing DVDs and not newly transferred with anamorphic enhancement for 16 x 9 sets. In spite of this issue, the newly available titles, the generous supplements included on each, and the reasonable retail price seemed more than enough to lure consumers to buy the set.

Under the executive in charge of production at Universal Studios Home Entertainment, Colleen A. Benn, former laserdisc producer and film historian Laurent Bouzereau produced all of the Universal Hitchcock DVDs, and wrote and directed substantial "Making of" documentaries of varying lengths for thirteen of the titles.

In the fall of 2005, Universal released the same fourteen titles in a handsome box-set and called it "The Alfred Hitchcock Masterpiece Collection." The set boasted remasters of all titles as well as previously unreleased supplemental material on a bonus fifteenth disc. Both *Vertigo* and *Psycho* were finally remastered with anamorphically enhanced 16 x 9 transfers. Is the new box-set with these features worth purchasing, or should one just hold on to the 2000 pressings? To help answer this question, the following is an analysis of the significant differences between the 2000 and 2005 DVD editions of each film, in chronological order by release date. These results were based on side-by-side comparisons on both standard 4 x 3 and large scale 16 x 9 television monitors, video projection units, and computer monitors.

The 2005 menus for each title, unlike the 2000 versions, play a brief snippet of Hitchcock's television show theme, Gounod's "Funeral March of a Marionette." Furthermore, each title has minor deletions of some superfluous supplemental features. Some supplements that were standard features on the 2000 discs—onscreen panels of information on the careers of "Cast and Filmmakers," DVD recommendation screen panels, and the Universal DVD newsletter via Universal Web Link advertisement page—have been deleted from all the new 2005 editions. The only other deletion is a key supplement from the *Rear Window* disc: a DVD-ROM facet that offers an interactive, printable version of the original screenplay is unfortunately not included on the 2005 DVD.

The 2000 DVD debuts of *Saboteur, Shadow of a Doubt, Rope, Rear Window, The Trouble With Harry, The Man Who Knew Too Much, The Birds, Marnie, Torn Curtain, Topaz, Frenzy,* and *Family Plot* include Bouzereau's specially produced "Making of" documentaries that are retained in the 2005 editions.

These segments contain interviews with many of the surviving principal cast members and filmmakers, industry professionals, critics, and academics. Most of the original 2000 DVD editions of these titles also offer additional interviews, photographs, and storyboards for individual titles, and in each case, those supplements have been retained on the 2005 additions. Finally, both DVD versions include the theatrical trailers for each title.

Saboteur (1942), the deft, paranoid thriller of mistaken identity and cross country intrigue, offers a wide-ranging visual landscape photographed in black and white by Joseph Valentinc. This picture marked the first collaboration between Hitchcock and Valentine as well as with associate art director, Robert Boyle. Shot in a spherical "flat" format with an aspect ratio of approximately 1.33:1, the film's visual style has roots in the contemporary crime films of the period with heavy shadows and stark, often high-contrast lighting schemes.

The 2000 DVD of *Saboteur* is a solid presentation of the film sporting a relatively accurate image transfer with good contrast. The digital 2.0 monaural audio, while slightly dense, is certainly satisfactory. The 2005 transfer is, however, an improved presentation of the film. Valentine's contrasting lighting and heavy use of shadow in the film is more pronounced, with a significantly brighter and sharper overall image presentation. The occasional dirt from the source material that was evident on the 2000 disc has been digitally scrubbed from the image. The 2.0 digital monaural audio is slightly clearer on the 2005 edition.

Generally known to be one of Hitchcock's personal favorites, *Shadow of a Doubt* (1943), the sinister tale of a brooding killer holed up in the sunny brocade of Thornton Wilder's Americana, was also photographed by Valentine with an aspect ratio of 1.33:1. Shot mostly on location in Santa Rosa California, the film has a cleverly contrasting photographic style, using high-key lighting setups as well as a more abstract noir-flavored lighting scheme.

The 2000 DVD has a generally accurate picture transfer and a solid, if slightly noisy audio transfer. The 2005 DVD is visually smoother and noticeably cleaner with the digital removal of much of the source material dirt that was sporadically evident on the 2000 edition. For example, when the opening title sequences on each version are run side by side, a marked difference in visible print dirt and sharpness is noticeable. The 2.0 digital monaural on the 2005 DVD is stronger with heavier bass and less age-related hiss.

Hitchcock's film-version of *Rope* (1948), Patrick Hamilton's hit play of murder and deceit among former college chums, marked his first use of color. This film, shot again by Valentine, was composed as a real-time event by using continuous, often moving camera takes and allowing for few perceived picture edits. Valentine brought in William V. Skall as a Technicolor assistant to ensure that the film's one set would have the appropriate hues of daylight change to give the illusion of time passing.

Both the 2000 and the 2005 DVD picture transfers are excellent. The 2005 edition is only slightly sharper, with some minor instances of print dirt visible on the 2000 edition now digitally removed. In terms of color timing and clarity, the two renditions of Valentine's work are nearly identical, although I have a slight preference for the 2005 DVD. The Technicolor hues are very well re-created in both versions. The 2.0 digital monaural tracks seem identical.

Rear Window (1954), perhaps the quintessential Hitchcock film, finds a homebound, bored photographer watching the windows of his neighbors, one of whom seems to have disappeared. Shot with an aspect ratio of 1.66:1 by Robert Burks, who had previously collaborated with Hitchcock on *Strangers on a Train, I Confess,* and *Dial M for Murder,* the film's famously saturated hues of summer in New York City are one of its hallmarks.

The restored materials from *Rear Window's* 1998 theatrical rerelease were used for the 2000 and also for the 2005 DVD. Both picture transfers offer generally accurate representations of Burks's canvas, thanks in part to the restoration elements. The colors are usually accurate, but too much grain does seem evident on both transfers. The 2005 version seems to be slightly sharper and is transferred at a moderately higher bit rate. Also, the 2005 version seems matted in a more appropriate framing. While both transfers seem tighter than true 1.66:1, the 2005 version feels slightly more centered. Both transfers are enhanced for wide screen 16 x 9 televisions and playback with slight letterboxing on the sides to keep the 1.66:1 framing ratio. The 2.0 monaural audio mixes are both solid and seem virtually identical.

The Trouble with Harry (1955), Hitchcock's low-key black comedy, finds the residents of a bucolic New England town concerned and bemused over the surprising discovery of a corpse. Burks returned as cameraman to photograph the pastoral grandeur of autumn in Vermont. The film, shot on location, has long been revered for its startling colors shot in the horizontal VistaVision format for projection at 1.85:1.

There's a distinct difference between the picture transfers on the 2000 and 2005 DVD versions. While both are enhanced for wide screen 16 x 9 televisions, have highly saturated hues, and are generally pleasing, the 2005 version is sharper with greater grain, illuminating more layers within the colors. The 2.0 digital monaural is fine on both DVDs, giving solid tonality to Bernard Herrmann's first score for a Hitchcock film.

Hitchcock's remake of his 1934 kidnapping thriller, *The Man Who Knew Too Much* (1956), finds a vacationing American family unwittingly involved in international espionage. Again using the "high fidelity" horizontal process of VistaVision for projection at 1.85:1, Burks shot the film on location in Africa, the United Kingdom, and on soundstages in Los Angeles.

The original DVD from 2000 was transferred from what appears to be source materials from the 1983 theatrical rerelease that had slightly "off" colors and a Universal logo in place of the original Paramount VistaVision fanfare footage. While Burks's panoramic use of long shots were now properly framed in the enhanced 16 x 9 transfer, the colors seemed to be less rich than intended, often running dark and inconsistent. The newer 2005 edition is a slightly better presentation of the film with sharper hues, but the transfer still suffers from occasional instances of color inconsistencies in what appears to be fading source materials. The original Paramount VistaVision fanfare, however, has been reinstated. While both discs have good 2.0 digital monaural tracks, the 2005 edition seems to have more punch, particularly in the climactic sequences in Albert Hall.

Hitchcock's epic meditation on the equally seductive and futile notions of romantic love, *Vertigo* (1958), remains one of the key fetish-objects of the cinema. Certainly one of cinematographer Burks's more beautiful VistaVision accomplishments for Hitchcock, the subtly diffused color and sweeping long shots of ocean-side vistas have helped give the film its legendary status.

After *Vertigo*'s 1996 restoration and theatrical rerelease, Universal released an excellent laserdisc edition in early 1997 using these new source elements. Issued as one of Universal's high-end "Signature Series" laserdiscs, a fine picture transfer was created with 1.85:1 letterboxing and a crisp stereo track in addition to a plethora of supplements. The supplements included a landmark audio commentary track with restoration team James C. Katz and Robert A. Harris, associate producer Herbert Coleman, screenwriter Samuel Taylor, Herrmann biographer Steven Smith, actor Kim Novak, art director Henry Bumstead, former director of publicity Herbert Steinberg, script supervisor Peggy Robertson, and Patricia Hitchcock O'Connell.

Also appearing on the benchmark laserdisc was Harrison Engle's thirty-minute documentary, *Obsessed with* Vertigo: *A New Life for Hitchcock's Masterpiece*, which takes a close look at the production and restoration of the film, including many interviews with key production members. The famed "foreign censorship" ending, which highlights the capture of Gavin Elster, was a key inclusion from the Universal vaults. Also included were production notes, cast and filmmaker profiles, theatrical trailers, and dozens of stills, drawings, storyboards, and advertisements. This excellent laserdisc was one of the most remarkable entries of that format's short history.

In the spring of 1998, the first DVD of *Vertigo* was released. The DVD package was a replica of the laserdisc presentation from the year before, with the same supplements, artwork, and navigation screens. It also presented the same image transfer that was engineered for the now surpassed laserdisc format. Unfortunately, a new anamorphically enhanced transfer was not created to make full use of DVD capability. It is also important to note that when the bulk of the Universal Hitchcock titles were released in 2000, the existing DVD of *Vertigo* was repackaged with new cover art to resemble the "Alfred Hitchcock Signature Collection" moniker.

Perhaps the most significant aspect of the 2005 DVDs is that *Vertigo* has been given an excellent new anamorphic transfer. The sharpness of detail in 16 x 9 viewing is instantly noticeable, giving the film the appropriate luster its restored elements make possible. Also, those purists who were upset at the 1996 audio restoration can now enjoy the film's original monaural track that has been included here along with the modern 5.1 mix previously available on the earlier DVD. The supplements from the benchmark laserdisc are all included, with the exception of the cast and filmmaker profiles. *Vertigo* has now been incarnated at the height of home video sophistication with this restored, enhanced transfer.

Released in 1960, *Psycho*, the monochromatic tale of madness and murder at a rundown motel just off the "old highway," is perhaps the cinema's most legendary shocker. Shot by John L. Russell, a veteran of Hitchcock's television show, the film has a spare, often stark visual quality that perfectly suits the narrative's grim tone. In 1998, an excellent laserdisc box-set of *Psycho* hit the market, letterboxed at the appropriate aspect ratio of 1.85:1 and closer than previous laserdisc transfers to Russell's intended contrasts. Also included were a plethora of supplements, making it one of the crown jewels of Universal's high-end laserdisc products, the "Signature Series."

The laserdisc offered the exhaustive ninety-seven-minute *The Making of* Psycho, the first of Bouzereau's documentary efforts to accompany a Hitchcock film. Like his later efforts, the segment featured principal cast members and filmmakers, industry professionals, critics, and academics. Theatrical trailers, newsreel footage, censored scenes, and an excellent archive of drawings, storyboards, and photographs were also included. Rounding out the box-set were advertising art and publicity material.

Just like the initial *Vertigo* DVD, the first *Psycho* DVD was released in 1998 as a replication of the "Signature Series" laserdisc. All the supplements were retained, and cast and filmmaker's galleries and a seventeen-page production notes section were added as additional bonus materials. Many of the artwork panels from the menu screens were also borrowed from the laserdisc. As with *Vertigo*, the picture transfer was the same as the laserdisc, not enhanced for 16 x 9 anamorphic screens, hardly making use of the available DVD technology. Like the *Vertigo* DVD, this transfer was also repackaged with different artwork in 2000 to match Universal's 2000 releases as part of the "Alfred Hitchcock Signature Collection."

The 2005 DVD presentation of *Psycho* has finally been upgraded to an anamorphic transfer with a sharper, cleaner image for widescreen 16 x 9 sets. With the exception of the routine deletions from the 2000 DVD as stated above, Universal has replicated nearly all the excellent supplements from the laserdisc and earlier DVD. Smartly, Universal has removed Bouzereau's feature-length documentary, *The Making of* Psycho, and put it on the set's bonus disc to make room on the DVD for a better feature presentation compression rate. Indeed, *Psycho* has been remastered at a higher bit rate, giving the film better contrasts and sharpness. The image also has less visible print dirt, thus making it more pleasing to the eye. The digital 2.0 audio seems identical to the original release, with much of the age-related hiss eliminated and capturing a surprisingly deep bass range.

Perhaps responding to the unbearably repressed natures of the good people of Bodega Bay when a stranger comes to town, the local birds turn violently against them in *The Birds* (1963). Robert Burks shot the visual effects-laden film with a broad spectrum of color in the soundstage and on location. Using a 1.85:1 aspect ratio, visible grain was part of the image design to help keep the effects shots seamless.

The 2000 "Alfred Hitchcock Signature Collection" DVD release offered a very good image transfer of *The Birds,* with a solid monaural Dolby 2.0 soundtrack. The image displayed a generally accurate rendering of Burks's palette with some occasional instances of source material wear. The 2005 image transfer is more impressive with slightly more realistic colors, a cleaner overall image quality, and a striking, film-like feel. As with the 2005 *Psycho* DVD, Bouzereau's feature-length documentary was moved to the box-set's supplemental disc to make more room for better compression rates, thus allowing the feature image to be clearer, making this disc a standout in the box-set. The digital 2.0 audio is nearly identical on both discs: clean and full-bodied with solid tonal range.

Marnie (1964), a disturbing tale of an elegant, compulsive thief and the man who tries to make her walk the straight and narrow, debuted on DVD in 2000, offering a very good, anamorphic image transfer with the correct 1.85:1 aspect ratio. Burks's soft, dream-like palette of primary colors and shadows finally looked close to what it should on home screens. Remastered in 2005 with bit-rates just slightly higher, the image transfer is an improvement in terms of framing: where the 2000 disc was slightly geared to the right, this transfer is framed more correctly to the center. Also, the image has a slightly softer quality that is truer to Burks's conception of the photographic style of the film. The most notable difference between the two discs is the 2.0 digital monaural soundtrack. The 2005 audio presentation seems fuller, with much more pronounced bass.

When a young American scientist pretends to defect and his unassuming girlfriend follows, spies and danger abound in *Torn Curtain* (1965). Shot by John F. Warren, a veteran of Hitchcock's television show, the film has a cool, dark sheen to it. *Torn Curtain* never looked as it should on home screens until the 2000 DVD, which boasted a 1.85:1 anamorphic image transfer with generally pleasing color balance and a solid digital 2.0 monaural audio counterpart. The 2005 DVD marks a marginal improvement. There appears to be less visible grain and, similar to *The Birds,* the new image transfer feels more true to the film, with cooler, more natural colors, although the bit rate seems nearly identical. The digital monaural 2.0 also is clearer with a more vibrant presentation of dialogue and sound effects.

Cold War antics among super-powers threaten to ignite international mayhem in *Topaz* (1969). Photographed by Jack Hildyard, *Topaz* has a vibrant, crisp color scheme. While widescreen 1.85:1 versions showed up occasionally on cable television broadcasts, it wasn't until the 2000 DVD release that *Topaz* was given its appropriate aspect ratio for home video, with an anamorphically enhanced transfer and color timings close to those of the original film. Like the 2005 DVD image transfer of *Torn Curtain*, this new version of *Topaz* is a marginal improvement over the solid 2000 transfer, offering cooler, more realistic colors. This newer transfer also leans toward being a shade lighter in most sequences. The digital 2.0 monaural audio seems slightly more clear, with more attention given to the film's score. Overall, the transfer is more pleasing, if not markedly different than its predecessor.

Frenzy (1972), the alternately brutal and amusing shocker that follows a serial rapist and murderer on the prowl in London, was shot by veteran British cinematographer Gilbert Taylor. Taylor's grim, often pale light shown on a sharp, realistic color palette has been well presented on both the 2000 and 2005 DVDs. The film's slick, gritty tones are generally well-realized on the 2000 disc, but like the 2005 transfers of *The Birds, Torn Curtain,* and *Topaz,* the 2005 *Frenzy* is sharper, with cooler, truer colors, making it a distinct improvement. The digital 2.0 monaural sound, with its standout bass presence particularly noticeable in the music just after the first murder, seems identical on both transfers.

A phony psychic stumbles upon a criminal plan that gets her more trouble than she bargained for in *Family Plot* (1976), the comic thriller about two very different couples. Hitchcock's final film was at last given a 1.85:1 transfer on DVD in 2000. Cinematographer Leonard J. South, former camera operator for over a dozen of Hitchcock's films, shot the film with quasi-realistic lighting setups and a fairly subdued color palette. Unfortunately, while the aspect ratio was correct, the colors seemed overly saturated and the overall transfer was disappointing, with too much visible film grain. The new 2005 transfer offers a generally cleaner, more pronounced image with less saturated colors, although there is still visible and occasionally excessive grain. While it's an improvement, *Family Plot* should look better than it does on both discs. These deficiencies could be the result of lackluster source materials or the deterioration of the original negative. (It is highly possible that *Family Plot* is one of the many mid-1970's American films shot on particular discontinued Kodak stocks that have been now noted to fade quickly.) The 2000 audio track is fine, but the digital 2.0 monaural seems a touch cleaner, with better music and effect separations on the 2005 DVD. John Williams's tongue-in-cheek score seems to benefit most from the cleaned-up audio track.

The fifteenth and final disc of the package is comprised of supplemental material, much of it unique to the 2005 edition. While hardly as packed as it could be with numerous newsreels, vintage footage, and Hitchcock ephemera, the disappointingly small array of extras are nevertheless of great interest. Bouzerau's excellent documentaries, *The Making of* Psycho and *All About* The Birds, that were left off the respective DVDs to create more compression room for feature transfers appear here and are the longest supplements. While the box-set has been rightfully criticized for not including more of the *American Film Institute's Salute to Alfred Hitchcock* (previously available on VHS and laserdisc at a more complete seventy-two minutes), the fifteen minutes offered gives an excellent glimpse of the evening, with charming speeches by Ingrid Bergman, James Stewart, and Hitchcock himself, accepting the Lifetime Achievement Award in 1979.

Also included is a thirty-four minute segment from the 1972 CBS television series *Camera Three*. Originally broadcast as *Camera Three's Masters of Cinema: The Illustrated Hitchcock* in two thirty-minute segments, the first features Hitchcock and film critic Pia Lindstrom (daughter of Ingrid Bergman) and the second, Hitchcock with film historian, professor, and collector William K. Everson. While slightly truncated from their original lengths, the segments feature both Lindstrom and Everson engaging with Hitchcock, who seems to enjoy the probing questions and works hard to answer them. To see him remarking thoughtfully on his own work and how it had changed over the years is fascinating. Ever the showman, he's garrulous and articulate with the two interviewers and clearly happy to have been invited.

The "Alfred Hitchcock Masterpiece Collection" is housed in a sturdy, wine-colored, velveteen box with four slip cases within that house three or four discs snugly. Each gatefold slip case is nicely designed with original poster art and advertising campaigns for each of the films. Tucked in among them is a thirty-two-page photo-booklet with brief, if unnecessary, introductions to each film and the director himself.

In the final analysis, it seems clear that however sufficient and well-received the original box-sets or single-units DVDs from 1998 and 2000 were, Universal's remastered "Alfred Hitchcock Masterpiece Collection," available in the box-set or as single units, is an overall better investment. In the brief history of the DVD medium, the compression technology in transferring image and sound to DVD has continued to grow, and in most cases these films have clearly benefited in these 2005 presentations.

As we move later into the first decade of the DVD format's reign, already home video formats are quickly going through changes while many studios scramble to decide which of the two dueling high definition DVD formats they will choose. One can only imagine what next level of home video transfer awaits these titles, whether it be the Blu-Ray format or HD-DVD. Currently, Universal Home Entertainment has made no comment on the digital format future for these titles, but for now we can revel in the generally excellent quality of this "Masterpiece Collection," as Hitchcock's films continue to fascinate, inspire, and entertain newer generations.

Book Reviews

Christine Gledhill, *Reframing British Cinema 1918-1928: Between Restraint and Passion*. London: British Film Institute, 2003. x + 214 pp. $70.00 cloth; $30.50 paper.

CHARLES BARR

Elveyesque! It's unlikely that this adjective has been applied to Hitchcock's work before now, and it's certain that Hitchcock himself would have been displeased by it. Christine Gledhill, in her absorbing book about the last decade of British silent cinema, uses it to describe the visual style of his last pre-*Blackmail* film, *The Manxman*. The reference is to Maurice Elvey. Born in 1887, he directed around 200 films between 1913 and 1957, almost all of them in Britain; at least 100 of them preceded Hitchcock's own first film as a director, *The Pleasure Garden*. Elvey represents exactly the kind of indigenous early British cinema that Hitchcock always ignored or denigrated in constructing a map of his own cinematic formation: he acknowledged influences from America, Europe (Germany in particular), and later the Soviet Union, and from British playwrights and novelists, but never from within silent British cinema, excepting only Alma Reville, who was still doing relatively subordinate jobs in the industry when she married him in 1926. Gledhill's perspective is quite different. Her book, based on years of close study both of films from that decade and of a wealth of contextual material, offers the most radical challenge so far to the Hitchcock version.

How did that version stay unchallenged for so long? By the time Hitchcock became a focus of serious scholarly attention, no one was much interested in his British roots: the denigration of the national cinema and the extreme privileging of the American films over the British, by François Truffaut and Robin Wood, in the two key publications of the 1960s, are too well known to need rehearsing. Maurice Elvey died in 1967, just before the English-language publication of Truffaut's interview book, and both Eliot Stannard, Hitchcock's regular silent scenarist, and Graham Cutts, the director with whom he worked on several Gainsborough productions, had died years before—not that anyone, then, would have been interested in any dissenting views they might have put forward on Hitchcock and his early environment. In 1978 came the first biography, *Hitch*, by John Russell Taylor, an "authorized" one on which its subject collaborated fully. With a deference that now seems rather ignominious, Taylor colluded in the Hitchcock version of his early years in the industry. Graham Cutts "was by all accounts not much of a director." Elvey is mentioned only in the context of *The Man Who Knew Too Much* in 1934, when he was evidently considered as replacement director after Hitchcock's old enemy C.M. Woolf decided it needed reshooting: Taylor records that Elvey "was cheerfully characterized by a colleague as 'the worst director in the world,'" and there it rests.

That colleague is not identified, but one wonders if it might have been Alma Reville. She, after all, has a script credit on two of Elvey's early sound films, *Sally in Our Alley* (1931) and *The Water Gipsies* (1932), and she had begun her film career, before the formation of Gainsborough Pictures in 1922, working for Elvey at the London Film Company, at a time when his regular scriptwriter was Eliot Stannard. She even had an acting role in Elvey's ambitious biopic, *The Life Story of David Lloyd George* (1918). Could it be that the early Reville-Stannard association helped influence Hitchcock's own initial choice of scriptwriter? Taylor makes no mention of these links, and he refers to Stannard only in passing. Of Cutts, he states disingenuously that none of his films seem to survive. On the contrary, many of them, starting with his second film *The Wonderful Story* in 1922, are, and were at the time, available in the archives in London; indeed, Rachael Low had already viewed and written about them for the 1918-1929 volume of her *History of the British Film* (1971). One gets the sense that the Hitchcocks were concerned to "cover their tracks," and that Taylor was happy to help them do so, by suggesting that their early British collaborators and contemporaries were too negligible to bother with.

Rachael Low, of course, had bothered with them, and her four-volume work on British silent cinema, begun soon after World War II, constitutes a wonderfully thorough pioneering achievement. However, although she wrote respectfully about Graham Cutts, she didn't exactly inspire scholars to follow her explorations; she gave a generally negative account of the aesthetic level of British films in the two decades before the rise of Hitchcock, writing of Stannard, Elvey, and many others as at best prolific journeymen. Even when British cinema history began to be perceived as a worthwhile area of study, the silent period—at least after *Rescued by Rover* in 1905—remained virtually closed off to research. Not much, other than Hitchcock, was easily available; Rachael Low had done the hard work, and surely no one would need to go there again.

How things have changed. Books on British cinema fill not just half a shelf, but a large bookcase. Even Robin Wood has ceased to be condescending about Hitchcock's British films. The Broadway Cinema in Nottingham—Alma's birthplace—runs a successful annual weekend event on British Silent Cinema, where Hitchcock is only one reference point among many. Year by year, it becomes harder to discount the significance of his roots not just in the British literary-theatrical culture of his youth, but in the British film culture also. I regret having connived in the facile denigration of the years 1905-25, in a chapter "Before *Blackmail*: British Silent Cinema," published in 1997 in *The British Cinema Book*, edited by Robert Murphy, but have since made partial amends in *English Hitchcock* (1999), mainly through foregrounding the importance of Eliot Stannard, whose career began in 1914, and have followed this up with a fuller account of his career in an essay on "Stannard and Hitchcock" for Andrew Higson's 2002 collection *Young and Innocent?: Cinema in Britain 1896-1930*. That volume does not contain much else directly on Hitchcock, but is still of interest to Hitchcock scholarship because of the way it continues to fill out the background to his early work. This is what Gledhill's book now does, in an unprecedentedly searching manner.

Gledhill is best known for her excellent work on melodrama. At the British Film Institute in the 1980s, she was involved in a long-term research project of which one outcome was the collection published in 1987, *Home is Where the Heart Is: Studies in Melodrama and the Woman's Film*; both the collection itself and, especially, her own long and wide-ranging Introduction, have had a real influence on the Film Studies agenda, at least in Britain. The book under review has its roots in the same research, in the course of which "the encounter with British films of the 1920s suggested a body of work more interesting, quirky and rich than was generally allowed" (1). Gledhill was inspired to embark on a systematic viewing of some 150 prints held in the British National Film Archive, along with a dauntingly thorough trawl through written material. She states her strategy at the start: "I wanted as far as possible to avoid cherry-picking the few titles already feted in the British historical canon: the silent Hitchcocks, Duponts and Asquiths"; instead, she explores the whole field, including "the lesser byways and backwaters of British film-making in this period" (1).

Anthony Asquith made only two all-silent films, *Shooting Stars* (1927) and *Underground* (1928), and E.A. Dupont only two British silents, *Moulin Rouge* (1928) and *Piccadilly* (1929), so essentially it is the far more "feted" Alfred Hitchcock, director of nine, who is being decentered. He is not exactly ignored: *The Manxman* is given nearly four pages, most of the preceding films are at least mentioned, and the index yields twenty references, eight of which, intriguingly, come under the heading "Hitchcock, Alfred: prefigured by earlier directors." There is a strong temptation to do what Gledhill abjured, and to "cherry-pick," looking up the Hitchcock references, and having a proper read only of the *Manxman* pages.

For non-British readers, the temptation must be all the stronger, since virtually none of the non-Hitchcock films referred to are accessible outside Britain, even in archives, and the abundance of close-packed material on the byways and backwaters of pre-1928 British theater and painting and popular culture will be even less familiar than it is to most natives. Moreover, neither Gledhill herself nor her publisher makes things easy for the reader. The BFI deserves high praise for putting all the resources of its archives at her disposal, and for publishing the results, but it has let her down badly with the production of the book itself. The text is squeezed into a tight two-column format, making it a strain to read, and incidentally giving a problem to anyone wanting to make marginal annotations. The number of illustrations, thirty-four, is ridiculously small for a substantial book that focuses so much upon analysis of pictorial conventions and of cinematic style, and deals with films that few readers will know. Many are printed too small, or in the wrong format; others are publicity stills rather than frame enlargements. *The Manxman* is granted a single still, one of the small ones, a landscape long-shot. If ever a book needed an abundance of frame enlargements, illustrating sequences as well as isolated moments, this one does, and it's hardly unrealistic to expect them: look at the BFI's own Film Classics series, where much shorter and cheaper books carry a generous number of illustrations, taken from the frame.

Nor is Gledhill's own verbal strategy always helpful in enabling one to visualize, in the absence of stills. For a number of key sequences, for instance from Elvey's *Mademoiselle from Armentieres* (1926), she uses the ponderous device of describing shots in order, without breaking up the page format, numbering them, in this instance, 1 to 30; twenty of these shots are labeled "repeat" and refer one back to earlier numbers in the table, so one has to keep looking back and forth and try to build up a mental picture of the cutting pattern, which, without a businesslike tabulation or chart, is (to me anyway) extremely difficult. However, take a piece of paper and create and fill in your own chart, and the sequence and its editing structure become clear, and make Gledhill's point very well, reinforcing the argument carefully built up about Elvey's distinctive and coherent pictorial style. This is characteristic of a book that is demanding but, when you persist, enlightening.

Reframing British Cinema divides neatly into two equal parts: "Co-ordinates" and "Conjunctions." Part One explores, in authoritative depth, the particular resonances that theatricality and pictorialism had acquired in British culture—both high and popular culture—by the start of the twentieth century, and how these helped to shape a distinctive filmmaking strategy resistant to the emerging "classical Hollywood" norms:

> Thus, despite awareness of the need for "punch," "pep" and "vim"—terms that attempted to catch the very different attractions of fast-paced American editing and acting—there is a reluctance to let go of the picture as the centre of pleasurable perception. (52)

The films of, for instance, George Pearson "represent a distinctive cinematic development of the national emphasis on the pictorial, acculturated image, taking film in a direction quite different from that consolidated in Hollywood" (54). Gledhill makes much of the distinction between the American term "movie" and the British "the pictures," noting that even the modernist critic Iris Barry called her 1927 book *Let's Go to the Pictures*, only to have the noun changed to *Movies* for its eventual U.S. publication. Both Pearson and Cecil Hepworth are quoted as arguing lucidly against the acceptance of a full "continuity" system, a term that was a focus for debate in the industry and the trade press in the early 1920s. Like Andrew Higson in *Waving the Flag*, Gledhill cautions us against seeing this, in a teleological spirit, as regressive or primitive; rather than trying, and failing, to emulate Hollywood on its own terms, these filmmakers were working out consciously different models whose distinctiveness could have been, and to some extent were, a selling point, at least in the home market. (She doesn't go into the crucial issue of how this market was distorted by the monopolistic tactics of American distributors, a problem not addressed by legislation until 1927).

This is how, at the start of Part Two, she summarizes the situation around the time Hitchcock entered the British film industry:

> Imagining film stories in terms of theatrical stages and pictures posed a challenge to a modernizing film industry seeking the capacity for narrative fiction now

established by Hollywood. In particular, pictorial framing and frontal shooting inhibited the scene dissection facilitated by analytic editing, on which depended the illusion of a seamless fictional world that was fast becoming the norm. However, out of the culturally conditioned mode of perception sketched in Part One, British film-makers developed a variety of strategies to handle the challenge of adapting theatrical staging and pictorial seeing to the needs of narrative cinema. (93)

The directors whose strategies are given closest attention are the two with whom Reville and Hitchcock respectively worked most closely at the star of their careers, the two whom the Taylor biography condemned without a hearing: Maurice Elvey and Graham Cutts. Elvey's film of 1918, *The Life Story of David Lloyd George*, has had several high-profile showings in Britain with musical accompaniment, thanks to its political interest and the drama of its rediscovery seventy-five years after its original suppression; some other Elvey films have been shown at the annual Pordenone silent film festival. What is needed now is to make these and some early Cutts titles more widely available. All I can say meanwhile, on the basis of what I have seen myself and on Gledhill's verbal account, is that she makes a convincing case for taking both these men seriously. It's easy to forget that Elvey's work earned him a contract in Hollywood, where he made five films for Fox in 1924-25 before returning to an environment he found more congenial.

As for Cutts: twenty years ago, in the course of research for an edited collection on British cinema, *All Our Yesterdays* (1986), I watched some of his films, and referred briefly, in the introductory survey chapter, to their dynamism and their sophisticated deployment of the look, so I can endorse Gledhill's detailed and nuanced analyses of these qualities. In the most recent of the Hitchcock biographies, Patrick McGilligan quotes Alma Reville on Cutts: "He wasn't really a pleasant man; he knew very little, so we literally carried him."

Pleasant or not, he made two of his key films, *The Wonderful Story* and *Flames of Passion* (1922), before Gainsborough was formed and the connection with Hitchcock, as designer and scriptwriter, began, so the question of "carrying" does not arise. Others, like *The Sea Urchin* (1926), were made after Hitchcock had gone off to direct. It's on the basis of these, more than the collaborations, that Gledhill makes the claim that

> In terms of pictorialism, Cutts's particular contribution lay in an instinctive sense of the power of the look, not only as a means of controlling others but as generator of projected internalised visions. . . . His films' insinuation under the skin of the public personae of British fiction anticipates and opens up the terrain Hitchcock would claim as his own. (114)

Another writer to take Cutts seriously is Anthony Slide. In *The Encyclopedia of British Film* (2003), he calls him "the finest of the country's directors in the 20s," which presumably includes Hitchcock. He adds that "It would have been nice to report that Hitchcock was influenced by Cutts, but their styles are so patently different." Gledhill would disagree, about the style and maybe the influence as well, but direct influence is not really the issue. What is surely now beyond dispute is that there was, at the least, a certain *affinity* between, on the one hand, Hitchcock and Reville, and, on the other, collaborators and contemporaries like Elvey, Cutts, Victor Saville, and the indispensable Eliot Stannard, and that their background in British culture, with the strong theatrical and pictorial elements that Gledhill analyses, was an important part of the formation of all of them.

And so to *The Manxman*. Gledhill's account of it makes much fuller sense when you come to it after a careful reading of the preceding chapters, rather than "cherry-picking" it: "The drama is enacted through a series of frontally shot portraits and group tableaux, the pace quickened when necessary through an Elveyesque flicker-book style of montage, homing in on and activating the emotional turning point of a pictorially realized situation" (119). While the term "flicker-book" (here as elsewhere) remains rather obscure, the affinity with some of Elvey's strategies, as previously outlined, is clearly brought out, and the elements of the pictorial and of tableau composition in *The Manxman* are undeniable. Gledhill sums up:

> *The Manxman* is a product of the poetics of British cinema, demonstrating both the rootedness of Hitchcock's techniques in its pictorial-theatrical practices and the powerful and distinctive cinematic language they can generate. This very excellence has served to obscure Hitchcock's aesthetic allegiances. (122)

Thanks to Gledhill, those allegiances, or at least an important branch of them, are obscure no longer.

John Orr, *Hitchcock and Twentieth-Century Cinema*. New York: Wallflower, 2005. viii + 207 pp. $75.00 cloth; $25.00 paper.

THOMAS LEITCH

No filmmaker is an island—not even Alfred Hitchcock, who identified himself with a genre of which he often seemed the sole and exclusive proprietor, told interviewers he saw other directors' films mainly for casting purposes, and produced a body of work whose major influence seemed increasingly to be that of his own earlier work. Although the foundational texts of Hitchcock criticism, from Rohmer and Chabrol to Robin Wood, isolated him by treating him either as the quintessence of commercial cinema or a unique case in its history, the tendency ever since Tom Ryall's *Hitchcock and the British Cinema* (1986; rev. ed. 1996) has been to place Hitchcock in a broader context of collaborators, filmmakers, and national movements in a more critical attempt to define his position within commercial cinema. Now John Orr, Professor Emeritus at the University of Edinburgh and author of *Cinema and Modernity* (1993), *Contemporary Cinema* (1998), and *The Art and Politics of Film* (2000), has produced a study whose title would seem to settle Hitchcock's place once and for all. The book does not live up to the promise of its title, but it is full of challenging and perceptive ideas, not least because of the problems that the title raises.

Orr's book is both narrower and broader than his title indicates. Its contextualizing of Hitchcock is not exhaustive but highly selective, as a survey of its chapter headings indicates. Looking both forwards and back, Orr considers Hitchcock's connections to David Hume, Weimar cinema, British fiction, the actors who appeared in his films, the French New Wave, David Lynch, and Robert Lepage. The list is strikingly arbitrary. Further, at least two of Orr's touchstones are well outside the province of twentieth-century cinema. If the contexts that best illuminate Hitchcock's work are so far-ranging, why not range further, for instance to music and the visual arts? Readers who see more in the first hundred years of film history than German silent cinema, Ingrid Bergman, the *nouvelle vague*, and David

Lynch will find Orr's title too general; readers who wonder why he is not exploring Hitchcock's relation to the surrealist paintings of Magritte and Chirico will find it too specific.

More to the point is the question of how representative of twentieth-century cinema Orr's contexts are. Here he must be given the edge over Peter Conrad, whose associations in *The Hitchcock Murders*, penetrating as they often were, often seemed more a function of Conrad's eccentric personal mythology than of any broader cultural critique. Whatever the limitations of Orr's analysis, the contexts in which he places Hitchcock are much more distinctive and clearly articulated than Conrad's. Any study that makes a sustained attempt to trace Hitchcock's roots in British philosophy, German cinema, and the English literary thriller, consider his casting and direction of iconic performers, and his influence on the New Wave and the neo-noir of Lynch and Lepage is making a significant contribution to Hitchcock studies.

The relation between Hitchcock studies and cinema studies generally, in fact, is the single most fascinating question Orr raises. Although his title may suggest that like Thomas Schatz in *The Genius of the System* he wishes to define Hitchcock as a representative but not unique figure within a broader institutional and historical context, the opposite is closer to the case. Orr sees Hitchcock as "a matrix-figure" who was "not only at the centre of his own cinema but of cinema as such" through whose films "much of the entire life of Western cinema has been nurtured and dispersed" (8). This Hitchcock is all too familiar: the figure who bestrides multitudes and incarnates all the leading themes and contradictions of commercial cinema in the West. Has there been a single major study of Hitchcock since Raymond Durgnat that has not seen the Master of Suspense as Master of the Universe?

It is hardly surprising, then, that on the vexed question of how deeply indebted Hitchcock was to the literary sources he professed to denigrate, Orr concludes that Hitchcock the taker is less important than Hitchcock the maker: "Often the source of his fiction is written fiction, but it is his experience of the world and his moulding (with his screenwriters) of that fiction that counts more" (41). What is both surprising and gratifying is the power and delicacy with which Orr traces individual connections between Hitchcock, the most representative exemplar of commercial cinema, and the outlying territories. He never traces a single connection, however familiar, without seeing it afresh.

Although Hitchcock's debt to Weimar cinema, established by his formative experiences working for Ufa in Berlin and Emelka in Munich, has been studied closely by Sidney Gottlieb and Joseph Garncarz, Orr gives the argument a novel and persuasive twist by contending that the deepest influence of the German *Kammerspiel* did not begin to manifest itself until Hitchcock came to America. *The 39 Steps,* Orr suggests, is a comic inversion of *Dr. Mabuse,* with the fearsome criminal's talent for disguise transferred to Hannay's man on the run. As the two émigré filmmakers' careers diverged, Hitchcock spreading his wings with bigger budgets and bigger stars, Lang hamstrung by increasingly studio-bound productions and a second-string repertory company, Hitchcock developed Lang's tropism for enclosed spaces more resourcefully than his master, especially in the one-set films *Rope, Dial M for Murder,* and *Rear Window*: "Compared with the monotony of Lang's office and home interiors, Hitchcock's *Kammerspiel* aesthetic would give his single interior an identity of its own, turn it in effect into a leading character in the film. Yet it is also a space in which the spectator is immersed" (63). Despite the obvious short-term impact Peter Lorre's performance as the psychotic child-killer Hans Beckert had on his casting in *The Man Who Knew Too Much* (1934) and *Secret Agent,* the real influence of *M,* Orr argues, was not displayed until *Frenzy,* forty years later, when Hitchcock would set a his own serial killer loose in what reviewers complained was a vanished Covent Garden in "an *M* reversal" which achieved its chilling effects "not by homage to early expressionism but through a ruthless reworking of New Objectivity cinema" (66, 67).

Lang is not the only figure who moves Hitchcock to inversion rather than imitation. Orr follows James Naremore in seeing Hitchcock, for all his generic similarities to 1940s film noir, as remaining outside its current. Setting up his discussion of Hitchcock and Lynch, who "turns Hitchcock outside in" (166) in *Blue Velvet, Wild at Heart, Lost Highway,* and *Mulholland Dr.,* he notes that *Suspicion* and *Shadow of a Doubt* both anticipate and invert noir's betrayal of a fall guy by a *femme fatale;* instead, Hitchcock turns the genre inside out by showing a fall girl betrayed into guilt-ridden complicity by an *homme fatale.* Even the trademark emphasis on an exchange of guilt Rohmer and Chabrol saw as central to Hitchcock is a departure from noir, "a guiltless genre" whose fallen heroes lament their tactical errors but never repent their moral flaws because "in noir all values are relative," whereas in Hitchcock calculated murder is "an amoral absolute" (157).

Perhaps the most original and compelling case Orr makes for Hitchcock's transformation of an admired influence is Graham Greene, whose assured mastery of an established genre, the literary thriller, stood in marked contrast to Hitchcock's more tentative mastery of the less sanctified art of cinema. Both Greene and Hitchcock admired John Buchan's novel *The Thirty-Nine Steps,* but their visions of what could be done with Buchan differed sharply. Greene sought to update Buchan's "flight-narratives" in the novelistic "entertainments" *Stamboul Train, A Gun for Sale,* and *Confidential Agent;* Hitchcock, as fond as Greene of trains as settings that moved rapidly even as they enforced a claustrophobic stasis on their passengers, increasingly "distanced us from his middle-class transgressors who were largely amoral and secular, letting us admire their technique and their sang-froid but disallowing empathy" (94). Within the context of this profound difference, Orr acutely traces the influence of *The Ministry of Fear* on *Spellbound* and considers Joseph Cotten's performance as the imperishable American innocent in *The Third Man* as a point-by-point inversion of his other signature role, Uncle Charlie in *Shadow of a Doubt.*

In Orr's hands, the question of influence becomes a complex network of relations, variously indirect and transformative, often reciprocal, but never symmetrical. He observes that the leading "directors who take Hitchcock in their own direction" — Chabrol, Rohmer, Resnais, Polanski, Lynch, Weir — "are all successors to him precisely because they are all *unlike* him. That is to say, they absorb him into the world of their *own* vision, because they have a starting point that is independent of his" (7). As a counterweight to Hitchcock's well-known centripetal imperative in producing and defining his own work, Orr offers Hitchcock the medium for a series of ever-changing transactions between the influences he inherited and those he bequeathed. Hitchcock may be the center of the cinema universe, but as a purely relational function, he lacks a center himself.

This insight is central to the first and most problematic of Orr's contexts for understanding Hitchcock: the eighteenth-century Scottish philosopher David Hume. Orr sees in Hitchcock "a key focus . . . on the *dramas of transaction* that changed predicament [of traumatic memory] generates. It lies in the external nature of relations that exist beyond the substance of related entities. As Gilles Deleuze has pointed out, in Hume relations are always external to their terms: human communication thus takes place through external relations and through the mediation of objects. These take priority over identity, not the other way around" (32). Hence the heroes in Hitchcock's most successful films "are not constant selves with clear identities in a hostile world but persons rapidly altered by a rapidly altering experience" (33). Orr illustrates this premise by considering Rose Balestrero's mental breakdown when her husband Manny is falsely accused of robbery in *The Wrong Man*:

> The film does not attempt to psychoanalyse her. Rather, it records the impact on her of changing relations that are beyond her control. Just as we see [Manny's] transformation from honest citizen to accused prisoner we witness her transformation from sanity into madness. . . . Yet if we see her breakdown, and harrowing as it is, the film does not try to

explain it. That is to say, it does not *explain* how she has become someone else, but it does *show* how she has become someone else. (34)

The point is well-taken and indeed central not only to *The Wrong Man* but to films as different as *The 39 Steps* and *The Birds*, whose characters are defined not by the core identities they assert but by the dramatically shifting relations with each other and a world that offers them such constant affronts. It is the nature of Hitchcock's films, Orr points out, that these affronts, traumatic as they may be, are often highly pleasurable, as they are in *The Lady Vanishes* and *North by Northwest*. Even when the characters suffer, Hitchcock allows viewers to enjoy their suffering by making it the stuff of black comedy in *Rope* or operatic excess in *Vertigo*. Speaking of the attacks in *The Birds* as "the high point of Hitchcock's art," Orr explains: "The attacks are in no way supernatural—there is no get-out clause here—and yet no convincing reason for them can be given." Here the audience shares both the characters' desperate pursuit of an explanation and their failure to find one. This project is quintessentially Hitchcockian: "His cinema leads us by varying degrees to the same endpoint. There will always be something new and different in experience to elude us, and yet we (audience and heroes alike) will always try to master it" (24, 25).

This formulation so clearly illuminates Hitchcock that it goes a long way toward justifying Orr's summons of Hume's radical eighteenth-century empiricism as the single most important touchstone in a book titled *Hitchcock and Twentieth-Century Cinema*. The problem is that Orr's formulation, penetrating as it is, does not establish anything unique about Hitchcock. It is certainly true, as he notes, that Hitchcock's "cinema of *figures*, not of characters," in which "it is the encounter not the self that is paramount," sets him apart from "the psychodrama of fullness and depth" in which Elia Kazan, Fred Zinneman, Nicholas Ray, Arthur Penn, and Douglas Sirk present heroes and heroines "search[ing] for deep, misunderstood selfhoods" (42). It is even true that this

character-centered cinema, incarnated by such Method-
trained actors as James Dean, Marlon Brando, Montgomery
Clift, and Paul Newman, has left a rich legacy in the characters
created by "Robert De Niro, Al Pacino, Dustin Hoffman, Meryl
Streep, Daniel Day Lewis, Sean Penn and many others" (42)—
though the increasingly iconic recent performances of De Niro
and Pacino suggest that this opposition may not be as neat as
Orr contends. But Orr's analysis of Hitchcock is equally
applicable to a much wider array of films, including *Rules of the
Game, Jules and Jim, Cries and Whispers,* and *The Conformist.*
Many of Orr's comments on Hitchcock would apply equally as
well to Antonioni's most celebrated films—*L'Avventura, La
Notte, Blow-Up, The Passenger.*

What Orr wants to claim as a distinctively Hitchcockian
empiricism, in fact, is more generally associated with the
thriller and an enduring minority tradition in Hollywood. The
generic matrix of the thriller, with its emphasis on doubling,
mistaken identity, pursuit, moral degradation, and traumatic
memory, predicates characters whose interactions precede
and shape their essences whether or not Hitchcock is at the
helm. More interesting is the Hollywood tradition of iconic
performers playing characters whose relationships define
themselves rather than the other way around. This tradition,
coeval with those of the Method's search for deep and
definitive psychological truth and the genre films of Howard
Hawks, which are shaped by the equally iconic but
apparently more self-determined performances of James
Cagney, Humphrey Bogart, and John Wayne, is aptly
represented by Orr's example of *Notorious.* But *Notorious* is
representative, not quintessential, and Orr never makes a
compelling case for defining this third strain of Hollywood
cinema, which has been more closely identified historically
with European cinema, as Hitchcockian.

But if he neither makes a convincing case for Hume's
radical empiricism as uniquely Hitchcockian nor installs it at
the heart of Western cinema, Orr succeeds in more
unexpected ways. He is an exceptionally deft and wide-
ranging close reader, as he shows in his analysis of the ways

the camera setups in the murder scenes of *Dial M for Murder* and *Frenzy* keep their viewers off-balance. In addition to adding new dimensions of interpretation to Hitchcock's greatest films—*Rear Window, Vertigo, North by Northwest, Psycho, The Birds*—he makes films like *The Manxman, The Paradine Case,* and even *Bon Voyage* central to the Hitchcock canon in new and compelling ways.

Orr's contexts also provide useful and substantial revisions of two of the hoariest clichés of Hitchcock criticism. He rejects both the terms homosexual and bisexual as adequate to describe the *"triangulation of desire* or love-triangle that works uneasily, or not at all, within heterosexual format" (15)—for example, in the love that the lawyer Philip has not only for Kate but for his successful romantic rival Pete in *The Manxman,* a love that makes him complicit with Kate, who shares his feelings, even before he seduces her while Pete is off at sea. And he makes brisk work of the canard that Hitchcock's cinema shows active men watching passive or fetishized women by introducing a fundamental distinction in "American Hitchcock"—"the gaze is institutional, the look individual"—adding that "the institution is the springboard to desire" (108). Orr warms to his subject in one of his few explicit criticisms of Hitchcock commentary:

> A whole generation of critics, who have misread Laura Mulvey, use Hitchcock to obsess with great pedantry about a generic male gaze on the female "subject." But they have entirely missed the point about the direction of his cinema. After *The Manxman,* with its triangulated gaze, the Hitchcockian genealogy runs from *female to male,* not the other way around. Three key variations of the female gaze rapidly follow *Rebecca* among Hitchcock's wartime pictures, in *Suspicion, Shadow of a Doubt* and *Spellbound.* With Cary Grant, of course, Hitchcock half-reverses it in *Notorious* but there establishes a parity of gaze and look between the two lovers. Only with James Stewart in *Rear Window* and *Vertigo* does it

> become fully male. In the meantime, however, he had
> generated a third variation—the gaze of *male on male*
> that comes out of *The Manxman* and finds fruition in
> *Rope* and *Strangers on a Train*. (85)

Although this passage is not likely to dissuade many anatomists of the male gaze from their faith in patriarchal hegemony, the complications it introduces into the debate are so welcome that it is a pleasure to see Orr forgo his customary reticence to take on his predecessors directly. Indeed one of his signal achievements is the general unobtrusiveness with which he engages Hitchcock scholarship without making his disagreements and departures an issue.

Orr is not immune from his own minor errors. In addition to Gus Van Sant's remake of *Psycho*, he cites two earlier sequels but forgets a third made for television. His reference to "Judy's eager impersonation of the affluent Madeleine at Scottie's bidding" (30) seriously misrepresents Judy's attitude toward Scottie's fatally misbegotten attempt to reconstruct his lost love in *Vertigo*. He misquotes Walter Neff's confession from *Double Indemnity* as "I didn't get the money, and I didn't get the girl" (155). He misidentifies Mrs. Van Hopper, the heroine's dragonish employer in *Rebecca*, as "Mrs. Van Stratten" (125). He misspells the names of the hero of *To Catch a Thief* and the hero and heroine of *Spellbound* as John Scobie, John Ballantyne, and Constance Pederson.

Yet these slips do no more to undermine Orr's authority than his attempt to define Hume's empirical skepticism as a uniquely Hitchcockian feature of the cinema or a title that promises both more and less than his book delivers. Like the director's heroes and his audience, Orr attempts to make sense of an impossibly large and contradictory field of experiences by imposing a pattern on them, presumably well aware that important as Hitchcock may be to cinema's first hundred years, he is in the end a MacGuffin. The value of Orr's Hitchcock, like that of the sculpture full of microfilm in *North by Northwest*, is not that he answers every question but that he provokes dialogue and drama more interesting than the MacGuffin itself. The paradox concealed in Orr's title is that the wider he casts his net for Hitchcockian resonances in twentieth-century cinema, the more likely it is that his discoveries will be discontinuous and episodic, as many viewers find *North by Northwest* itself. If both Hitchcock as a filmmaker and each of his films imply not so much a hegemon as a system capable of assimilating and generating provocative ideas in a pleasurable way, Orr's fascinatingly selective survey of touchstones is truly and rewardingly Hitchcockian. Not the least of its considerable achievements is that it makes it impossible to take the phrase Orr uses to describe Hitchcock's impact on neo-noir—"a pure Hitchcock legacy" (174)—without a healthy grain of salt.

Michael Walker, *Hitchcock's Motifs*. Amsterdam: Amsterdam University Press, 2005. 512 pp. $37.50 paper.

Stephen Mamber

Michael Walker's *Hitchcock's Motifs* is likely to wind up on any fairly short list of essential Hitchcock books. The importance of this book lies in its aspiration to comprehensively chart recurring elements in Hitchcock's films from objects to situations to character types to certain settings and even to some types of weather. Not all of the arguments in the book are convincing, and some of Walker's rather idiosyncratic readings and at times curious methods might leave one puzzled or dissatisfied, but there is more than enough solid explication here to make the book extremely useful.

Walker distinguishes between motifs, which he defines as concrete elements in a film, and themes, which he calls "more abstract," but the rationale for what he chooses to include for discussion here is not always clear. Overall, though, the book is a nice compendium of some familiar Hitchcock subjects (handcuffs, food, keys, staircases) and others that seem fairly fresh (home movies, confined spaces, lights, portraits). The alphabetical listing, perhaps rather than suggesting an exhaustive list, makes the book read like a series of essays on selected topics. This organizational structure enables the sections to stand independently, and this allows for some diversity of approach from section to section, partly, one assumes, due to the differences between the motifs under discussion.

Walker does, however, connect various sections by adopting a print version of a hypertextual link; for example, when Roger Thornhill's phone call to his mother in *North by Northwest* is discussed in the "Mothers and Houses" section, because it comes from a phone booth, there is an arrowed reference: >CONFINED SPACES. But not every phone booth call in every Hitchcock film is similarly noted or linked, nor is the example mentioned above a very significant instance of a confined space, leaving one with the sense that the connections commented on are somewhat erratic, or at least somewhat arbitrary. Every reader of this book will no doubt come up with likely candidates for links that perhaps should have been included. For example, one would expect a discussion of hand washing in the Hands section to be linked at least to Water, if not also to Guilt. It should be said that Walker, while perhaps employing this linking device a bit sparsely, doesn't seek to detail exhaustively every occurrence of a selected motif when they appear in other sections. Too many arrowed references would make the book a patchwork of needless diversions, but by using the device at all he may be making no more than a gesture to a sometimes fashionable hypertext method. (See, for example, James Burke's *The Pinball Effect* to get an idea as to how this sort of thing can be done rigorously.) It would already be well understood that discussing individual motifs is a process of isolation for the sake of analysis. Virtually any such motif would almost inevitably be potentially linked to others. But to do that linking here (and suggest that the reader might jump from this spot immediately elsewhere) does damage to the exploration of a specific motif in itself. So these references wind up being more diversionary than enlightening, and I think the reader does best to ignore them. Maybe someday in an electronic version, and with many more such links added, this method could be helpful. For now, the half-hearted nature of the linking enterprise serves mainly to get in the way. On the other hand, one of Walker's strengths is to stick to each motif and examine the specific topic with considerable concentration, and he may have used the links as a welcome diversion.

Walker specifically excludes visual motifs, which themselves would certainly make for a few good Hitchcock books, as he acknowledges (17). While occasionally visual devices will interest him, I think it is fair to say that motifs lead him to a kind of content analysis; his discussions start from content rather than visual elements. Perhaps the unifying idea here is that Walker's emphasis on interpretation leads to content analysis of motifs (and it is typical of those who search for meaning to ignore style/visual design). One description of his method he offers is that he is using motifs to "trace an interpretive path" through a film, though what constitutes interpretation will certainly vary from case to case. It shouldn't take nearly four hundred pages for his principle interpretive method to be stated explicitly, but it is indeed not until page 399 that he finally says "a psychoanalytic approach is the most productive way of analyzing Hitchcock's motifs." Of course psychoanalytic readings (of various sorts) abound prior to that point, and on page 50 he announces that his general argument is that "a psychoanalytic reading of Hitchcock's motifs helps reveal the resonances, undercurrents and associations." Why this should be so would likely have required a bit of Hitchcock critical history, which is not his principle subject, and he does have his own take on what aspects of this method most interest him.

In general, identifying Oedipal overtones is a key aspect of his psychoanalytic approach. Certain films where doubles figure (e.g., *North by Northwest*, *Spellbound*, and *Shadow of a Doubt*) are identified as Oedipal narratives (151), and an "implicit Oedipal structure" is central to several films where Falling is the motif in question (243). Even a MacGuffin can "mark a moment of Oedipal tension" (301), by which point one may feel that Oedipal trajectories may turn up wherever one chooses to look for them. There's a bit of stuffiness to his psychoanalytic leanings—he's openly reliant on Wollen and Modleski and a few others, but one feels that he has little sympathy for Bellour or Žižek. Indeed, Walker's book can probably be taken as a measure of how mainstream psychoanalytic readings of Hitchcock have become. Psychoanalytic critics often criticized or abandoned what were perceived to be the constraints of auteurism, but in Walker's hands psychoanalytic interpretation becomes a matter of reading auteurist motifs.

For the most part, this approach is perfectly acceptable, though each reader will likely reach a point where he or she feels that this method is getting out of hand. Mine most certainly comes in the discussion of Keys and Handbags (275), when he first argues that "the use of the handbag undoubtedly sexualizes the scene in *Dial M for Murder*" of key stealing, and then feels compelled to explain "that there are two 'pouches' suggests the labia, and Tony's deft fingering would seem to hint at foreplay, with the key as the clitoris." Another example of what I feel is an overstretched interpretation comes when Walker argues that in *North by Northwest*, the statuette is "symbolically pregnant with Vandamm's and Leonard's child: the MacGuffin is their baby" and that Leonard dropping the statuette when he is shot is "like a miscarriage" (357). It can be a relief when Walker is a little more conventional with regard to symbolic meanings, as when he resorts to *The Penguin Dictionary of Symbols* to suggest a range of associations with staircases (351).

As befitting one with a strong psychoanalytic orientation, Walker is also greatly interested in, and very good at discussing, the effect of motifs upon male-female relations in Hitchcock films. As he says in the excellent section on Hands, "my basic point remains: that the hands motif in Hitchcock serves as a pretty good guide to the gender politics of his films" (235). When he discusses two instances in *Stage Fright* of close-ups of Eve's and Jonathan's hands, he is sensitive to how hands are related to male and female power, and also how they are linked to questions of guilt. He then goes on to show how hands express significant moral patterns: for example, he notes that male hands often relate to murderousness, though he also finds some instances of rescuing male hands. His approach to a motif often goes from a psychoanalytic argument to a more general consideration of how a motif indicates particular inflections that mark significant characteristics of Hitchcock's work as a whole, not just in terms of a psychoanalytic or gender issue.

Psychoanalytic and symbolic readings are by no means the sole critical arrows in his quiver. In many instances Walker functions in an exemplary way as a traditionally interpretive critic when he teases out the meanings from motifs. Sometimes (even often) he can be truly skilful and original in this endeavor, as when in exploring the jewelry motif he can work out five subcategories of its appearance, two minor and three major, and provide thorough, solid discussions of key instances, especially in *Vertigo*. While reading through the book, one gets the feeling that Walker has been cataloguing these motifs and elaborating these interpretations for years, and has now really worked through their significance. It is this careful and long-standing attention to detail that makes the book both at once so useful and so personal.

One is certain to have likes and dislikes among the entries, but the range of topics gives the work a pleasant diversity: if one topic seems labored, it will soon be followed by a fresh motif. Walker seems to realize that this sort of approach has ample room for occasional levity, as when we're told in the "Dogs and Cats" section that the German shepherd accompanying the police in *Frenzy* to arrest the wrong man "clearly cannot in any way be blamed" (145). One fears though, that on the subject of dogs, he is serious, so much so that in his index of motifs at the end of the book, he cross-references Charles Barr's *English Hitchcock* so that the reader can know "when he mentions the motif and I don't" (467). That we might want to keep track of the disagreements between these two estimable critics with regard to significant dog appearances on a film-by-film basis may be a little more detail than even the dedicated reader might wish to have provided.

Of far more importance unquestionably is the frequent appearance of the police in Hitchcock's films, a topic Walker deals with quite thoroughly. One of Walker's interesting repeated strategies is that regardless of motif, he will always include a section on how the one in question relates to the police ("Staircases and the police," "Water and the police," and so on). This establishes a useful element of continuity, and also an effective way of arguing for the centrality of a particular motif. Were this done too much, the notion of motifs could break down somewhat, but returning to an interest in the police is a convincing method of testing the significance of each motif, as well as a means for him to have at least one form of continuity from section to section. Like the attempt at hypertext linking mentioned earlier, too much of this linking of motifs to other subjects could get in the way, but with these returns to the role of the police each time he is at least maintaining a critical consistency that serves a useful purpose. While there might have been other topics that could have appeared in each section, Walker's overriding idea is that we can see how important his chosen motifs are because we can always look at how they are inflected in terms of how each interacts with the police. This results in enjoyable conclusions, such as the one in the "Blondes and Brunettes" section, that "The moral for cops is clear: stick to brunettes" (86). Furthermore, by showing that the topic of the police can be a way to look at each of his motifs, he provides a useful validation for the idea that the study of motifs can bring new perspectives to our thinking about Hitchcock.

One particular talent of Walker's is his ability to link moments in widely separated films. I would say that this is even one of the principal pleasures of the book. Walker's real argument about Hitchcock might actually be labeled, to use the often dreaded word, auteurist in nature. Finding continuities in Hitchcock's body of work through a repeated and sophisticated deployment of motifs is the fundamental argument of his book, whether he chooses to foreground this aspect of his enterprise or not. While he occasionally admits that motifs "serve to indicate Hitchcock's own auteurist position" (46), Walker seems either reluctant to acknowledge this as a central tenet of his method or implicitly assumes that the reader will be aware of it without further reminders and accepting of it without strenuous argumentation. We could label Walker a "post-auteurist," in that he is assuming that (at least with Hitchcock) we no longer need to fight this old critical battle, and that if we're reading this book in the first place, we have an interest in continuities in Hitchcock's work.

Throughout the book, Walker is truly insightful in not just identifying how motifs are repeated, but in teasing meanings from Hitchcock's return to old interests. Seeing that Cathy carrying caged birds in *The Birds* mirrors Stevie doing the same in *Sabotage* (and also properly citing Susan Smith for discussing this too), Walker argues for a common victimhood expressed through this means, and continues his parallels between the two into several other areas. He then neatly transitions to

contrasting the birthday party in *The Birds* to another children's
birthday party scene, in *Young and Innocent*. Merely noticing the
repetition of such scenes would be quite an accomplishment,
but it is only a starting point for purposeful comparisons
between the reappearances of the motifs.

Walker's occasional analyses of motifs that Hitchcock
shares with other filmmakers are usually extremely
interesting. In a quick survey of cut hands (229), after
mentioning Lang and Mamoulian, he discusses a scene in
Hathaway's *Niagara* where Joseph Cotten cutting his hand
suggests castration (as do his other examples). He links this to
an example in *Frenzy*, where the breaking of a glass is also
linked to castration, but he then goes on to discuss other
examples of damaged hands in Hitchcock that do not follow
the common patterns of all these films, thus breaking
Hitchcock out from the pack. There is an even fuller
discussion elsewhere of portraits in films by others (320-21),
including a breakdown into what Walker sees as four key
categories of their use, and even of some literary antecedents
of portrait use. (Walker is especially interested in films such as
Pandora and the Flying Dutchman in which portraits are
associated with death.) Here too, though, "Painted portraits in
Hitchcock's films fit into these traditional associations, but
also take things further" (322).

Later with the motif of rain, he links Hitchcock to a
director you wouldn't expect to see him connected to: Frank
Capra. After discussing Capra's regular use of rain as a
romantic motif ("Rain, for me, is an exciting stimulant, an
aphrodisiac" [394]), he discusses Hitchcock's shared interest
in rain, albeit used for very different (not romantic) ends.
Comparisons like this between Capra and Hitchcock make
Walker's ideas of Hitchcock's "inflection" of a motif even
clearer, as most of the time we don't know how much Walker
is arguing that Hitchcock is unique with regard to a given
motif. What constitutes an inflection for Walker, though, may
at times be very slight. He argues, for instance, that the
appearance of rain in the flashback sequence of *I Confess*,
when Logan and Ruth take refuge in a gazebo in the rain,

"seems prompted by Ruth's wish to seduce Logan" (395). Maybe this isn't Capra-romantic, but the scene is certainly erotically suggestive. So it's good that Walker compares Hitchcock at times to other directors in terms of their approaches to certain motifs, even if here too, we don't always have to agree entirely upon the distinctions he makes.

One general problem with motifs is that what one says about a film while looking at a certain motif can lead to different interpretations of the same elements when one shifts focus to another motif. This happens to Walker even within separate categories of a single motif. In a thoughtfully argued section on Guilt and Confession, where he separates Catholic overtones from Transference of Guilt, the same circumstances receive alternative readings. Speaking of *Vertigo*, he first says that "Judy forgets how dangerously exposed she is, and her death is not intentional" (206), but then asserts a few pages later, when we've moved to another aspect of guilt, that "it's as though Judy's guilt causes her death" (212). I guess Judy can both forget her dangerous circumstances and still feel guilty enough to cause her own death, but this seems sufficiently at odds with itself for Walker to have explored the apparent contradiction. And to complicate things further, while earlier discussing another motif, Endings and The Police, Scottie (rightly, I'd say) gets his share of the blame (156). A reasonable conclusion is probably that, hypertext-like jumps aside, sections are best read on their own for what they tell us about the specific motif under examination, even if seeming contradictions can arise within sections about a single motif. The ending of *Vertigo* (like many moments in Hitchcock) is of course deeply complex, and Walker's varying viewpoints ultimately serve more to enlighten than confuse.

How to determine that a motif is even in evidence may be a problem too, particularly if stylistic arguments are not often brought to bear. Is the tracking shot near the end of *Shadow of a Doubt* as niece Charlie descends the staircase really a repetition of the hand motif (224)? Walker is divided enough to reference the jewelry motif here as well, but if the presence of her hand (which the ring is on, and it is the presence of the ring that really does seem the most important thing about the track-in) makes this example significant, then wouldn't one say the same of the elaborate crane shot in *Notorious* down to Alicia holding the key at the start of the party? As Walker acknowledges at the beginning of the Hands section, Philippe Demonsablon in his early *Cahiers du Cinéma* article about Hitchcock motifs listed some thirty-five instances of the hands motif, and there are many more. What would be helpful here, or maybe at the outset, would have been a little further laying out of just what constitutes a motif. Is it the repeated appearance of an object? A certain kind of action? Repeated scenes? It's all these and a little more. Walker often has specific objectives behind his highlighting a motif—objectives that could bear a little more direct examination. In the case of hands, Walker is fairly straightforward, saying that his main interest is to use this motif "as a means to examine key aspects of the sexual politics in Hitchcock's films" (221). This still suggests that the motif exists separate from his interpretation of it—a somewhat dubious smokescreen of neutrality. Whether a motif is one of hands or of jewelry depends ultimately upon where one wants to go with it.

Walker's lack of interest in visual devices as motifs may be part of a general preference of his to talk about the content of shots rather than issues of style. This preference even leads him entirely away from frame enlargements as either support for arguments or illustrations for his book; instead, he claims rather idiosyncratically that "[publicity] stills are better than frames from films to illustrate the motifs," arguing that one of these "always includes more of a given scene, and thus sets the elements, including any motifs, in context" (21). It is arguable whether this is so, but at the very least this attitude strongly suggests that how an object is photographed in a film is not Walker's highest interest. While he can speak in died-in-the-wool auteurist terms of "the principle that all Hitchcock's films interconnect with one another, so that visual echoes from one film to another are always significant" (134), his particular interest in motifs as thematic content (again, rather than as evidence of style) makes his approach unique. This preference may also account for his general avoidance of semiotic issues, although connecting motifs to codes to some extent would certainly be a possible direction of critical inquiry. (He prefers the Peter Wollen of the rather Freudian "Hitchcock's Vision" to the never-mentioned *Signs and Meaning*, for instance.) The only reference to any semiotic activity is of "restricted and elaborated codes" discussed by Basil Bernstein (27); Metz doesn't even warrant a mention. We should, of course, allow Walker his preferences, but should also be aware that others might be inclined to go down different paths in examining and interpreting Hitchcock's motifs.

The orientation toward content rather than style also makes him far less likely to discuss narrational issues. On the subject of flashbacks, for instance, Walker argues that Hitchcock uses them rarely (202). However this is not quite true. There are significant flashbacks in *Stage Fright*, *I Confess*, *Spellbound*, and *Marnie*, not to mention an abundance of other films with flashback sequences (like Scottie's dream in *Vertigo*). Is this narrative technique not worthy of being labelled a motif (especially if one like "Endings and the Police" is included)? One has to conclude that this sort of thing is not what Walker is really all that interested in. Consider his treatment of the MacGuffin. His analysis of this device is extremely well done, but he is not particularly concerned with its narrative functions. He sees it more in terms of character functions, such as its role as an "overvalued object" (299), and insightfully notes that "the characters who carry the MacGuffin in their heads are oddly enduring eccentrics" (305). And, Walker argues, MacGuffins can "mark a moment of Oedipal tension for the hero," as occurs in several films (301). None of these are exactly a form of narrative analysis, but Walker is at least sensitive to narrative devices as they affect characters and their circumstances.

Walker is groundbreaking early on in outlining a critical approach that seems to be quite promising for Hitchcock studies and perhaps for farther reaches of film study in general. In his initial overview, he quite daringly presents two of what he calls "Diagrammatic representations," one of motifs mapped by locations, and the other of motifs mapped by characters (47-48). These reminded me somewhat of Franco Morretti's book *Atlas of the European Novel*, where Dickens and Zola, among others, are also diagrammatically represented. Besides providing almost literal overviews of all the motifs he is exploring, the diagrams indicate multiple linkages of the motifs that wind up suggesting a map (or two) of the Hitchcock world. Seeing which sets of motifs link heroes to villains (instead of two heroines) or which connect to domestic spaces is a very fresh way of considering these issues. The prodigious effort behind this aspect of his enterprise is worthy of close consideration by the reader.

He is also to be commended for including, even if in an appendix, some discussion of Hitchcock-directed episodes of the *Alfred Hitchcock Presents* television show. It's also to his credit that he acknowledges that he has only been able to see slightly less than half of the episodes Hitchcock directed, as this probably leads to some rather skewed summary assessments. His overall conclusion that "four of the nine" episodes he looks at connect to issues of homosexuality (though only one "implicitly positive") is perhaps a case of a limited sample distorting one's sense of the prevalence of a motif. Even so, that he pays attention to these important and generally neglected works is another indication of his scrupulous attention to how Hitchcock's motifs play out throughout his entire output.

In the end, it may be Walker's idiosyncrasies and distinctive critical preferences that make this project so winning, as a more pedestrian or even-handed accounting of motifs would be excruciatingly dull, which Walker is certainly not. His thorough digestion of massive amounts of Hitchcock scholarship, his deep knowledge of the full body of Hitchcock's work, and tremendous quantities of fresh ideas about these basic building blocks and central ideas, make *Hitchcock's Motifs* a delightful and highly significant as well as personally charming book.

Nicholas Haeffner, *Alfred Hitchcock*. New York: Pearson Education Limited, 2005. ix + 125 pp. $14.95 paper.

SIDNEY GOTTLIEB

In *Alfred Hitchcock*, part of the Pearson Longman "On Directors Series," Nicholas Haeffner sets himself the usual impossible goals for a short critical study of a major filmmaker, attempting to provide a "comprehensive introduction to Alfred Hitchcock's major British and Hollywood films" (back cover blurb) that is accessible to students and general readers, sophisticated and argumentative enough to appeal to critics and professors, and alert and responsive to the vast realm of commentary and debate on Hitchcock, let alone the far reaches of Hitchcock's own work—all this in slightly more than 100 pages. Much to his credit, he has more than a little success in each of those areas, and the reader of this book will come away with much solid information about Hitchcock's life, career, and persona, a good grounding in what Hitchcock had to say about his approach to filmmaking, and a useful exposure to some of the key issues in Hitchcock criticism. At the same time, Haeffner rushes so quickly from one topic to the next that his arguments are sometimes sketchy, and the book is filled with bold assertions that need more careful qualification and with critical promises left unfulfilled as he points us one way and then goes in another.

The centripetal and centrifugal thrusts of the book are evident right from the opening pages. The heart of the introductory chapter is a concise overview of Hitchcock's family background, early experiences making films in England, move to America, and later career as director, producer, and public figure. Here as elsewhere, Haeffner nicely focuses not only on key elements of Hitchcock's cinematic style, illustrated by brief references to memorable moments in particular films, but also on Hitchcock's broader notion of what films should do and what kind of films should be made, illustrated by quotations from his writings and interviews. But all this is framed by what to me are tangential remarks about whether Hitchcock is a genius (he has Donald Spoto's *The Dark Side of Genius* in mind), swipes at psychological approaches to his life and work (a topic he will return to in a later chapter), cryptic and undeveloped comments about how Hitchcock's films are "preoccupied with relationships, most especially between people and the everyday objects of their perception" (1), and a concluding statement about the need to consider not only the "higher-minded claims made for his films" (12) but also their industrial and cultural contexts, a worthy objective, but one pursued somewhat intermittently.

The remainder of the book is organized thematically rather than chronologically. In chapter 1, he discusses some of the major components of "Hitchcock's Heritage," particularly the influence on him of melodrama (especially as found in novelists like Dickens, Marie Belloc Lowndes, and Daphne du Maurier, and filmmakers like Griffith), the thriller, early German cinema, Russian theories and examples of montage, and the cinema of attractions, linked to fairground settings and popular culture and audiences. Brief comments at the beginning and end of the chapter link all these elements to Hitchcock's self-conscious dedication to forging a "British middlebrow cinema" (14) that crossed social and cultural barriers and appealed to all audiences.

A substantial part of chapter 2 on "Authorship and Reputation" examines Hitchcock's careful cultivation and control of his image through publicity, including personal appearances, interviews, and writings; the boost to his career as a result of being adopted as one of the key examples of an auteur by the *Cahiers du Cinéma* critics; and the ways in which at various points he became trapped by his reputation. A definition of the major elements of auteurism then provides a somewhat lurching transition to a consideration of distinctive aspects of Hitchcock's *mise-en-scène* and editing, which in turn provides a transition to the next chapter's discussion of his "Fascinating Design." Here Haeffner rightly stresses Hitchcock's attraction to formalism, supported by quotations from Hitchcock himself as well as some of his key formalist-minded critics, especially William Rothman, Peter Wollen, Eric Rohmer, and Claude Chabrol. While the chapter title promises a treatment of image and sound, Haeffner spends most of his time on the latter, and redresses the typical neglect of this critical element of Hitchcock's work by careful analyses of the sound design of several films. He does this so well that I wish he had done more of it; but I also wish that he had devoted equivalent attention, as promised, to image and the broader structural design of Hitchcock's films. I have no reservations about agreeing with Haeffner that, in the words of Rohmer and Chabrol, Hitchcock was "one of the greatest inventors of form in the entire history of cinema" (quoted 45), but this high praise needs to be constantly confirmed by patient analysis.

Haeffner balances his attention to Hitchcock's formalism by turning next to "Realism and *The Wrong Man*." I think that he is onto something very important when he asserts that in general "Hitchcock's films show a keen interest in documenting everyday activity" (58), a claim usually supported by reference to the early British films but which applies to later ones as well. And while by no means neglecting the prominence in Hitchcock's films of fantasy, non-realistic special effects, and recurrent attempts to render interior feelings and disordered perceptions, Haeffner reminds us that "many of Hitchcock's films show an awareness of contemporary events within the real world" (58). All this adds deep texture to Hitchcock's films, as well as social and political dimensions that his viewers need to be more aware of. But instead of pursuing these very promising observations by a demonstration of how they can be illustrated across the full range of Hitchcock's work, he focuses instead primarily on *The Wrong Man*. This is both logical and ironic: logical because *The Wrong Man* is indeed in many ways "the most self-consciously realist of all Hitchcock's films" (61), but ironic because in being so it seems atypical, and in fact failed with audiences, Haeffner says, because it was not the kind of Hitchcock film that they expected and therefore broke an implicit contract with them. Haeffner's interpretation of the film is insightful and well developed, but moves us no closer to understanding the far reaches of Hitchcock's realism.

The following chapter on "Hitchcock and Women" is somewhat rambling, but perhaps necessarily so because he tries to cover numerous aspects of this complex topic (including representations of women in the films as well as Hitchcock's own real-life relations with women), survey some of the major critical treatments of the subject, defend Hitchcock from recurrent charges of misogyny, and indicate an awareness of the frequency in the films of manipulative and abusive men and victimized, vulnerable, as well as stereotyped women, some horrifying and others perversely attractive. He challenges what he takes to be Spoto's caricature of Hitchcock as a "cruel and bitter man who took pleasure in inflicting pain on women" (69), on and off the screen, and Laura Mulvey's description of the limited types of "gaze" available to characters within and spectators watching Hitchcock's films by following the lead of critics like Robin Wood, Tania Modleski, and Robert Samuels in showing how Hitchcock carefully sets up "an oscillation between identification with and objectification of women" (80). Not surprisingly, Haeffner focuses largely on later films like *Vertigo* and *Marnie*, but also refers at least briefly to many earlier films as well to illustrate Hitchcock's lifelong attention to women as subject and object.

Perhaps the least satisfactory chapter is on "The Uses and Abuses of Psychoanalysis." He first offers a brief but informative survey of the representation of psychoanalysis in several key films, which calls attention to a recurrent concern of Hitchcock's—one dealt with far more extensively and persuasively in an essay by Jonathan Freedman in *Hitchcock's America*, cited by Haeffner. But for the most part the chapter presents a superficial and in some places mistaken and misleading picture of what psychoanalytic theory and analysis (whether Freudian or Lacanian) entails, which is then used to support an impassioned critique of "the dominance of psychoanalytical interpretations of Hitchcock's films" (91). I am sympathetic to the aims of this critique and share Haeffner's impatience with criticism that mechanically and monolithically reduces all films to inscriptions of "the insistent logic of Oedipus, the phallus, anality, the law of the father, castration, voyeurism, fetishism, scopophilia and the *objet petit* à" (91). But to spend so much time railing against what the chapter title calls the "delirium of interpretation" is to remain transfixed by it, and especially in such a short book I wish that Haeffner had used this space practicing the kind of criticism he admires, rather than caricaturing the method he wants us to abhor and avoid.

The next chapter, in fact, takes the former approach, and to good effect. The result is an interesting discussion of "Audiences and Identification," which proceeds without an "over-use" of what Christopher Williams calls "the clumsy club of ideology" (quoted 92) and the predictable repertoire of spectatorship studies maneuvers and yet still manages to say insightful things about Hitchcock's pleasurable and rhetorical manipulation of his audiences, didactic and moral intentions, and skilful involvement of his films' spectators in the lives and perceptions of the characters onscreen. Unfortunately, as happens in key places elsewhere in the volume, this brief chapter ends with a tantalizing restatement of the importance of a subject—in this case, Hitchcock's "subtle understandings and negotiations of the art of spectatorship" (102)—substituting for a more satisfying detailed discussion.

The book ends with a discussion of "Hitchcock's Legacy," using *Psycho* as the primary bearer of this legacy—a case not much strengthened by Haeffner's focus on how Hitchcock's *Psycho* begat three inconsequential sequels and two works of quite limited interest: a "postmodern pastiche of the original" (111) by Gus Van Sant (spelled throughout the chapter as Van Sandt), a failure in almost all ways but which continues to live primarily as an adjunct to most critical discussions of Hitchcock's film; and Douglas Gordon's *24 Hour Psycho*, for all its length basically an art-house flickering "moment." A short introductory book on Hitchcock may well require a detailed treatment of *Psycho*, even to the exclusion of discussions of other arguably "better" and "more important" or "more Hitchcockian" films, so I certainly do not begrudge Haeffner his choice here, and he does include much useful material about the production circumstances, music, and marketing of the film. But he pays hardly any attention to what makes the film so captivating and significant in terms of its themes or its style, and this means not only that his treatment of *Psycho* is incomplete but that his attempt to end the book with a strong statement of Hitchcock's lasting importance and influence is hamstrung. Even a sketchy treatment of Hitchcock's legacy should, I think, attempt to take into account much more than what Haeffner mentions here, and if we are to tie this legacy to particular films, I would expand the short-list and include *Vertigo*, arguably the Hitchcock film that most haunts and influences serious contemporary filmmakers.

Finally, I wonder if Haeffner's concluding reassertion of Hitchcock's ongoing relevance, importance, and influence might not be balanced by at least some attention to a more sober and qualified assessment of the dynamics of his legacy. I am not quite as confident as Haeffner that Hitchcock's films "show little signs of diminished appeal for a new generation" (113), that his "reputation as a popular entertainer is unassailable" (113), and that "At the start of a new millennium, Hitchcock's films . . . constitute a cultural institution, reassuring and dependable" (114). I would, instead, describe Hitchcock's status in the way that Haeffner rightly describes the films: as in some ways unstable, problematic, "unsettling and disturbing" (114). Hitchcock is not the same cultural and cinematic icon that he once was, and even studies that, like Haeffner's, acknowledge and praise his perennially fascinating artistry might also acknowledge and trace the ongoing shifts, shadings, and even recession of his reputation and image in the new millennium.

Philip J. Skerry, *The Shower Scene in Hitchcock's* Psycho: *Creating Cinematic Suspense and Terror*. Lewiston, New York: The Edwin Mellen Press, 2005. 409 pp. $129.95 cloth.

MICHAEL HEALEY

One's opinion of Philip J. Skerry's *The Shower Scene in Hitchcock's* Psycho: *Creating Cinematic Suspense and Terror* will likely depend in large part on whether the reader appreciates the author's "postmodern" (3) approach. Following critics such as Linda Williams and Paul Monaco, Skerry argues that *Psycho*—and the shower murder sequence, in particular—represents the dividing line between classical and postmodern cinema. His book "weave[s] multiple perspectives and voices into the fabric of the text" (2) in an attempt to create an appropriately unconventional narrative structure, mixing formal analysis, cast and crew interviews, effusive claims for *Psycho*'s cultural significance, and a compilation of accounts by viewers recalling their first experiences of the film. This unusual, varied design is connected explicitly to Skerry's interest in audience response and the film's wide-ranging influence, but also implicitly to the shifting system of character alignment within the film.

Approximately half of the text appears in the form of traditional, critically-oriented chapters, but nearly as many pages are devoted to interviews (there are six, in all) and a concluding "memory" chapter, "The First Time." The latter includes reminiscences of first viewings of *Psycho* by a few notables such as director Wes Craven and Hitchcock biographer Patrick McGilligan, but is comprised mainly of anecdotes by individuals identified as teachers, attorneys, retired electrical engineers, or in two cases simply "Film Buff." Skerry never explains how he collected these stories and statements, which seems uncharacteristic, as he's not shy about inserting himself into the other chapters, whether it be references to his acquaintance with screenwriter Joseph Stefano and actress Janet Leigh or an explanation of how he approaches teaching Hitchcock to "students from a wide variety of ages, backgrounds, educational levels, and cultural experiences" (3) and the effect of his teaching experience on this book's methodology. I suspect that many of the contributors must be friends, family members, students, and colleagues of the author. Regardless, their stories attest to remarkably similar reactions, with most members split into two camps: either they did not expect the shower murder and were completely terrified when it occurred, or they knew something was going to happen but were nevertheless completely terrified when it occurred. A secondary variation among the male viewers would be whether they admitted their fright to their companions.

When taken as a whole, these testimonials of a seemingly unified response that seized the majority of theatergoers offer convincing support of Hitchcock's famous declaration that he played the audience like an organ. However, I cannot but wonder to what extent these memories have been shaped by the passing years and the discussion *Psycho* continues to generate. This is certainly not Skerry's fault, but there's a suspicious lack of variety in these reports. For instance, a number of viewers describe gasps and shrieks during the frenetic stabbing montage, followed by stunned silence as Marion Crane's life drains away. Did no one laugh, even if as an expression of nervousness? Were there no smart-alecks ready with wisecracks to defuse the tension? If not, then Hitchcock must have been even more skilled at manipulation than we generally believe. Yet it may be more illuminating to suppose there were diverse individual responses—rather than only the avowed group reaction—which may have melted away with the years. Perhaps these contrasting sensations or postures (laugher, aesthetic distance, distraction, anger) exert a weaker hold on memory because they are inconsistent with the master *Psycho*-viewing narrative. Each account eagerly supports our understanding of the film as a uniquely overwhelming event, but when read one after another, they imply that an array of possible human responses has been filtered over time, and now only the archetypal experience remains, which everyone professes to have shared. Was everyone truly affected the same way by the shower scene, or does it only appear so in retrospect?

The interviews inspire more confidence in their credibility perhaps because much of the material is well-known, at least in Leigh's and Stefano's chapters. Yet Stefano is such a modest, contented talker that I did not mind encountering familiar tales such as Hitchcock's interest in Stefano's psychoanalysis or how the director complimented the young writer by telling him that "Alma loved" (67) a draft of the early scenes. Leigh, on the other hand, adopts a combative stance, which makes her interview (to which I will return) the most interesting of the set.

Skerry also includes less dramatic conversations with *Psycho* crew members Hilton Green (assistant director), Danny Greene (sound editor), and Terry Williams (assistant to editor George Tomasini), as well as with Amy Duddleston, who edited Gus Van Sant's 1998 *Psycho* remake. Some new information, albeit minor, is revealed throughout. Danny Greene swears that a roast beef, rather than a melon, was the source of the shower scene's slashing sound effect. In an exquisite touch reminiscent of the *Alfred Hitchcock Presents* episode "Lamb to the Slaughter," the young technician took it home from the set, and his wife cooked it for dinner the following day. Less cheerful is Hilton Green's moving account of Hitchcock's last years, including a frightening telephone call when the ailing director fell in his office. The longtime assistant director also offers insight regarding the difficulties that could arise on the set, such as when the typically composed Hitchcock dressed him down after a repeated failure to capture a desired flare effect for the scene where Lila discovers Mrs. Bates's corpse in the fruit cellar.

The book's highlight is the interview with a prickly, sometimes antagonistic Janet Leigh, who does not hesitate to voice her disagreement when she feels the author is off the mark. Though Skerry remains polite and respectful toward Leigh, their dialogue dramatizes the conflict between an academic approach and a less high-minded appreciation of the film. Most memorably, when Skerry suggests a Freudian spin on the shower scene, the actress responds with a none-too-polite word for "balderdash." She makes it clear early on that their conversation will not be simply a rehash of the usual anecdotes and platitudes when she questions the necessity for his project: "[There's] only one thing that confuses me . . . there have been so many books on *Psycho*. I find it so odd— not odd, exactly, but what are they thinking? . . . What I'm interested in is how your publisher would think that you're going to find out something new about the shower scene" (24). That's an interesting sentiment for Leigh to express, seeing as she, too, wrote a book on *Psycho*. Is her objection partly territorial? Skerry does not pose a new reading of the shower scene or of the overall film, it's true, but one could argue that his aims are not first and foremost critical. Including lengthy interview transcripts, for instance, suggests that one of his key intentions is to compile an archive of primary material. However, the work does include scores of pages dedicated to close readings of scenes or shots, and the plentiful details from *Psycho* and other Hitchcock pictures accumulate to foster an expectation that they will be unified. I was frustrated by the relative absence of interpretation throughout.

Lacking an overarching thesis, Skerry's reflections— regardless of their quality—cannot be considered more than a collection of observations, many of which will be familiar from the work of earlier critics such as Robin Wood, V.F. Perkins, Robert Kolker, and Linda Williams. His title notwithstanding, Skerry offers meticulous readings of many scenes in addition to the shower murder. He overdoes it with some of the earlier pictures, settling frequently for protracted description instead of critical analysis, but he accomplishes nice work with *Psycho*'s first act. His attention to specifics of montage and *mise-en-scène* reveals telling details such as the alternating profile shots when Norman (Anthony Perkins) shows Marion (Leigh) to her room: Marion stands at the left side of the frame, her image reflected by a dressing table mirror in the background. Norman stands near the doorway, facing her, but his answering shot does not include a corresponding reflection. His "Mother" half is not present in this exchange, and thus his character is shown to be incomplete. When he returns carrying sandwiches and milk after arguing with "Mother," Norman's upper body can be seen reflected in the window of Marion's room, reinforcing his split personality. Such observations are astute, but Skerry does not organize or amplify them so as to contribute anything substantial to the abundant critical literature.

Nor do his claims regarding *Psycho*'s historical context and cultural impact—arguably the book's main theme—offer a significant advance in our understanding of this canonical film's stature. The Leigh interview's position as the second chapter of Skerry's book allows their differences of opinion on this matter to affect one's assessment of all that follows. The disagreement is not resolved entirely in Skerry's favor, either. He contends that, as much or more than any other film, *Psycho*'s initial release led to the downfall of the Production Code and set the standard for subsequent treatment of sex and violence onscreen. This is a dubious assertion when rendered so baldly, and some discussion of 1950s Hollywood beyond Hitchcock's filmography would have strengthened Skerry's historical argument. He introduces other contexts, such as the rise of television culture and the Baby Boom, but (excepting general references to the Code and the waning studio system) Skerry is oddly silent regarding the film industry.

The shower scene may seemingly come out of nowhere, but *Psycho* itself did not. Skerry does a fine job dissecting scenes from earlier Hitchcock pictures (especially *Blackmail* and *The Wrong Man*) that prefigure the shower murder, but I would have liked the author to demonstrate what set the director apart from his contemporaries in this period. There was a growing interest—and success—in representing onscreen violence and sexuality throughout the 1950s. *Psycho* may very well be that movement's capstone, but Skerry does not prove that; he merely asserts it. Onscreen brutality became more prevalent throughout the postwar period from the extended, exhausting bar fight in *Treasure of the Sierra Madre* to *The Man from Laramie*'s salt flats whipping scene, not to mention the relentless late noir films such as *The Big Heat* or *Kiss Me Deadly*. Other than the shock of killing off its main character less than halfway through the film, what is it that distinguishes *Psycho* and leads to our continued fascination with it? Skerry is right to point to the film as a defining moment in cultural history, but he provides few answers for the reader who wishes to know why that may be.

Leigh draws a fine distinction when Skerry trumpets *Psycho*'s sweeping influence during their interview. The actress argues that if such is the case, then Hitchcock's followers have not heeded one of his most important lessons. The shower murder is neither gory nor shocking for its own sake. The violence is primarily formalistic rather than the product of spurting blood or other explicit details. Leigh points out that "You didn't see anything. *Psycho* was the perfect example of how imagination works miracles. . . . [Now] they've taken away the imagination. An audience doesn't have to think anymore, isn't given the privilege of imagining anymore" (30). She cautions against "blaming" Hitchcock for propelling cinema into a more explicit period, as the shower scene only suggests nudity or a knife tearing flesh rather than showing either one outright.

Skerry contends that *Psycho* changed everything, yet that is not a self-evident truth. If he wants the reader to side with him instead of with Janet Leigh, then he ought to back up his claims with examples from other pictures. He need not perform shot-by-shot analyses, but excepting other Hitchcock movies and the notorious Gus Van Sant remake, he hardly mentions any specific films produced after 1960 until the penultimate chapter. Even then, his examples are limited primarily to the later *Psycho* pictures, *Simpsons* and *Looney Tunes* parodies, broad references to the slasher film genre, a bug-spray commercial, and obvious offspring such as Brian De Palma's *Dressed to Kill*. As one of his stated criteria for *Psycho*'s greatness is its impact not only within the film industry but on the culture at large, his failure to illustrate that premise—one of the book's main themes—seems a significant lapse.

Robert J. Yanal, *Hitchcock as Philosopher*. Jefferson, NC: McFarland and Company Inc., 2005. 206 pp. $35.00 paper.

LISA BROAD

Robert J. Yanal introduces *Hitchcock as Philosopher*, an inquiry into the epistemic implications of Alfred Hitchcock's film *oeuvre*, with a general exploration of the philosophical potential of narrative cinema. In accordance with what he terms "Customary Metaphilosophy" or CMP, Yanal argues that, "beyond presenting characters that illustrate general truths about human nature" (4) or expounding on philosophical topics, genuinely philosophical films and filmmakers engage with matters of morals and/or metaphysics at the level of form and narrative.

Drawing on Aristotle's *Rhetoric*, Yanal proposes that maximally philosophical filmmakers like Hitchcock use their films to pose and/or defend solutions to moral and metaphysical quandaries in much the same way that philosophers like Hillary Putnam and Jean-Paul Sartre employ fictional scenarios to illustrate their arguments. He explains that both cinematic and philosophical fables lay the groundwork for inductive reasoning by presenting (or representing) singular, concrete examples of universal, abstract ideas.

Although the extent of Hitchcock's philosophical acumen and ambition is unclear, in Yanal's view his approach resembles that of Ludwig Wittgenstein, whose arguments rely heavily on examples that must be interpreted by the reader. In the interest of closing the inductive gap between the singular scenarios presented by the films he discusses and the general truths that they suggest, Yanal intends the subsequent fourteen chapters of *Hitchcock as Philosopher* to serve as "philosophical studies that enable the reader to see the meaning of the example" (7).

Following its encouragingly straightforward methodological introduction, the body of *Hitchcock as Philosopher* is subdivided into three major parts entitled "Deception," "Mind," and "Knowledge," which consist primarily of thematic interpretations of the twelve major Hitchcock films

Yanal deemed sufficiently philosophical. (Given Yanal's identification of philosophy with the areas of morality and metaphysics, his explicit rejection of *Rope* as devoid of philosophical implication is very peculiar.) Yanal identifies his target audience as "fans of Hitchcock and fans of philosophy" (10). For the benefit of the philosophy fans, Yanal includes frequently over-generous plot summaries that he invites his more film-savvy readers to skip. For the Hitchcock fans, Yanal begins each of the three parts with disappointingly brief introductory chapters that sketchily summarize—in three pages or less—the basic philosophical issues he touches on in the course of his analysis.

In the preliminary chapter to the section on Deception, Yanal introduces his readers to the figure of Descartes's "evil deceiver." However, he is less concerned here with the philosophical implications of epistemic limitations than with the psychological impact of worldly deception on neurotic heroes and heroines who disobey Descartes's proscription to submit the will before the intellect. For instance, in the chapters on *Rebecca* and *Suspicion* Yanal hypothesizes that the heightened susceptibility to deception exhibited by the heroines of both films stems from emotional insecurity. He argues that Mrs. de Winter's anxiety about her own fitness as a wife ultimately leads her to doubt Maxim's love for her and misconstrue his relationship with Rebecca. Similarly, Lina's feelings of inferiority leads her to close her eyes to evidence of her husband's deception and to take an unwarranted attitude of certainty towards his innocence. Though Yanal fails to make a case for *Suspicion* as a Cartesian allegory, he does undertake a philosophically interesting discussion of the film's testament to the fundamental instability of suspicion relative to doubt and belief. He also mounts a novel defense of the film's much criticized ending, arguing that it leaves the fictional truth of many of the film's events and Lina's fate tantalizingly ambiguous.

Noting their shared preoccupation with themes of doubt and deception, Yanal identifies the first two parts of *Rebecca*, preceding the shipwreck, as an enactment of Descartes's *First*

Meditation. However, the thematic resemblances he discerns between the two works fail to provide sufficient evidence for identifying *Rebecca* as a genuinely philosophical film. For, while Descartes seeks to explore the possibility of indubitable knowledge in the face of human cognitive and perceptual fallibility, Hitchcock can most instructively be viewed as interrogating the possibility of love in the face of emotional weakness and insecurity. Both achieve their distinct objectives admirably, and there is a certain pleasing similarity in their approaches, but to conflate psychology and epistemology in the course of overstating that similarity does neither any favors.

With respect to *Rebecca's* denouement, Mrs. de Winter's freedom from doubt and deception is brought about, primarily, by her own willingness to trade a doomed romantic union for a functional companionate one. As Yanal explains, "She comes to a decision—what Wittgenstein would call an 'acknowledge-ment'—about her role in her marriage" (28). While I take no issue with Yanal's interpretation of Mrs. de Winter's decision or of its consequences for her marriage, I am unsure what to make of his allusion to Wittgenstein here. Aside from a brief opening quote from *On Certainty*—"Knowledge is in the end based on acknowledgement"—it is the only such mention in the chapter. In the absence of any explanation, it serves to generate more questions than it answers. How does Wittgenstein define acknowledgment? Why does he posit acknowledgement as the basis of knowledge? What does any of this have to do with Alfred Hitchcock? As Yanal notes in the introduction: "Reading [*Rebecca*] with or through Descartes and Wittgenstein is not a diversion from the narrative; it is a way *into* the story. In this way I hope to be consonant with Hitchcock's intentions" (8). First, given the brief and isolated nature of the reference, it is unclear whether Yanal has truly succeeded in reading *Rebecca* through Wittgenstein. Secondly, the fact that Wittgenstein would call Mrs. de Winter's decision to become her husband's helpmate an "acknowledgement" does little to illuminate the intentions of either Hitchcock or Wittgenstein without supplementary information.

In the chapter on *Vertigo*, Yanal continues his focus on the self-deception that can result from an increased suscepti-bility to deception by others. However, in contrast to the heroines of *Rebecca* and *Suspicion*, it is not insecurity but romantic obsession that allows Scottie to lose himself in the hall of mirrors inhabited by Madeleine Elster and Carlotta Valdez. Although he undertakes a brief discussion of Scottie's similarity to Descartes's "dreamer" figure, Yanal's primary point of comparison in this chapter is not expressly philosophical, but literary. He hopes to "show that Hitchcock is mounting a critique of the romantic hero . . . [by] pointing to the romantic hero's willingness to accept illusions" (52). Yanal bases his argument on the similarities between *Vertigo* and the medieval myth that provides the basis for Wagner's *Tristan and Isolde*. Yanal argues convincingly that Hitchcock was familiar with the myth and intended to refer to it, and that Scottie, who happens to be self-deceiving, possesses some of the same traits as Tristan, a romantic hero. However, he fails to demonstrate that all or even most romantic heroes are self-deceiving or that Hitchcock takes a critical stance towards the figure of the romantic hero for this or any other reason.

In the chapter on *North by Northwest*, Yanal offers evidence for and comments instructively on the film's privileging of theatricality, illusion, and artificiality, arguing that the film constitutes a cinematic apologia for deception, or at least an ode to its potential pleasures. (Yanal's hairsplitting dispute with George Wilson over the difference between illusion and deception is less instructive.) He notes that the Professor—the "principal-deceiver" responsible for both the disruption and the romance that enters Roger Thornhill's life after he is mistaken for George Kaplan—might be viewed as a more benevolent counterpoint to Descartes's "evil spirit." Yanal also views the Professor as a stand-in for Hitchcock himself, noting, after Wilson: "Perhaps Hitchcock *is* showing off his prowess: as a great manipulator of fictional characters and real audiences. And perhaps Hitchcock is also saying that deceivers have their good sides" (78). In this way, by arguing that *North by Northwest* constitutes a reflexive exploration of the illusionistic/deceptive potential inherent in both film and modern culture, Yanal takes his first tentative step toward attributing something like actual philosophical intent to Hitchcock.

Yanal opens the second section on Mind with the briefest of introductions to the Cartesian and Wittgensteinian positions on "incorrigibility" and "privileged access." (Insofar as he allows out-of-context quotes to carry most of the explanatory burden, the section on Wittgenstein is vague to the point of incomprehensibility.) In Yanal's view, *Shadow of a Doubt* and *Strangers on a Train* provide solutions to the problem of knowing another mind and "are in this sense Wittgensteinian and anti-Cartesian" (82). He opens his analysis of both films by describing numerous instances that point to doubling as a central formal and thematic motif before going on to point out several similarities between Young Charlie and Uncle Charlie and Guy and Bruno. To this end, I agree with Yanal's objection to Robin Wood's interpretation of Uncle Charlie's death as accidental. That Young Charlie is or has come to be capable of violence when threatened strikes me as both true and necessary.

In the chapter on *Shadow of a Doubt,* Yanal notes that it is the special affinity between the two Charlies that allows Young Charlie to discover her Uncle's secret, regardless of his numerous deceptions and the ignorance of her family and community. Despite some compelling textual and extra-textual evidence to the contrary—especially the subjective insert of waltzing widows that accompanies Charlie's receipt of the ring—Yanal points to the film's pervading realism as proof that this affinity is not telepathic but analogical. Drawing on Hume's *Dialogues Concerning Natural Religion*, he explains: "I can try to derive my knowledge of another's thoughts and feelings from consideration of my own thoughts and feelings—if I and the other are similar enough, that is. When two things, X and Y, are similar in certain respects, it is frequently the case that they are similar in other respects as well" (94). According to Yanal, Young Charlie's similarity to her uncle gives her an "epistemic edge" that allows her to construct a picture of his true nature.

Insofar as this analogical interpretation—which he applies in a similar fashion to the question of Bruno's and Guy's intimate mutual knowledge in *Strangers on a Train*— seems to provide a plausible realist theory of the way in which similar characters can acquire knowledge about each other's innermost thoughts, Yanal has succeeded in characterizing these films as anti-skeptical fables in support of the possibility of knowing other, similar minds by analogy. Thus, both *Shadow of a Doubt* and *Strangers on a Train* are revealed to be maximally philosophical films, and Hitchcock a philosophical film director. In addition, Yanal's convincing interpretation of the dramatic camera movement in *Shadow*'s library scene and his level-headed refutation of Robin Wood's "incest hypothesis" mark the chapter on *Shadow of a Doubt* as one of the more successful chapters of the book.

Their interpretive achievement notwithstanding, both chapters perpetuate a serious philosophical error. After irresponsibly implying in the introductory chapter that all anti-Cartesian theories are Wittgensteinian and vice-versa, Yanal only makes matters worse when—not once, but twice—he introduces chapters containing an argument that is both anti-Cartesian and anti-Wittgensteinian with a quote from the *Philosophical Investigations*. Yanal's analogical theory is anti-Cartesian in that it holds that other minds are not entirely opaque and that the incorrigibility of first-person reports is problematized by the possibility of deception. And it is also anti-Wittgensteinian in that it relies on an assumption of privileged access, which as Yanal himself notes, Wittgenstein resoundingly rejected. As I've noted earlier, Yanal's insufficiently rigorous treatment of Wittgenstein, which will most likely leave philosophy fans cold and Hitchcock fans confused, is one of the most serious drawbacks of *Hitchcock as Philosopher*.

While the chapter on *Psycho* expands on the Mind section's preoccupation with the theme of doubling, it largely dispenses with the problem of other minds in favor of exploring the nature of the divided self: "In *Psycho* people take on different personalities with dire consequences for themselves and others. The personae Marion Crane and Norman Bates adopt take them over; each loses sight of who he or she is" (119). For Yanal, Norman's extreme psychosis problematizes the analogical theory. As similar as he and Marion may be in certain respects, she lacks the "epistemic edge" that might alert her to the threat he poses: "The mistake the other character's make in trying to understand Norman Bates is to think of him as motivated by normal needs: filial devotion or sex or money. But Norman isn't like other people" (123).

As Yanal points out, part of *Psycho's* unsettling effect results from the psychological and emotional discomfort that accompanies identification with a figure like Norman. This discussion offers an interesting explanation for *Psycho's* and Hitchcock's unique ability to challenge preconceived notions concerning the mechanisms of identification, but its epistemic implications are rather limited. (A fragment of Locke's "puzzle case" from *An Essay Concerning Human Understanding*, which makes a baffling appearance during the discussion of spiritual possession, is the only expressly philosophical material in the body of the chapter.) As Yanal notes, *"Psycho* is a film about the dangers of becoming another mind" (125), a problem whose solution falls outside of the domain of epistemology.

Yanal continues his exploration of psychology with a tandem discussion of *Spellbound* and *Marnie*, Hitchcock's "therapy films," each of which hinges on an individual's attempt to aid a romantic partner in the recovery of a traumatic memory containing clues about a mysterious death. However, these films are not devoid of philosophical interest, in that they offer a Freudian challenge to the notion of privileged access by raising the possibility of repressed or unconscious memory: "Coming to remember—to pull something from memory—is, it would seem, a paradigm case of coming to know one's mind, directly. But in the case of repressed memory, the subject is barred from direct access to it—this is the point of departure for both films" (135). Although he misses a great chance to compare Freud's and Wittgenstein's views on privileged access and incorrigibility, Yanal does succeed in identifying the films' most important philosophical implications. In addition, his discussion of point-of-view in *Marnie's* flashback sequence is both novel and illuminating.

In the final and most successful section of *Hitchcock as Philosopher*, Yanal explores the implications of "Problematic Knowledge" from both ethical and epistemological/skeptical perspectives. Although he begins the chapter on *Rear Window* with an apt and unambiguous quote from Aristotle's *Metaphysics* on the desirability of knowledge and the primacy of sight, he takes the main thrust of his analysis from the distinction between aesthetic and ethical approaches to knowledge as detailed by Kierkegaard's *Either/Or*. He argues that throughout the majority of the film, "Jeff and Lisa live aesthetic lives, by which I mean (a) that they thrive on looking and being looked at, and (b) that they avoid commitment especially of the marital sort" (151). In Yanal's view their interest in Lars Thorwald stems not from an ethical wish to see the guilty punished, but from pure aesthetic curiosity. In this respect they have much in common with the film's audience. For Yanal, the narrative of *Rear Window* charts Lisa and Jeff's transition from an aesthetic existence toward a more (although not fully) ethical one.

In contrast to the vagueness that characterizes many of the earlier chapters, here Yanal undertakes a clear and focused explanation of both the aesthetic and ethical modes of being and the context in which they appear in Kierkegaard's writing. While Yanal provides no evidence that Hitchcock was aware of the philosopher's work, his Kierkegaardian reading of *Rear Window* generates a novel and compelling interpretation, which he supports with generous textual evidence. First of all, his analysis helps to highlight and explicate the moral parallel the film seems to draw between uncommitted romantic relationships and voyeurism, by viewing both as the result of an aesthetic attitude toward others. Secondly, Yanal's reading puts a finer point on Hitchcock's reflexive critique, by identifying the detached passivity of film spectatorship with the detached amorality of the aesthetic existence.

In the chapter on *The Man Who Knew Too Much* (1956), Yanal takes Jean-Paul Sartre as his philosophical touchstone. Following a perfunctory comparison between the American and British versions of the film, he reads the McKennas' dilemma through an excerpt from "Existentialism and Humanism" on the ultimate impossibility of determining the value of the life of an individual with respect to the value of the well being of the nation or community. Since both versions of the film leave the collective interests at stake somewhat unclear, Yanal undertakes an interesting discussion of the political situation at the time each was produced. Despite the film's more-or-less happy ending, in Yanal's view it is impossible to say whether the McKennas made the "correct" decision, since the outcome relied so heavily on chance. Ultimately, Yanal's interpretation fails to reveal anything terribly interesting about the film and most likely could have been formulated without reference to Sartre. It also seems somewhat out of place in a section on knowledge. However, insofar as Yanal's analysis highlights the film's *moral* stance, he is still able to make a strong case for *The Man Who Knew Too Much* as a philosophical film.

Hitchcock as Philosopher concludes with a discussion of *The Birds*, arguably Hitchcock's most philosophically interesting film. Yanal views *The Birds* as an unconventional horror film, which diverges from the typical generic pattern primarily in its failure to provide a singular scientific explanation/ resolution for the bird attacks. As Yanal notes, "The problem is that many explanations of conflicting types are offered" (185). After providing what seems like an exhaustive list of all the hypotheses offered by the film's characters as to the cause of the attacks, Yanal divides them into three groups: Natural, Preternatural, and Theological.

In Yanal's view, the preternatural explanation is presented as the most convincing one, and the characters that espouse it are also presented in the most sympathetic light. However, as

Yanal notes, the preternatural explanation ultimately explains very little: "Once the uniformity of nature is demonstrably upset, as it is in *The Birds*, there is no explanation forthcoming. . . . *The Birds* is not about fear of the unknown, but fear of the unknowable" (189). Yanal's analysis of *The Birds*, though fairly conventional, is also one if the best and most rigorous in the book. However, he would have done well to better integrate or to entirely dispense with the "Postscript on the film's sources," awkwardly appended to the analysis. (The chapters on *Rebecca*, *Vertigo*, and *Strangers on a Train*, end with similar addenda.) A stock comparison between the film and the du Maurier story, it does nothing to further Yanal's philosophical objectives and, in the absence of a concluding chapter, serves to end the book on something of an anti-climax.

These criticisms notwithstanding, *Hitchcock as Philosopher* is a refreshingly straightforward, engaging volume that is sure to interest philosophically-minded readers approaching Hitchcock and film studies for the first time. Several of Yanal's film analyses—notably of *North by Northwest*, *Rear Window*, and *The Birds*—are quite effective in exhibiting Hitchcock's work in a philosophical light, and will appeal especially to analytically-inclined Hitchcock fans weary of stock film theory and psychoanalytic interpretations. However, the book as a whole lacks the focus and ambition necessary to truly distinguish itself within either the vast arena of Hitchcock scholarship or the growing field devoted to tracing the philosophical implications of individual films and their medium. Perhaps if Yanal had opted to treat fewer films with greater philosophical rigor his volume might have come closer to realizing its significant potential.

Jerome Silbergeld, *Hitchcock with a Chinese Face: Cinematic Doubles, Oedipal Triangles, and China's Moral Voice*. Seattle: University of Washington Press, 2004. 146 pp. + DVD. $29.95 paper.

MARSHALL DEUTELBAUM

Despite the promise of its title, only the first of the three films Silbergeld analyzes in depth in *Hitchcock with a Chinese Face*, Lou Ye's *Suzhou River* (*Suzhou he*, 2000), with its purposeful echoes of *Vertigo*, has a direct Hitchcock connection. Silbergeld justifies the inclusion of the two other films, Ho Yim's *The Day the Sun Turned Cold* (*Tianguo niezi*, 1994) and Hou Hsiao-hsien's *Good Men, Good Women* (*Haonan haonu*, 1995) simply because of their use of doubles, a Hitchcockian motif, rather than because of any direct link to Hitchcock's films. For this reason, I will limit this review to his discussion of *Suzhou River*.

Suzhou River was awarded the Grand Prize in the 2000 Tokyo Filmex competition. According to the Tokyo Filmex website, during the question and answer session that followed the film's screening, Lou Ye denied that there was any connection between it and *Vertigo*, saying: "I like Hitchcock a lot, but wasn't thinking of him at all when I made this film." A brief description of the film may convince viewers otherwise: A man (Mardar) falls in love with the woman (Moudan) he is supposed to take care of, but is unable to prevent her from falling to her death. Some years later, obsessed by his memory of her, he returns to search for her in the city where this event happened. By chance he encounters a woman (Meimei) who closely resembles her. However, the woman denies that she is Moudan. Other similarities to *Vertigo* include the consistent association of the two women with green lighting and clothing; the occurrence, at times, of music on the soundtrack that sounds like Bernard Herrmann's score for *Vertigo*; and the fact that the same actress plays the roles of both women.

Silbergeld, a professor of Chinese Art History, explains Lou Ye's incorporation of these elements from *Vertigo* as an example of *fang*, a "transformative imitation," in which the

artist's aim is "to develop *creatively* on borrowed material . . .
often leading in directions quite different, unimagined, or
even contrary to the original work" (13, 15). Thus the ways in
which *Suzhou River* differs from *Vertigo* are equally important
as the similarities: there is no character in the film comparable
to Elster; Mardar has no disability; and Moudan's apparent
death is not part of a plot to deceive Mardar. Furthermore,
Moudan is herself, not someone made up to resemble her;
Meimei is actually not Moudan, though she resembles her;
and Mardar, unlike Scottie Ferguson, turns out not to be the
film's protagonist.

The film's protagonist, only revealed as such at the film's
conclusion, is the unnamed and almost entirely unseen
narrator, Meimei's lover, who appears to relate the story of
Mardar and Moudan as it was told to him, more or less, by
Meimei. The man is a freelance videographer and his
narration is related from his point of view by a jittery
subjective camera whose captured images are filled with
ellipses and jump cuts. The effect is like watching a
postmodern *Lady in the Lake*. Thus as Silbergeld notes, the
elements borrowed from *Vertigo* are incorporated into a
noirish tale told in voiceover that is set in the dilapidated
warehouse district around Shanghai's Suzhou River.

And in an unexpected twist that illustrates how Lou Ye
creatively refashions the material from *Vertigo*, Mardar's
search for Moudan is not an end in itself. Rather, Meimei is
so astonished by his dedication to finding his lost love that
she stages her own disappearance to test whether the depth
of the narrator's love for her is its equal. She asks him
whether he would search as devotedly for her if she
disappeared, and although he assures her that he would, she
doubts his commitment and disappears, leaving a note with
her challenge: "Find me if you love me." Despite his
previous assurances to her, the narrator justifies his decision
not to search for her with the cynical attitude that "nothing
lasts forever."

Silbergeld succinctly sums up the transformation of the
material from *Vertigo*:

In *Suzhou River* virtually the entire film is turned into a MacGuffin. We're long interested in the hero's pursuit of the reincarnated heroine before we discover in the last moments of the film that the moral of this tale is best embodied neither by the vanished girl, . . . nor by the reincarnation she is supposed to be, but instead by someone she evidently was not but *now* becomes. Meimei, as spectator, is so transformed by the events we have all been watching that she confirms the lasting meaning of the film: fidelity matters more than identity, and in the end optimism rises to challenge the pervasive cynicism of contemporary Shanghai. (17)

The film's ultimate aim, he suggests, is to offer contemporary Chinese viewers a model of idealized personal commitment as an alternative to the selfish, cutthroat economics encouraged by China's embrace of free-market competition:

Suzhou River, in its pattern of betrayal, loss, and pursuit of recovery, is less concerned with the intricacies of crime-solving . . . than it is with overcoming a collective neurosis, with encountering and transcending a corrupting cynicism that originates . . . in the social sphere. . . . It is, indeed, a cry for a society that in recent times has swung broadly from corrective political frenzy to impersonal economic fervor to become more romantic, more idealistic, more personal, for people to become more concerned (even obsessed) with each other rather than remain trapped by materialistic ideologies. (18)

Silbergeld's extensive knowledge of traditional Chinese art and literature, as well as of contemporary Chinese society, enhances our cultural understanding of Lou Ye's Hitchcockian appropriation. Nevertheless, inveterate Hitchcockians will have to decide for themselves whether one of Lou Ye's alterations to the plot of *Vertigo* is either an inventive narrational strategy or merely a bit of a cheat.

When Mardar first encounters Meimei, she already resembles Moudan in both her facial features and her dress. Mardar only remarks on her facial resemblance to Moudan. Viewers, however, are more struck by her dress—and her occupation—as more likely signs of her true identity because they appear to fulfill Moudan's threat to Mardar just before her death that, if he does not leave her alone, she will return as a mermaid to haunt him. Meimei entertains the patrons of the bar where she works by swimming in a large bowl dressed as a mermaid. While Mardar never makes a comment about this, viewers will also notice that Meimei's mermaid costume is the same as the costume of a mermaid doll that Mardar gave to Moudan as a birthday present. A frame enlargement appears in the text of the moment in the film when we first see Moudan with the doll held triumphantly in an outstretched hand (24).

Given Meimei's appearance as a mermaid, anyone familiar with *Vertigo* will be shocked by Mardar's sudden certainty that she is not Moudan, as well as by his decision to search elsewhere in Shanghai for her. That he searches for Moudan and finds her in one of only three convenience stores in the city that sell Buffalo Grass Vodka is a further surprise that may seem unmotivated. Yet another look at the frame enlargement shows that at the same moment Moudan holds the doll in one outstretched hand, she holds a bottle of Buffalo Grass Vodka in her other outstretched hand. The film, in other words, offers two signs of Moudan's identity. Perhaps viewers forget the vodka because all the business involving the mermaid is so visually striking. In retrospect, however, because the mermaid is associated with a curse, while the vodka is associated with the occasion when the couple first acknowledged their love, the vodka seems— symbolically, at least—the more compelling sign to follow, even if her rediscovery as a convenience store clerk is so undramatic. I suspect that the more familiar one is with

Vertigo, the more disappointing will be this sudden deviation from its pattern. Perhaps during the question and answer session at the Tokyo Filmex Lou Ye denied any conscious connection between his film and *Vertigo* because he sensed that an awareness of its partial presence in his film would distract viewers from *Suzhou River's* dramatic focus.

Charlotte Chandler, *It's Only a Movie: Alfred Hitchcock: A Personal Biography*. New York: Simon and Schuster, 2005. 368 pp. $26.00 cloth; $16.95 paper.

SUSAN WHITE

Professional biographer Charlotte Chandler's *It's Only a Movie* is a sympathetic portrait of Alfred Hitchcock as director, socialite, family man, *raconteur*, and prankster. As is the case in her well-regarded biographies of Groucho Marx, Federico Fellini, and Billy Wilder, Chandler here takes advantage of her vast Hollywood network and many years of interviewing to lay before her reader both old chestnuts and original commentaries on the director's life and works by those who witnessed them firsthand. That Chandler doesn't attempt to place her own research in the context of other Hitchcock biographies and interviews is both refreshing and frustrating. Those familiar with the other biographies, eager to know what new information and insights Chandler has to impart, may find tedious her faithful repetition of Hitchcock's stock comments about himself. But because Chandler herself knew and spoke at length to Hitchcock and his collaborators, her narrative of his life has its own integrity and a newness that should not be overlooked. The book features an extraordinary range of interviews with individuals who worked with or knew Hitchcock from the beginning of his career until his death and benefits from Chandler's knowledge of Hitchcock's opus and familiarity with his milieu.

Despite its scope, *It's Only a Movie* comes off at times as loosely woven and even unambitious, in that Chandler rarely attempts to address directly—in her own authorial voice—the controversies about Hitchcock so thoroughly hashed over by his other biographers. Detractors and admirers of the director are given their due in the book's interviews, creating a sense of good sportsmanship and balance in its presentation of a disturbingly complex and contradictory personality. Many reviewers have described this sympathetic biography as "intimate," not in the tell-all sense of Spoto's *The Dark Side of Genius*, but because of Chandler's apparent ability to inspire trust in her interviewees, who come off as candid and relaxed. Chandler's narrative voice is indeed low-key, usually eschewing obvious authorial commentary. She does, however, frame interviewees' remarks with an eye toward giving Hitchcock—as a "genius" or simply as a decent if fallible person—the benefit of the doubt in situations where evidence indicates that he treated others shabbily at best. Fortunately, even as it is polite to a fault with Hitchcock, the book manages to reveal at many junctures how Hitchcock's ambivalences and reserve may have caused pain to others, even as it divulges that some collaborators have softened their initially harsh assessments of their working relationships with the director. The book proceeds more or less chronologically, with occasional flashbacks and flashforwards, covering, if sometimes rather spottily, Hitchcock's entire life and career.

Chandler's skill as an interviewer is in evidence throughout the book. Rather than repeating verbatim the habitual comments made about Hitchcock by his collaborators, she creates an atmosphere where her interviewee can be thoughtful and reflective. For example, both Donald Spoto and Patrick McGilligan emphasize the negative aspects of John Gielgud's working relationship with Hitchcock and repeat what he said to interviewers while he was starring in *The Secret Agent*: "Hitchcock has often made me feel like a jelly, and I have been nearly sick with nervousness" (Spoto, *The Dark Side of Genius: The Life of Alfred Hitchcock*, 152; McGilligan, *Alfred Hitchcock: A Life in Darkness and Light*, 183). Chandler reports a more mellow assessment made later in Gielgud's life:

I think now it was my own inexperience with the film medium which was responsible for my insecurity and subsequent stiffness. Then, too, I didn't feel I was good-looking enough to be a screen leading man, especially with someone as beautiful as Madeleine Carroll. But when I saw the film rather recently, I was struck by how well we all played together . . .

> For many years, I stopped making films entirely, and I blamed Hitchcock for this, but it wasn't his fault. Looking back, I realize that I didn't have much confidence in my talent as a film actor and, when I first saw the film, I thought my performance was rather poor. When I saw it decades later, I was stunned—by how young I looked.
>
> Actually, I rather enjoyed working with Hitchcock. He was a great joker. Now, I love the film and treasure my appearance in it. (101-02)

The homosexual overtones of films like *Rope*, *Strangers on a Train*, and *North by Northwest* have been frequently dealt with by biographers, critics, and gender theorists. McGilligan cites at length the fascinating perspective brought to bear on *Rope* by Arthur Laurents, the film's screenwriter, who also happened to be living with Farley Granger during the shooting of the film. Spoto also quotes Laurents on the film's "homosexual element" (*Dark Side of Genius*, 304). Farley Granger discloses to Chandler information that is less scandalous than the Laurents material, but is quite significant for interpretations of *Strangers on a Train*:

> We never discussed any homoerotic attraction Walker's character had for me, but I think Hitch did that with Walker, and he just wanted me to act kind of normal and not be aware of too much undercurrent. Of course, Hitch understood all of this, and he knew what he could do, and what we could do. He had a light touch. (196)

If Chandler had had the opportunity to interview Walker (who died in 1951, the year *Strangers on a Train* was released), I have no doubt that she would have gotten the whole story.

Regarding *North by Northwest*, Martin Landau, who was apparently not interviewed by either Spoto or McGilligan for their Hitchcock biographies, proves to be both amusing and informative in his long conversation with Chandler. Like Granger, Landau was willing to discuss the homosexual implications of his role:

> Leonard was written as a henchman, but I chose to play him as a gay character, because Leonard felt the need to get rid of Eve Kendall. I felt it would be very interesting if he were jealous of her beyond just being a henchman. But this was 1958, so I played it very subtly. (250)

Like Hitchcock, Chandler has a "light touch," and is very adept at shaping her public persona, playing the double role of first-person narrator and of compassionate ear to those she interviews. Chandler the interviewer is polite but frank, a Hollywood insider who remains unassuming, familiar with film history but with no pretense of being a critic. To some degree her authorial persona mirrors Hitchcock's blend of reserve and bluntness, but one senses that she is going out of her way to be non-threatening, surely the only way she could gain the confidence of gun-shy celebrities. While this interviewing technique can be valuable, one sometimes feels that she is playing Hitchcock's game of cat and mouse too much as the mouse. She seems to acknowledge unpleasant facts about Hitchcock's public and private behavior in the interest of subsequently downplaying them.

In a characteristic warding-off gesture, the book opens on an interview with Hitchcock in which he acknowledges his own embarrassment about the shape of his body and his discomfort with sex. The reader unfamiliar with the fierce debates inspired by Hitchcock's sexual and professional behavior may not see in this more than a disarming moment of self-revelation by a very shy man. Read in the context of the Hitchcock biography industry, however, this is a strategic opening move in a book that seeks to some extent to perform a course-correction regarding how Hitchcock is to be remembered by his public. As discussed above, conversations that Chandler reports are frequently used as an opportunity for interviewees to set the record straight about an incident or relationship that has raised red flags in earlier Hitchcock biographies. Chandler does not assign herself the task of correcting Spoto's excesses, as does Patrick McGilligan in his more comprehensive biography. Instead she gives Hitchcock and others the opportunity to air grievances, express belated admiration, or simply to recount happy memories surrounding a film's production circumstances—and then she moves on in a brisk, no-nonsense manner to the next episode.

The direction of Chandler's course-correction is above all to place the events of Hitchcock's life in the context of the warmth and normality of his family life. Her excellent relationship with Alma and Patricia Hitchcock made this referencing of the happy family both convincing and (one suspects) inevitable. Touchy subjects are raised in many of the interviews—Hitchcock's distaste for Method actors (and perhaps most actors), his cruel practical jokes, his perhaps inappropriate behavior with Tippi Hedren—and often are quickly followed up with a quote from Alma or Patricia in which the best face possible is put on what must have been difficult personal and professional situations. Considering that the book opens on Hitchcock's intimate thoughts about his own body and quotes his naughty version of his name many times ("Hitch, without a cock"), one can hardly accuse the book of avoiding the issues about his sexuality that have obsessed other Hitchcock biographers. Chandler even-handedly reports Hitchcock's deal-breaking exchange with Evan Hunter regarding the rape scene in *Marnie*—"Evan, when he sticks it in her, I want the camera right on her face" (273)—and doesn't hesitate to quote Melanie Griffith's harsh assessment of the Master of Suspense: "He was a motherfucker. And you can quote me" (272).

For better or worse, raking up old scandals is not what Chandler is about. She is more interested in assessing the overall impact of Hitchcock's life. One must, in other words, read between the lines to understand the Hedren-Griffith perspective on Hitchcock. The accusations of sexual harassment frequently bruited about are not explicitly repeated here, but they do lie iceberg-like under the surface, making me wonder if it might not have been preferable for Chandler to confront in more depth the problems created by Hitchcock's growing power and his ambivalences rather than introducing them and moving on. One senses that, despite her gameness, her willingness, like Carole Lombard, to "use the language men use with each other" (Hitchcock's observation about Lombard, quoted on page 133), Chandler would find it distasteful to elaborate upon the more salacious details of Hitchcock's relationships with others, or to dwell upon possible unkindnesses—that is, unless they have already become part of Hitchcock's discourse on himself. Indeed, we are very often told, in Chandler's underplayed prose, what seems to be the Hitchcock family's official version of events:

> Hitchcock sometimes may have fallen in love with one of his leading ladies, as she appeared onscreen, playing her part, a role that was partly his own creation. Then, when the film wrapped, so did his relationship to the character. Thus, Alma could say to me that she had never been jealous of any actress who appeared in her husband's films. (283)

In his films, television programs, and interviews, Hitchcock created worlds where judgment and guilt induce feelings of ultimate dread. It is of course ironic that his tremendous talent and achievements, which led to a certain, occasionally abused, "power and freedom," have left him open to the judgments and speculations of so many, and one senses that Chandler empathizes with the vulnerability of Hitchcock and his family to the public eye. To a certain extent Chandler's is an impossible task. Without going into the philosophical problems regarding truth and history, it is intuitively obvious that human beings are inconsistent and that the authority of our lives' witnesses may come from many sources. Certainly, for example, Janet Leigh's deep respect for "Mr. Hitchcock," as reported by Chandler, has as much the ring of authenticity as any of the reports on Hitchcock's lack of generosity towards his colleagues. The endearing Hitchcock is as real as the monstrous one, and as enduring. Chandler cites a telling anecdote by Patricia Hitchcock:

> It was just a very normal life at our house. My father was a wonderful father, so dear and funny. He liked it when I was mischievous. He was. Sometimes when I was very young, I would wake up and look in the mirror, and he had drawn a clown's face on me. This happened a lot. He never woke me, and I never knew who I would be. (99)

This episode bears witness to a human relationship that is as complex and moving as any I have ever observed. One finds here in embryonic form all the elements of exuberance, control, disguise, paternal ambivalence, and shock that Hitchcock deployed and critiqued in his films, and which, as elements of his personality, inspired both strong dislike and endless affection. For the moment I'm happy, like Chandler, to dwell on the latter, without losing sight of the former.

Contributors

Charles Barr is Emeritus Professor of Film and Television at the University of East Anglia in Norwich, England, where he taught for many years, and he recently took up a two-year appointment as Visiting Professor of Film and Media at the University of Washington in St. Louis. His publications include *English Hitchcock* and (in the BFI Classics series) *Vertigo*.

Lisa Broad is a second-year doctoral candidate in the New York University Cinema Studies Department.

Marshall Deutelbaum is Professor Emeritus at Purdue University and co-editor of *A Hitchcock Reader*.

Sidney Gottlieb is Professor of Media Studies and Digital Culture at Sacred Heart University.

Michael Healey is nearing completion of his M.A. degree at New York University's Cinema Studies program. His essays and reviews have been published by *Senses of Cinema*, the *Hitchcock Annual*, and *PopMatters.*

Thomas Leitch teaches English and directs the Film Studies program at the University of Delaware. His books include *Find the Director and Other Hitchcock Games*, *The Encyclopedia of Alfred Hitchcock*, and the forthcoming *Film Adaptation and Its Discontents: From* Gone with the Wind *to* The Passion of the Christ.

Stephen Mamber is a Professor in the Critical Studies Program of the UCLA Department of Film, Television, and Digital Media.

Leland Poague teaches film in the Department of English at Iowa State University. He is co-editor of *A Hitchcock Reader*, and most recently edited *Frank Capra: Interviews*. His book *Another Frank Capra* is just out in paperback from Cambridge University Press.

Angelo Restivo is Assistant Professor and Director of Graduate Studies in the Moving Image Studies program at Georgia State University. He is the author of *The Cinema of Economic Miracles: Visuality and Modernization in the Italian Art Film*.

Kenneth Sweeney is the Program Administrator for the Department of Cinema Studies at New York University. He is a contributing writer for *American Cinematographer Magazine*, where he writes DVD reviews.

Jacqueline Tong was born in Hong Kong. She received her undergraduate degree from Oberlin College and is currently pursuing a graduate degree in Contemporary Cinema Cultures at King's College (London).

James M. Vest is Professor of French, interdisciplinary studies, and cinema at Rhodes College. He has published several articles on Hitchcock's French connections, as well as a book on the subject, *Hitchcock and France*.

Michael Walker is a retired teacher who is on the editorial board of *Movie* magazine. He has contributed to *The Movie Book of Film Noir*, *The Movie Book of the Western*, and *Alfred Hitchcock: Centenary Essays*. His book *Hitchcock's Motifs* was recently published by Amsterdam University Press.

Susan White is Associate Professor of Film and Comparative Literature in the Department of English, University of Arizona, and Film Editor for *Arizona Quarterly*. Her recent work focuses on violence, masculinity, and acting in the films of Hitchcock, Kubrick, Nicholas Ray, and Anthony Mann.